Ground War

T0355208

Ground War

Courts, Commissions, and the Fight over Partisan Gerrymanders

NICHOLAS GOEDERT

OXFORD
UNIVERSITY PRESS

OXFORD
UNIVERSITY PRESS

Oxford University Press is a department of the University of Oxford. It furthers
the University's objective of excellence in research, scholarship, and education
by publishing worldwide. Oxford is a registered trade mark of Oxford University
Press in the UK and certain other countries.

Published in the United States of America by Oxford University Press
198 Madison Avenue, New York, NY 10016, United States of America.

© Oxford University Press 2022

Library of Congress Control Number: 2021925678
ISBN 978-0-19-762663-4 (pbk.)
ISBN 978-0-19-762662-7 (hbk.)

DOI: 10.1093/oso/9780197626627.001.0001

1 3 5 7 9 8 6 4 2

Paperback printed by Marquis, Canada
Hardback printed by Bridgeport National Bindery, Inc., United States of America

For Sumin and Arcadia

Contents

Acknowledgments

This book has been over a decade in the making, during which the entire field of redistricting took many unexpected twists and turns, requiring rewrites and restructurings that sometimes seemed endless. As with any project of such scope and duration, it would not have been possible without the help and support of many people along the way. Those listed here represent only a small sample.

I am first indebted to the late Prof. Roy Schotland, whose mentorship in election law seminars at Georgetown led me down the career path of studying the empirical implications of election institutions. I am thankful to the Princeton University Department of Politics for their initial encouragement of my project in the early stages, especially my dissertation advisor, Brandice Canes-Wrone; my other advisors over the course of my graduate career, including Nolan McCarty, Aaron Meirowitz, Chris Achen, and Tali Mendelberg; and all of the American Politics graduate students and faculty who deepened my development as a scholar, both in my coursework and at the weekly research seminars where I was given the chance to present my own ideas and delve into those of my colleagues.

I would like to thank the Department of Political Science, the College of Liberal Arts and Human Sciences, and the Policy Destination Area at Virginia Tech for lending their institutional support for both this project and my research over the past five years. I am especially grateful to the empiricist group within our department, including Aaron Brantley, Karen Hult, Eric Jardine, Caitlin Jewitt, Jason Kelly, and Karin Kitchens, for their valuable feedback on my manuscript prospectus and several of the analytical chapters. Additional thanks to Robert Hildebrand for help with rendering the book's graphics and maps, and Conrad Briles for proofreading.

I am also grateful for the engagement and encouragement of the participants of a manuscript workshop I held in 2019. Daniel Bowen, Keith Gaddie, Alex Keena, Nolan McCarty, and Nick Stephanopoulos each provided thorough critiques of my initial draft that proved invaluable toward getting me over the hump toward final submission. And I would like to thank my editor, David McBride, for his patience and persistence in seeing the book through to review and publication during a very difficult time.

Most important, I am grateful for the unconditional love and support of my family throughout my life and during the years spent on this project, especially my wonderful parents, Jim and JoAnn.

I dedicate this book to my beautiful, kind, and generous wife, Sumin, who has encouraged me in all aspects of my life every day for the past five years, and my daughter, Cady, whose birth provided the ultimate deadline to finish my writing and whose miraculous growth provided inspiration for me to see it through to the end.

1

Introduction

A Tale of Two Gerrymanders

Partisan gerrymandering, the drawing of legislative district lines to deliberately advantage one political party, has been present and controversial in American politics since before the ratification of our Constitution. Throughout the past several decades, the propriety, legality, and effectiveness of partisan gerrymanders has bounced back and forth in a wide-ranging debate among legislators, scholars, judges, and citizens.

Yet over the course of the past decade, a series of legislative, electoral, and judicial events have given this issue a prominence it has never before seen, especially as it applies to the U.S. House of Representatives. In the 2010 midterm elections, a concerted effort by Republicans to win state legislative seats ("Project REDMAP," described in detail in Daley 2016) gave one party unprecedented control over the redistricting process in the majority of large swing states, including Florida, Michigan, North Carolina, Ohio, Pennsylvania, and Virginia, following the 2010 national census. These partisan gerrymanders aided in a strikingly "antimajoritarian" outcome in the 2012 congressional elections, in which Republicans won a large majority of congressional seats despite winning fewer congressional votes than Democratic candidates at the national level. The intuitive unfairness of these results led to a burst of litigation against partisan gerrymandering in all of the affected states and others over the course of the next several years. In 2015 through 2018, reform advocates won a series of victories in the state courts and lower federal appellate courts, leading to brief optimism that the ultimate solution might lie in the court system. But this optimism was crushed in the summer of 2019, when the U.S. Supreme Court held in *Rucho v. Common Cause* that partisan gerrymandering claims were a political question that the federal courts should have no role in deciding.

This is a book about the harms caused by the gerrymandering of the U.S. Congress and the role that courts and voters should play to solve them. Justice Roberts's majority opinion in *Rucho*, essentially foreclosing the possibility that federal courts can remedy partisanship in the drawing of legislative maps, was deeply disappointing to advocates of redistricting reform. But the decision was not unreasonable or unprincipled. Indeed, the issues of political fairness involved in districting are nuanced and multidimensional and do not lend themselves to

Ground War. Nicholas Goedert, Oxford University Press. © Oxford University Press 2022.
DOI: 10.1093/oso/9780197626627.003.0001

judgment by a simple, one-size-fits-all standard. A gerrymander may be viewed through an entirely different lens across two different states, two different voters, or two different election cycles. The pathologies of partisan gerrymandering, and indeed legislative control of the redistricting process itself, are real. But they are not confined to an easily measurable bias in an election result. For these reasons, this book argues that the more appropriate actors to address the fairness of a map (or the process of drawing a map) are the voters within each state, not the U.S. courts.

Although gerrymandering has received the greatest attention in the most recent decade, the problems presented by districting and the effectiveness of solutions can be most clearly drawn by contrasting two cases from the early 2000s: a partisan map in Pennsylvania that landed in the Supreme Court and a bipartisan compromise in California that led to citizen revolt at the ballot box.

Pennsylvania, 2001–2010

For the first half of the 2000s, Pennsylvania Republicans might have believed they had found the perfect gerrymander. At the beginning of the decade, the Republican-controlled legislature, with assistance from national party figures such as Karl Rove and Chairman Tom Davis of the National Republican Congressional Committee, crafted a map "designed so effectively to change political outcomes in Pennsylvania that it began to be referred to by Democratic state legislators as a 'massacre' and by a local Harrisburg newspaper as 'the most partisan congressional gerrymander of this young century, and among the worst in the last several decades of the earlier millennium'" (Douglas 2016, 199–200). After yielding a 12–7 GOP majority in the elections seventeen months earlier, the map was upheld in 2004 by the U.S. Supreme Court in *Vieth v. Jubelirer*. In this case, a 5–4 conservative majority held that no standard yet existed that would allow the courts to fairly adjudicate the harms caused by partisan gerrymanders.

Yet that same map must not have seemed so perfect to Republicans in 2006, when Democrats regained control of Congress by flipping thirty-one seats that included four Republican-crafted districts in Pennsylvania. While this was a strong night for Democrats on many fronts, their gains were not spread equally across the country: Democrats also gained two seats drawn by bureaucrats in Iowa and two seats drawn by a nonpartisan commission in Arizona, but the balance of the delegation in California, where the map had been approved by both parties working in close concert, remained unchanged.

The Pennsylvania map was aggressive in seeking to maximize the Republican advantage, eliminating a district in each of Pittsburgh and Philadelphia and placing six Democrats in districts with other incumbents. But in drawing such a bold map, the governing party did not anticipate the partisan shifts that their state would experience over the decade, particularly as voters in suburban Philadelphia increasingly identified as Democrats. Few of the Republican-held seats could be called truly safe: George W. Bush received 52% of the vote or less in seven of these twelve seats in the 2000 election. So the Republicans, relying on the moderate party brand remaining viable in many of the suburban swing seats, were buried under the Democratic tide of 2006. Four incumbents were defeated that year, some by scandal and others simply by changing demographics, with a fifth losing in 2008.

Republicans in Pennsylvania, attempting to win more than two-thirds of the seats in an evenly matched state, gambled on assembling swing districts that they hoped to win merely by running moderates or popular incumbents. So it is unsurprising that things did not go as planned for Pennsylvania Republicans when the tide turned against them. Had the mapmakers not been so willing to take risks, dividing pockets of moderates into Republican districts in order to eliminate as many Democratic seats as possible, some of their doomed incumbents might have survived the massacres of 2006 and 2008.

Pennsylvania voters were able to reverse the result of the partisan gerrymander at the ballot box in 2006 and 2008. But their failure to achieve relief from the courts in 2004 also ensured that this reversal was short-lived. The Republican wave of 2010 restored the map to a five-seat GOP advantage, and this majority was further exaggerated by another Republican gerrymander in 2012. That year, Republicans in Pennsylvania won thirteen of the state's eighteen seats despite losing the congressional popular vote. Again, Pennsylvania voters turned to the courts, but this time, the state courts. In 2018's *League of Women Voters v. Pennsylvania*, opponents of partisan gerrymandering finally won a major court victory. The Pennsylvania State Supreme Court reversed the congressional map on *state constitutional* grounds, and Democrats achieved an even split of the delegation under the court-drawn map in the 2018 midterm elections. Nevertheless, this decision narrowly applied only to Pennsylvania, and when the U.S. Supreme Court rejected a series of challenges to partisan gerrymandering in *Whitford*, *Rucho*, and *Benisek*, nationwide relief in the court system remained elusive.

Because of the ambiguous lessons we might draw from it, the Pennsylvania congressional map of the early 2000s has been a touchstone allowing many scholars to arrive at very different conclusions about partisan gerrymandering. In their book *Gerrymandering in America*, McGann et al. (2016) argue that the success of Pennsylvania's map at the Supreme Court in the *Vieth* case caused states to feel less constrained about drawing partisan maps in the next decade, leading to much more aggressive and successful partisan gerrymanders after the 2010 census. But in his book *Drawing the Lines*, Seabrook (2017) uses the backfire of the same Pennsylvania map in 2006 and 2008 as evidence of inherent electoral constraints that limit the ultimate effectiveness of partisan maps.

California, 2001–2010

At the same time that Pennsylvania lawmakers were drawing the partisan maps that would win in court but backfire at the ballot box, California legislators were drawing a map that was much less legally controversial yet arguably just as pernicious and more effective. During the 1990s, a court-ordered plan kept the partisan balance close in California for most of the decade, but leftward trends finally caught up to Republicans in 2000, when Democrats flipped four Republican districts in that cycle to take a 32–20 advantage in seats. California gained one seat in the 2000 census, and Democrats held control of state government. Many expected the party to use this power to significantly expand their majority.

But the Democrats did not use this opportunity to draw an aggressively partisan map. Instead, they felt pressure from both the right and the left to be much more cautious. If they drew a map to gain as many seats as possible, they risked a Republican-backed ballot proposition to change the redistricting process and the prospect of serious primary challenges from state legislators forced to retire due to legislative term limits. Thus, leaders of the state congressional delegations of both parties reached an agreement to draw a map that would ensure the reelection of almost every incumbent. Over the objections of almost half the Democrats in the state legislature, the plan passed with roughly even support from both parties.

While one might expect a map produced by bipartisan compromise to be a story of triumph for pluralist and deliberative democracy, those involved in the process describe something else entirely. Congressman Alan Lowenthal (2019, 4), a California Assembly member at the time, recounts:

> I found this process to be very upsetting. More reminiscent of the Tammany Hall political machine than twenty-first-century governing, incumbent elected officials held private meetings behind closed doors and literally selected their own voters. Those officials prioritized political expediency and incumbency protection over any criteria that considered natural boundaries, compactness, or cohesive communities of interests.

In a review of recent California reforms, Eric McGhee (2015, 7) described the maps as "a set of plans that largely preserved the status quo by making districts less competitive, especially for Congress, while seeming to satisfy no one but the authors."

The map worked exactly as expected. In the 2002 general election, every incumbent won with at least 58% of the vote, and the Democrats held a 33–20 advantage in the delegation. And over the course of the decade, these seats remained safe for incumbents. Out of 265 congressional elections that took place in California under this map, the incumbent party was defeated only once, and Democrats had gained just one additional seat by 2009. Even in the face of the Republican tide in 2010, Democrats held on to all thirty-four of these seats, a sign that the map was resilient to tides in both directions.

So, unlike in Pennsylvania, large swings in public sentiment seen in the second half of the 2000s were unable to subvert the intentions of the legislature in drawing California's congressional map. And also unlike in Pennsylvania, California citizens did not turn to the court system for a solution but instead used their direct power of referendum, and did so repeatedly. Even in the absence of unilateral partisan motivations, "good government organizations began to see redistricting as a question of effective representation, [and] argued that the lack of competition in the new districts protected extreme partisans in the legislature" (McGhee 2015, 7). An initial reform effort led by Governor Arnold Schwarzenegger to place redistricting in the hands of retired judges narrowly failed in 2005. But in 2008 and 2010, a series of ballot initiatives successfully transformed California's electoral process, including 2010's Proposition 20, which took the power to draw congressional district lines out of the hands of the partisan state legislature and put it into the hands of a commission. California was not the first state to adopt a redistricting commission, but it did adopt unique selection and deliberation procedures to encourage an unprecedented degree of independence and citizen involvement.

The results of adopting a commission were immediately apparent, as congressional elections became demonstrably more competitive and responsive. California has seen triple the number of close elections in the 2010s compared to the previous decade, and the 2018 midterms saw a dramatic disruption in the political split of the delegation in response to strong partisan tides, as Democrats flipped seven seats previously held by Republicans.[1] At the same time, California became a model for redistricting reform across the country, as four states adopted redistricting commissions by ballot referendum in 2018, many clearly borrowing procedures and criteria for Proposition 20.

The Lessons of Pennsylvania and California

The examples from Pennsylvania and California demonstrate a clear contrast in both the problems presented by legislative gerrymandering and its potential solutions. The recurring "countermajoritarian" outcomes in Pennsylvania congressional elections show that partisan gerrymandering presents real norma-tive problems to the functioning of a representative democracy. Yet the map was also ultimately responsive to the ongoing demographic changes in the state and short-term swings in voter preferences in successive wave elections at the end of the decade. By comparison, the map in California was *not* drawn to advantage one party or the other. But even when parties come together to draw a mutually agreeable map, as California Democrats and Republicans did in 2001, the results can be just as normatively offensive as the worst of partisan gerrymanders, arriving at a map that is completely immune from changes in the makeup of the electorate or the will of the voters.

Pennsylvania and California also show two very different avenues for pursuing reform. Democrats in Pennsylvania went through the federal court system and had their claim not just rejected but rejected with such force that many argue the case incentivized even worse partisanship going forward. Their suit did nothing to prevent an even more egregious partisan map ten years later. Democrats again pursued litigation, and this time finally succeeded in 2018. But they succeeded in state court, not federal court, under narrow state constitutional grounds that did nothing to alter the future gerrymandering process, instead only imposing some superficial constraints.

California's voters chose to pursue a public referendum rather than litigation. In doing this, they received immediate and permanent relief through the crea-tion of an independent redistricting commission in 2010. While the results in Pennsylvania were only getting worse, the results in California were strikingly better, mostly eliminating bias in the delegation, increasing competitiveness, and improving the congruence of representation.

These two outcomes exemplify the two major paths to gerrymandering re-form. And as this book will argue, one path has clearly emerged as superior. Even prior to Justice Roberts shutting the door on federal litigation in 2019, re-lief from the courts has always been unpredictable, superficial, and temporary. By contrast, nonpartisan commissions have provided enduring, structural, and effective solutions, even in the face of partisan criticism. And although these commissions have most often been enacted by public referendum, potential for this sort of reform exists even where citizen initiatives are not available. I hope that this book might contribute to the political will to accomplish this.

Plan of the Book

Throughout this book, I make the argument that although partisan gerrymandering harms American democracy in several important ways, the more realistic way to fight it lies in changing the process at the state level by adopting nonpartisan commissions rather than through the court system. The argument requires an understanding of the political theory behind districting and representation, the jurisprudential background and legal history, the empirical evidence for the historical and recent effects of gerrymandering, and recent political reform movements. And so it proceeds through each of these topics as follows.

In Chapter 2, I discuss the theory of how gerrymandering works, with emphasis on two dimensions of the issue that are sometimes neglected. First, many equally valid yet often competing claims can be made about the quality of one's representation, and a map or electoral process that responds well to one claim may fail to accommodate others. Second, an electoral map is not static, and resulting delegations may change dramatically over its life. So when evaluating a map, we must anticipate the range of possible outcomes that it may produce.

In Chapter 3, I discuss the legal arguments surrounding several recent prominent cases on partisan gerrymandering, in each instance trying to distill the most important claims made by the plaintiffs into an easily or universally applicable test. I then apply each "stylized test" to the facts of the other cases, concluding that no single test or standard will resolve all cases in a satisfying way.

In Chapter 4, I use historical evidence from the past fifty years of congressional elections to examine the conditions under which partisan, nonpartisan, and bipartisan gerrymandering has encouraged or suppressed competitive elections and partisan turnover. Here I find that while partisan gerrymanders discourage close competition when the national environment is close to even, they create a lot of close elections and turnover under strong tides averse to the gerrymandering party. In contrast, I demonstrate that nonpartisan commissions tend to foster the most close elections, while bipartisan agreements consistently generate the fewest, regardless of partisan tides.

Chapters 5 through 7 use a new measure of bias and responsiveness to show both the multiple harms created by partisan gerrymandering in the current era and the potential for nonpartisan commissions as a flexible solution. This measure, historically weighted efficiency gap (HWEG), estimates bias under a wide range of electoral conditions for any given state, leveraging national historical election data, along with results from congressional and statewide elections in each state. Unlike other measures in common use, HWEG can be used to easily visualize the situations under which any map will be most biased and/or responsive, as well as synthesize average bias and responsiveness under a weighted average of conditions, regardless of the state's underlying partisan balance. In Chapter 5, I discuss the motivation for my measurement and detail how it is calculated, using several illustrative examples. In Chapter 6, I apply the measurement to all partisan gerrymanders in the 2010s decade. I find that these states all violate important democratic norms, but not all in the same ways.

Rather, partisan gerrymanders in competitive states are severely biased when the election is close but somewhat compensated through responsiveness to changes in public opinion, while gerrymanders in noncompetitive states show a more understated bias but at the cost of an almost total lack of competitive elections under all conditions.

In Chapter 7, I apply this measure to five cases of states adopting a more non-partisan approach. From this, I draw two important conclusions. First, each of these states has made a different but deliberate decision to privilege some norms or goals over others, such as competitiveness or geographic stability. And so the results produced by each commission vary significantly. But each commission state has also tended to produce mostly unbiased maps that also promote democratic responsiveness. Thus, commissions have largely succeeded at not only remedying the immediate harms observed under all classes of partisan gerrymandering but also adapting the particular preferences embodied in the political culture of their state.

In Chapter 8, I summarize the findings of the previous chapters but also look to the future. Specifically, I examine recent efforts by citizens and legislatures to combat partisan gerrymandering as possible models for action nationwide. While the likelihood for a solution in the court system may still be dim, the prospects for reform at the state level have never been higher. And this is not just the more likely venue for action, but the more appropriate and effective one.

2

The Theory behind Gerrymandering

Drawing Districts in the United States

In almost every nation in the world with some democratic electoral structures, representatives are chosen at least in part by dividing the country into geographic districts. In U.S. federal elections, these districts are the fifty states for the U.S. Senate and 435 single-member districts contained within those states for the House of Representatives. Elections for state legislatures are also mostly conducted using single-member geographic districts, with a handful of states using multimember districts for one legislative house.

As I will detail in Chapter 3, the U.S. Constitution requires that congressional and state legislative lines be redrawn into equal population districts following the national census that occurs every ten years. I refer to this legally mandated process as *redistricting,* and the fact that states periodically must redistrict is not in and of itself in dispute. However, as redistricting is mostly done by the elected branches of our state governments, several political factors tend to seep into this process, leading invariably to conflict and controversy. The use of the redistricting process to achieve some political goal is generally referred to as *gerrymandering.* This book deals specifically with *partisan gerrymandering,* which I define as the use of redistricting to achieve the electoral goals of one political party, such as increasing the likely number of representatives elected from that party, or maximizing the likelihood that a party will elect a majority of representatives.

Partisan gerrymandering has been practiced and disputed for centuries, with state legislative gerrymandering predating the ratification of the Constitution and evidence for congressional gerrymandering seen in elections for the first Congress, in 1788 (Hunter 2011). The word "gerrymander" itself emerged in 1812 when a political cartoonist effectively coined the term by pointing out that a Massachusetts state senate district engineered by Governor Elbridge Gerry resembled a salamander.[1] Its effects and possible remedies have been debated at least as far back as the late nineteenth century (e.g., Sterne 1869; Dillon, Smith, and Woodruff 1892). But in recent years, it has been at the forefront of our political and legal debate.

Ground War. Nicholas Goedert, Oxford University Press. © Oxford University Press 2022.
DOI: 10.1093/oso/9780197626627.003.0002

How Does Partisan Gerrymandering Work?

The basic logic of partisan gerrymandering is that voters may be distributed across districts in such a way that one party's votes are more efficient than another party's in electing representatives. This is because the probability of electing a representative within a single-member district does not increase linearly with the proportion of voters who vote with the party. If you increase the proportion of Democrats in a district from 45% to 55%, the likelihood of electing a Democrat will increase significantly. However, increasing the number of Democrats from 10% to 20% (or from 80% to 90%) will likely have no impact on the partisan outcome in a district, despite the fact that the absolute number of voters moved in each example is the same.

The principle that marginal votes matter much more in competitive districts than in noncompetitive districts motivates the two central strategies of partisan gerrymandering: *packing* and *cracking*. These essentially involve moving the favored party's voters into competitive districts and moving the disfavored party's voters into noncompetitive districts. Under the practice of *packing*, voters from the disfavored party are *packed* as much as possible into a small number of districts. For example, if a district is already 70% Democratic, it costs Republicans almost nothing electorally to remove Republicans from the district and instead pack it further to make it 80% or 90% Democratic. Displaced Republicans can then be moved to other districts where they are more likely to swing an election result.

Under the practice of *cracking*, voters from the disfavored party with enough voting strength to win a district are *cracked* across several districts, so that they constitute a minority in every district. For example, suppose three neighboring districts are 60%, 60%, and 0% Democratic, respectively. These districts are likely to elect two Democrats among them. If gerrymandering Republicans were to instead *crack* the Democrats in the first two districts so that they are evenly spread across all three districts (40% in each), Republicans would likely win all three seats despite no change in the underlying electorate.

These concepts are often easier to understand visually, and so toy state examples with a small number of voters and districts are commonly used in the popular media to explain the basic mechanisms of gerrymandering. For example, a graphic showing competing gerrymanders originally posted on Facebook by Steven Nass as "How to Steal an Election" circulated across the internet in 2015, eventually appearing in some form on news organizations such as the *Washington Post* and *Huffington Post* and advocacy groups like FairVote.[2] An adapted version of this graphic, depicting the division of fifty people into five districts of different configurations, is shown in Figure 2.1. The graphic describes

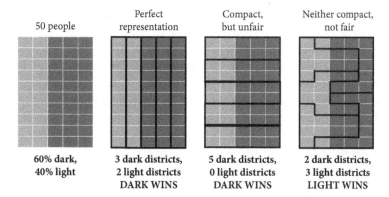

Figure 2.1 Popular Toy State Gerrymandering Example: Three Different Ways to Divide 50 People into Five Districts

Source: Adapted from Christopher Ingraham, "This Is the Best Explanation of Gerrymandering You Will Ever See," Wonkblog, WashingtonPost.com, March 1, 2015, www.washingtonpost.com/news/wonk/wp/2015/03/01/this-is-the-best-explanation-of-gerrymandering-you-will-ever-see and "This Is How Gerrymandering Works," Reddit, February 28, 2015, www.reddit.com/r/woahdude/comments/2xgqss/this_is_how_gerrymandering_works/; original concept by Steven Nass.

one example of the "light" party being "cracked" across all five districts and another example of the "dark" party being "packed" into two districts. It also simply depicts two of the most intuitively troubling outcomes: one in which a significant minority of voters are completely excluded from the delegation and one in which one party wins a clear majority of the vote but a minority of the seats (the *countermajoritarian* outcome).

The example in Figure 2.1 (which I will refer to as the "Nass toy model") presents an easy shortcut to thinking about a few of the representational problems presented by gerrymandering. But it also ignores several important realities of the American political system and political life. First, even a fair map using single-member districts will not distribute seats proportional to a party's vote. Note that the only map described as "fair" in this example is one in which the blue party is virtually guaranteed to win 60% (three out of five) seats given 60% of the vote. Yet we will see in Figure 2.2 that in a typical congressional election, a party winning 60% of the vote should expect about 70% of the seats even absent intentional partisan gerrymandering. So the "fair" map in the toy graphic would actually be slightly historically biased toward the minority party.

Second, the American electorate is not unchangeable. Throughout our history, wave elections favoring one party have been regular occurrences, with a reverse wave sometimes following shortly thereafter (e.g., Democrats went from winning the congressional popular vote by 11 points in 2008 to losing it by 7 points in 2010). The toy graphic seems to assume an entirely stable electorate and gives no consideration to the fact that if one or two voters in each district were to change their minds in the "unfair" maps, the results might be entirely different. In contrast, in the one "perfect" map, every district is entirely saturated with voters from the same party such that no plausible shift in public opinion would likely cause a change in the delegation. The fact that this map would likely be entirely unresponsive to changes in voter preference in either direction is also not given any weight in the assessment of this map as "perfect."

Finally, there may be many other considerations besides the partisan makeup of a delegation that voters value in deciding whether a map is "fair," including the backgrounds and qualities of the actual member elected and the policy and legislation that the resulting body produces. But in the interest of simplicity, none of this is incorporated into the toy graphic. Instead, the sole measure of fairness appears to be the partisan balance of a single election iteration compared to pure proportional representation.

The remainder of this chapter outlines three ways in which this toy model of gerrymandering and its associated judgments about fairness in representation are inadequate. Each of these challenges an assumption implicitly made in the Nass model, as follows:

1. *The assumption of singular interests.* This assumes that voters care only about the partisan makeup of the legislative body or their delegation to the exclusion of other factors. But there are many different types of competing claims that a citizen might reasonably make about how the quality of representation should be assessed, which might invoke such considerations as the individual elected to the seat, other demographic characteristics of representation, or the actual policy emerging from the legislature. Thus the fairness of representation should be considered along several dimensions beyond the partisan division of a delegation in a particular election or which party wins the majority of a delegation.

2. *The assumption of proportional representation,* This assumes that the most just or effective method of assigning seats to a political party is always in proportion to the party's share of the vote. But even if we are measuring only the partisanship of the delegation, it is inappropriate to use proportionality as the only fair benchmark. Particularly in single-member district systems, elections historically overrepresent majority parties when translating votes to legislative seats, even when there is no partisan motivation or bias involved. And there exist strong normative arguments why this overrepresentation may be desirable.

3. *The assumption of an unchanging electorate.* This assumes that the partisanship of the electorate is stable across time and that voters rarely change their preferences in a way that might demand a corresponding change to their representation. But it is inappropriate to assess the results of one election as though they are a permanent state of government. The idea that government will be responsive to changes in the will of the public over time may be at least as strong a republican principle as the idea that a government will reflect the will of the public in a single instantiation of an election.

The conclusion of the chapter enhances this toy model in light of these additional considerations to show how the initial conclusions it draws are faulty and incomplete. The remainder of the book explores this deeper understanding of the synergy between districting and representation legally and empirically.

Diverse Norms of Representation: Challenging the Assumption of Singular Interests

Assessing the effects of a gerrymander requires us to develop some concept for how to measure what is "good" or "bad" about a specific map, or what is "fair" or "unfair." To do this, we might begin by thinking about what a citizen or voter might want or claim from their government and how we might want our government to address these claims.

In any election or government outcome, some voters will be happy with the results, other voters will be unhappy, and still others will be happy with some facets of the result and unhappy with others. The election and policy process will naturally involve "winners" and "losers," and the concept of majority rule is rooted in the goal of maximizing the number of winners and minimizing the number of losers. But democratic politics is certainly not as simple as assuming that a voter will be happy if they voted for a winning candidate and unhappy if they voted for a losing candidate. There are many different ways in which a voter might feel represented or unrepresented by their government, and thus several different normative claims that citizens might make on their government. Each of these claims might require a different kind of measurement if we are going to assess the true quality of an electoral system in general or a legislative map specifically. There are countless possible variations of these claims, but I will list five important "representation norms" that might feasibly be conceptualized and measured.[3]

Policy/Median Representation

In a republican system of government, public elections are for the most part seen not as an end in their own right but as a means toward electing representatives who will vote on policies to benefit the voting public. Thus a voter might feel that they are fully represented by their government only if their preferences are ultimately enacted into policy; in a majoritarian system of government, this might be defined at the electoral stage as having their interests represented by the median legislator, who has the power to determine party control of the body. In the case of a state legislative body, it might be very appropriate to judge a gerrymander by the composition, and the resulting legislator, of its median district. We might think of this as the probability that a voter's interests will be in majority control of the legislature. And the concept of the median *legislator* as pivotal to policy has been used in several instances to evaluate representation systems. For example, Gilligan and Matsusaka (2006) argue that the fairness of a districting scheme be assessed by the distance of the median legislator from the median voter, and Krehbiel, Meirowitz, and Romer (2005) use average distance from the median delegation member as one of two welfare measures in simulation results.

In the case of a congressional map, where a single state elects only a small portion of the legislature, it might not be as sensible to assign particular importance to the median district or legislator. Nevertheless, several scholars suggest judging the constitutionality of a partisan gerrymander by its median district election result, even in the case of congressional maps, discussed in more detail in Chapter 5.

Compositional Representation

As an alternative to the policy median norm of representation, the compositional measure of representation judges a map by the entire composition of its resulting legislature or delegation. The "compositional" norm of representation contrasts with the "policy median" norm in that it does not hold any particular member as pivotal but rather considers the ideology of every member of the legislature equally in assessing how well a voter is represented.

We can observe a broad interpretation of compositional representation in the early twenty-first century debate over majority-minority districting. For those advocating that districts be drawn where a racial minority will have an effective majority, it is not enough that Democrats have majority control of the chamber or the delegation; it also matters *what sort* of Democrats are elected, and electing members that more closely reflect the ideologies of minority constituents can be worth sacrificing some probability of majority control. We see this debate among liberals in the U.S. Supreme Court decision *Georgia v. Ashcroft* (2003). In *Ashcroft*, Georgia Democrats, including African American leaders, drew a state legislative map that reduced the number of districts with large Black majorities but dramatically increased the number of districts with substantial Black "influence" (30–50% Black voting-age population). The hope was that by spreading Black voters around, African Americans might not maximize their "symbolic" representation (in terms of the number of Black legislators) but would maximize their "substantive" representation (by electing more Democrats who would vote in their interests). The U.S. Attorney General and Georgia Republicans charged that this was a violation of §5 of the Voting Rights Act, as reducing the number of clear majority-minority districts constituted retrogression.

The Court found for the State of Georgia (and thus the state Democrats) by a 5–4 vote, with the five conservative justices siding with the Democrats, and the four liberal justices siding with the Republicans. There was thus a disagreement between liberal politicians and liberal judges as to whether "influence districts" constituted sufficiently equal representation for minorities. Perhaps most succinctly representing the deep ambivalence of the Black community in this case, Congressman John Lewis, a civil rights leader, supported the Georgia plan and testified in its favor in the *Ashcroft* case but went on in 2006 to advocate for an amendment to the Voting Rights Act that would overturn the Court's ruling upholding the map (Issacharoff et al. 2007).

Under this nuanced conception, the identity and ideology of every single legislator are important to determining whether and to what extent a voter feels compositionally represented. But in the context of partisan gerrymandering, we might simplify this into merely measuring the partisan composition of a delegation. Under this measure, each additional Democrat elected contributes equally to the satisfaction of Democratic voters. This is the assumption that largely underlies most measures of partisan bias that do *not* use the 50/50 point as a pivotal measure, including the efficiency gap measure that is incorporated into later chapters.

Personal/Dyadic Representation

In addition to the shape of the legislature as a whole, we might also think it is important for many voters to feel "personally" represented by the person or persons representing the district in which the voter lives. The contrast between "personal representation" and "virtual representation" dates back at least as far as the early stages of the American Revolution. Arguing against the claim of "taxation without representation," members of the British Parliament countered that although American colonists had no direct power to elect members of Parliament, their interests were still "virtually represented" by other members who voted in line with American interests. Regardless of whether the British were in fact looking out for the American colonies, the modern question here is whether the voter gains anything by having one or more representatives under their direct electoral control, personally assigned to represent their interests, or whether it is merely important that the voter have *someone* in the legislature defending those interests.

The fact that single-member districts allow for such direct "dyadic" representation may be an advantage of the American plurality-rule system over systems employing proportional representation or even multimember districts.[4] In an electoral system such as Israel's, where votes are cast for party lists rather than individual candidates, voters may be able to more closely match their interests with one of the many parties represented nationwide in the legislature, but voters will not have individuals specifically designated as their representative, and thus no individual specifically accountable for their activities to a discrete group of voters. "Constituent service," the responsiveness to individual voter requests in interacting with government, is almost universally seen as an essential job of a U.S. legislator, and this responsibility will be almost entirely absent under a party-list model. For this reason, the complicated mixed-member models used in Germany might seem to best balance this interest, with the overall partisan composition of the legislature being based on national vote proportions, but with each voter also being assigned to a single district with a single representative elected through plurality rule.

In the gerrymandering context, we might ask: Should a voter care that their individual representative disagrees with them on most issues, as long as there are a sufficient number of agreeable members elected from other districts? Scholars advocating for "safe districts" in fact use the satisfaction of voters with *their own representative* as a crucial metric in their argument (see Buchler 2005; Brunell 2008). Brunell argues that safe, noncompetitive districts promote better democratic representation because they allow large majorities of voters to elect representatives they are happy with, regardless of the overall balance of the legislature.

One can see this inherent trade-off within the context of majority-minority districting by comparing *Gomez v. Watsonville* (1988) to *Voinovich v. Quilter* (1993). *Gomez* provides an example where a court rejected a remedy to vote dilution because it failed to provide sufficient personal representation to minority voters, despite the fact that the map achieved reasonable virtual (proportional) representation. In *Gomez*, Latinos represented 37% of the voting-age population, and the plaintiff's proposal drew two majority-Latino districts (out of six) but still left the majority of the Latino population spread throughout the remainder of the majority-white districts. The district court rejected this map, arguing that although the plaintiff's proposal may represent Latinos proportionally, it would still not enable enough individual voters to elect a member of their group. Moving more Latinos into majority-Latino districts probably would not have increased the total number of Latinos on the city council compared with the plaintiff's plan (in fact, it may have made the members in the other districts less responsive to Latinos), but it might have allowed more Latinos to feel that their *personal* representative (not just those in other districts) represented their interests.[5]

By contrast, the *Voinovich* plaintiffs complained that an Ohio state legislative map packed too many African Americans into overwhelmingly Black districts. This map also achieved sufficient proportionality, but here plaintiffs wanted to trade feeling actually represented by a member of their group for increased influence on the overall composition of the legislature. To the *Voinovich* plaintiffs, being a member of a very safe majority-Black district represented not a democratic or expressive good but simply a wasted vote. It would seem that these plaintiffs were content to feel only "virtually" represented so long as the overall composition of the legislature was proportionate.

Discursive Representation

A fourth potential dimension of representation acknowledges that not all political outcomes are determined by formal moments of public election, legislative organization, or bill ratification. Rather, politics and policy are also formed gradually and informally through political *discourse*. This could include organized legislative debate, unstructured negotiations between legislators, political debates and campaigning covered in the news media, and even discussion of politics among friends and family. Through the process of political discourse, viewpoints might be heard, considered, and even become influential or decisive without the need for the legally prescribed elections or legislative process. But in order for a viewpoint to be heard, the viewpoint must first be permitted in the debate. The inclusion of a viewpoint in the discourse might be termed *discursive representation*.

I use the term "discursive representation" here as advanced by Dryzek and Niemeyer in their 2008 article with that title; it is related to "the politics of presence" discussed by Canon and others working on racial representation. Dryzek and Niemeyer use the example of the completely unelected Bono (lead singer of the Irish rock band U2) as a discursive representative for Africa in open public dialogue. But within the framework of the U.S. Congress, I will confine my definition to debates within the American legislative process. In this case, while other measures of representation may assume that each additional marginal legislator contributes equally in their ability to represent an interest, we might also imagine that a single voice within a deliberative body can be uniquely powerful. Indeed, Dryzek and Niemeyer argue that "there is no need for proportionality in discursive representation" (485). But unlike "personal" representation, there is no need for a voter's interests to be represented discursively by the legislator they elect from their own district; that voice just needs to be present somewhere in the body.

The relevance of this dimension to the representation of racial minorities is probably best exemplified by drawing examples from the U.S. Senate, which in recent years has often had either zero or one African American member. Canon (1999) recounts an instance when Carol Moseley Braun, the lone Black member of the Senate, was able to convince seventy-four colleagues to vote against renewing a patent on a Confederate flag insignia, defeating a measure that would have sailed through in a nongermane amendment were it not for her passion.

Moseley Braun's 1998 defeat left the Senate without a Black member, a loss that became particularly relevant on January 6, 2001. During the counting of electoral votes, twenty representatives, most of them members of the Congressional Black Caucus, rose to file objections to the electoral votes of Florida. However, such objections had to be sponsored by both a representative and a senator, and no senator was willing to sign on as a cosponsor. Vice President Al Gore was forced to rule each of these objections out of order. Thus, while the presence of a single African American senator might not have been able to affect the ultimate outcome of this election, it is almost certain that the "discourse" within the Congress would have taken a very different turn.

Two recent examples also show the potential influence of a single member representing a unique discourse on the national political debate. In June 2018, Alexandria Ocasio-Cortez, a twenty-eight-year-old Latina former bartender and self-described socialist, defeated Democratic Party Caucus Chair Joe Crowley in the congressional primary for the safely Democratic 14th District in New York. Despite her limited experience and seniority, Ocasio-Cortez immediately became a nationally recognized political figure and was able to inject ideas such as the "Green New Deal" into the political dialogue. Largely because of her unique background and perspective, she was able to exert an influence on the direction of the Democratic Party disproportionate to the de jure power of a single freshman member of Congress. This is likely because people of similar background or belief found a *discursive* representative in her, regardless of whether they were residents of her district. Ocasio-Cortez was not formally their representative in the legislature, but rather their representative in the dialogue. And for this purpose, having a vote in Congress is much less important than having a voice that would be heard by the media and other leaders.

On the other side of the political spectrum, Congressman Justin Amash, a Michigan Republican, made national news in May 2019 with a series of Twitter posts advocating beginning an impeachment inquiry of President Donald Trump. During his congressional career, beginning in 2010, Amash had built up a reputation as a consistently libertarian and sometimes iconoclastic member of his party's caucus. His tweets were quickly hailed by many in the media as a rare sign of an independent and thoughtful perspective on Trump's presidency among Republican legislators, and many called on Amash to run for president on the Libertarian Party ticket. Like Ocasio-Cortez, Amash's formal legislative power within his caucus was likely very small, and his stance likely did little to increase the actual chance of President Trump's impeachment. But his choice to represent a dialogue unique among members of his party made him appear to be the representative of dissatisfied Republicans and Libertarians across the country, and perhaps caused many conservatives to look at the allegations against the president from a fresh perspective (though it also precipitated Amash leaving the Republican caucus a short time later).

In this way, discursive representation also intersects with a notion that Mansbridge (2003) refers to as "surrogate representation," in which a voter who does not feel well represented by their formal representation instead finds some sense of representation in a member from another constituency. Mansbridge cites Barney Frank, the first openly gay member of Congress, as an example of a surrogate representative for many in the gay community in the late twentieth century. We might also see Frank as representing a unique background that gave him influence on the dialogue surrounding gay rights during this period disproportionate to his formal role in Congress.

When thinking about discursive representation, we are thus almost always considering the diversity of viewpoints represented within the parties, or perhaps representatives outside the major parties. Thus the way an electoral system facilitates robust primary elections or third-party participation may be more important than the balance of seats between the major parties. For example, a system of pure proportional representation might facilitate discursive representation in one way by allowing small parties relatively easy entry into the legislature. But the American system of allocation of geographic districts to each state might facilitate discursive representation entirely differently by guaranteeing that the perspective of each state is represented in the national legislature (and even more so in the U.S. Senate).

Responsive Representation

All of the definitions discussed so far have assumed that we can measure the quality of representation by looking at a single snapshot in time. Yet merely through the process of holding regular and frequent elections, our electoral system assumes that the composition of our legislature should change over time, presumably in response to changes in either the makeup or the attitudes and positions of the electorate. Thus a voter might reasonably claim that being well represented demands not only that the legislature or their representative resemble the voter at a particular moment in time, but also that the legislature or representative should *change* when the opinion of the voter changes. We might generally term this *responsive* representation, the idea that changes in the electorate should correspond to changes in the delegation.

When we should expect change in a responsive system might vary under different conceptions of the voter-representative relationship. Mansbridge (2003) delineates two different conceptions of responsive representation, one forward-looking and another backward-looking. Under "promissory representation," the representative makes promises during the election about future performance, and then is judged by the voters in future elections based on whether promises were kept. Under "anticipatory representation," the representative once in office attempts to act in a way that will satisfy future voters, potentially allowing the representative to anticipate changes to the electorate. But in both cases, a failure by the representative to meet their normative obligation should lead to a change in representation in the next election cycle.

Both of these concepts might qualify as responsive variants of personal representation, in that they cover the dyadic relationship of voters to their own representative. But we might also conceive that the election system as a whole be responsive to shifts. An example of this might be the theory of "responsible party government," popularized in works like Ranney (1962). Under this conception, the normative obligation of an electoral system is twofold. First, it should enable the election of a party to power that will allow the party to enact its policy agenda. But second, and just as important, it should allow voters to displace the party in power with a different party, which could then enact a different agenda, if and when voters become dissatisfied. Scholars during the mid-twentieth century worried that the fractured nature of U.S. electoral and party systems, in contrast to parliamentary systems in Europe, had made responsible party government impossible by discouraging internal party unity and encouraging divided government. Seeking to measure responsive representation might thus involve measuring the ease with which a change in vote translates into a change in representation, either on an individual seat or a policy majority basis.

Relationship to Substantive and Descriptive Representation

Much of the normative scholarship surrounding redistricting, most commonly as it relates to racial gerrymandering, has discussed representational claims along yet another axis: the potential conflict between *substantive* and *descriptive* representation. While these are both very broad concepts with many possible definitions, *substantive* representation is, loosely speaking, the match between the voter's policy preferences and the policy outcomes of the legislature (or at least the power and activities of a member in actually implementing policy), while *descriptive* representation is the match between descriptive demographic traits of the voter and their representation (most often racial or ethnic identification, but this could include gender, religion, economic class, etc.). In the racial gerrymandering context, this is most often expressed as the possible trade-off between drawing a smaller number of majority-minority districts likely to elect a member of a previously underrepresented racial minority, or drawing a larger number of coalition districts likely to elect a white representative who will be responsive to the policy preference of the minority (see, e.g., Lublin 1997; Cameron, Epstein, and O'Halloran 1996; Shotts 2001; Casellas 2010).

Each of the concepts I have outlined may be defined in such a way as to model representation along a single ideological or partisan dimension. But descriptive representation implies that a second dimension, such as the race of the representative, must be considered not merely as an instrument for representation along the first dimension. As such, no single one of the representation norms is an exact substitute for this concept of descriptive representation. Rather, three norms (compositional, personal, and discursive) encompass various facets of what might be valued as descriptive representation, in contrast to the strict policy median definition, which comes closest to most definitions of *substantive* representation.

Specifically, descriptive representation demands that a particular voice be included in the governing body, whether or not that voice is ultimately decisive in policy outcomes. Under discursive representation, that voice can come from anywhere in the legislature and can be but a single voice among many. Under compositional representation, a single voice still has value, but it gains proportionate value as its numbers grow (and loses value as its opponent's numbers grow). And under personal representation, it is important that the voter have a direct electoral connection to the voice that they elect, that is, that the voter is personally empowered. So the concepts I have outlined are all informative on the debate between substantive and descriptive representation, despite not clearly representing either side in a single measure.

Nonrepresentational Normative Considerations

Beyond the quality or fairness of representation, there might be other normative considerations that come into play in considering an aspect of the electoral system. These might include ease of citizen participation or trust and confidence in government. While both of these are likely to increase as perceived quality of representation increases, each might also be influenced by other factors. For example, consider the geographic shape of a district. If a district is very strangely shaped or does not follow well-known existing boundaries, it may be more difficult for voters to know who their representative is, and thus to acquire relevant information necessary to participate in the process. Additionally, very strangely shaped districts may naturally cause citizens to be more suspicious of the motives behind their creation. Even in cases where there is no difference in the representation or policy that a map produces, voters may trust their government less when it is created by a suspicious-looking map rather than an aesthetically pleasing one.

Some of these considerations, especially district compactness and congruence with existing political boundaries, are frequently given the shorthand label "traditional districting criteria." As we will see in Chapters 3 and 7, both courts and reformers proposing guidelines for commissions often place great weight on these "traditional" criteria, perhaps because they are easily evaluated and understood by the practitioners and the public, in contrast to the nebulous and multidimensional representational interests I have described. Nevertheless, as I discuss further in the concluding chapter, I put relatively little weight throughout this book on the inherent value of pleasing-looking districts, as the actual geographic distribution of voters tends to be messy, and districts are meant to represent those people. But it is important to acknowledge the arguments in favor of criteria like compactness that a pure focus on representation might not capture.

Translating Votes into Seats: Challenging the Assumption of Proportional Representation

On a purely intuitive level, it may strike us that the fairest way to translate the votes a party receives in a national legislative election into seats in the legislative body would be to give each party a proportion of the seats roughly equal to the proportion of votes the party received. Such a system would typically be termed "proportional representation," and some form of this is common in many national legislatures, especially in continental Europe and Latin America (see, e.g., Golder 2005).

Yet legislative elections in the United States have never assigned legislative seats to parties on the basis of proportional representation. Rather, elections to the House of Representatives are always assigned only a single winner, almost always the individual candidate who receives the most votes in the general election. Parties are usually relevant to the extent that they are assigned a ballot line in the general election round, but the total number of votes that candidates from a party collectively win is never relevant when awarding seats.

Such a system may be called "single-member plurality" (SMP) rule or "first past the post," and is predominant in the English-speaking world. In such systems, it is very common, to the point of being the rule rather than the exception, for the party winning the most votes to win a substantially *greater* percentage of the seats than proportionality would award them. This is often seen as a feature rather than a bug of SMP systems, as it makes it more likely that effective and stable majority governments will be formed.[6] Several studies have found that in specific political systems there is a ratio that regularly predicts the way votes will translate into seats in an SMP system. More complicated models include the "cube rule" or a logit or probit relationship. But analysis of more than a century of elections suggests that a very simple ratio of seats to votes (sometimes called a "swing ratio") fits the U.S. House of Representatives extremely well.

Edward Tufte (1973) performed an analysis of congressional elections between 1900 and 1970 and found a long-term swing ratio of 2.09. That is, for every 1% increase in vote share, a party can expect on average to win an additional 2% of seats. Writing in the 1970s, Tufte also found evidence that "a persistent bias has favored the Democratic party" and that "in the last few elections, the swing ratio has decreased considerably" (543).

Yet with the benefit of fifty years of additional election data, we can observe that the 2:1 swing ratio seen in the first two-thirds of the twentieth century has held firm, and evidence for any long-term bias in favor of one party is scant. Figure 2.2 plots the two-party Democratic share of the aggregated popular vote for the House of Representatives against Democratic seat share for each of the twenty-five elections from 1972 to 2020. Elections from each decade are shown in a different color and shape. A linear regression of Democratic vote advantage against seat advantage yields the result shown in Table 2.1 (with the regression line shown by the dashed line in Figure 2.2).

The relationship of seats to votes over the past five decades in House elections has been almost exactly 2:1, with a very insignificant bias in favor of the Democrats of 0.14%. Thus the swing ratio found by Tufte at least as far back as 1900 has continued into the present day. While no bias is found across the five-decade data set, we do see in Figure 2.2 some evidence of bias within subsets of the data. Elections prior to 1994 tend to fall above the regression line, indicating Democratic bias, while elections after 2002 tend to fall below the line, indicating Republican bias. A regression analysis of elections just since 2002 shows a bias in favor of Republicans of 1.8%, significant at $p < 0.05$. So just as Tufte found evidence of Democratic bias in his most recent data, we see some evidence of Republican bias in our current century. This recent bias may be partially due to nonintentional factors, most prominently the geographic sorting of partisans. But the greater number of Republican partisan gerrymanders during the past two decades is also a likely culprit, as much of the rest of this book explores.

Table 2.1 Linear Regression of Seats to Votes in U.S. Congressional Elections, 1972–2020

Democratic Vote Advantage	
Democratic Seat Advantage	2.00***
	(0.19)
Constant	0.0014
	(0.0071)
R-squared	.84

Notes: Standard errors in parenthesis. Both variables are coded as Democratic proportion of vote/seats over 0.5.

*** p<0.01.

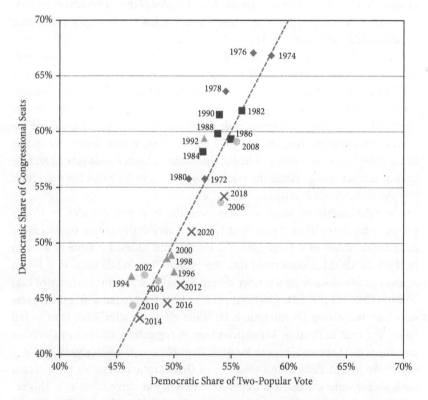

Figure 2.2 Relationship of Seats to Votes in U.S. Congressional Elections, 1972–2020

So we might draw three basic conclusions about the past fifty years of congressional elections from the graph in Figure 2.2. First, there has been some short-term bias in the overall assignment of seats to each party based on vote share, but almost no long-term bias. Second, there has been significant variance even in the short term in the vote share for each party. The two-party Democratic vote has ranged from 46.3% (in 1994) to 58.5% (in 1974), and just between 2008 and 2010 it fell from 55.5% to 46.5%. Finally, congressional elections are very responsive to changes in this vote share, but in a long-term predictable way, closely resembling a 2:1 seats:votes slope. Among the representation norms discussed in the previous section, this hyperresponsiveness might be seen as being a benefit to *responsive* representation and perhaps *policy median* representation (since larger working majorities may facilitate the policy process) but harmful to *compositional* representation (since the legislature will not proportionately represent all groups) and perhaps *discursive* representation (since small minorities may be completely shut out).

Fairness and Countermajoritarian Outcomes

It is clear that in the American system of legislative elections, proportional representation is neither guaranteed nor expected, and perhaps not even desirable. Yet there are still *some* deviations from proportional representation that intuitively strike us as more unfair than others. One example may be when a significant *minority* of the population is *completely excluded* or almost completely excluded from representation. For example, consider a party that wins 30% of the vote but 0%, or even only 5%, of the seats. This is going to violate not only our sense of proportionate or compositional fairness but also our desire for discursive representation, the idea that all major points of view should at least have some voice in the decision-making process.

Another example of intuitive unfairness would be a *countermajoritarian* outcome (sometimes called an *electoral inversion*), in which a party receiving a *majority* of the vote *fails to receive a majority* of the seats. For example, when one party win 55% of the vote but only wins 45% of the seats. The 50% threshold in a representative body is uniquely important in most legislatures, as a majority of legislative votes is typically required to enact policy. Thus a party winning 55% of seats, compared with a party winning 45% of seats, may achieve substantive policy victories with frequency far disproportionate to their seats share, thus violating our sense of fair policy median representation. Additionally, a countermajoritarian outcome violates our most basic understanding of the principle of democracy, which is that the option with the support of a greater number of voters should prevail over the option with the support of fewer voters.

Nevertheless, there are some situations in which policy-median representation, and thus the potential for a countermajoritarian outcome, should be a
predominant fairness consideration, and others in which it should be largely
ignored.

Consider these two elections results drawn from recent American history:

Example 1: Party A wins 52% of the two-party vote, and 62% of seats.
Example 2: Party B wins 49% of the two-party vote, and 57% of seats.

Intuitively, Example 2 probably strikes you as less "fair" than Example 1, even
though Example 1 deviates more from proportionality. And in these particular
cases, you would probably be right to find Example 2 more normatively troubling. Both of these are examples from recent American presidential elections,
with the "seats" being seats to the electoral college. Example 1 is from 2012, when
Barack Obama won a small popular vote victory but an electoral college blowout.
Example 2 is from 2016, when Donald Trump won the electoral college despite
losing the popular vote to Hillary Clinton. In 2012, given that the popular vote
winner also won the electoral college majority, no one gave a second thought
to the *size* of that majority, and in fact electoral college blowouts are quite frequent. But the 2016 outcome was extremely controversial, spurring a national
debate over abolishing the electoral college and leading several states to adopt
a "Popular Vote Compact." Our different reactions to these two situations are
indeed quite sensible. "Representation" in the electoral college is only a vehicle
to electing a single executive, and so while Democrats in 2016 may have gotten
significant electoral college "representation," this representation proved substantively useless in gaining policy influence over the executive branch. And thus
whether the outcome is "majoritarian" or not may reasonably be our primary
fairness consideration.

However, consider these two additional examples:

Example 3: Party B wins 52% of the two-party vote and 75% of seats.
Example 4: Party B wins 47% of the two-party vote and 64% of seats.

Following the logic of Examples 1 and 2, we might intuitively find Example 4
less fair than Example 3, because only Example 4 is countermajoritarian, despite Example 3's being a greater deviation from proportionality. Yet the context in these examples is very different from the previous two. Both of these are
results of Republican congressional gerrymanders in the 2012 election cycle.
Example 4 is from Michigan, where Democrats won the vote majority but
only five of fourteen seats, while Example 3 is from Ohio, where Republicans
won the narrow majority and twelve of sixteen seats. Each representative in

both states represents a discrete constituency, and voters in these constituencies may rightly care deeply about the individual they elect. But it is also true that the composition of a *state's* delegation to the U.S. Congress is not substantively meaningful to determining policy outcomes, except as it contributes toward the national partisan majority. And in 2012, this *national* partisan outcome was indeed countermajoritarian, with Republicans winning 53% of national seats despite winning only 49% of the two-party vote. Yet while the state outcome in Michigan was itself countermajoritarian and Ohio's was not, Ohio's map contributed *more* to the countermajoritarian outcome at the national level, with Republicans winning three to four seats more than might be expected under a fair map, compared to winning two more than expected in Michigan.

So in the case of state congressional maps, we should probably value each marginal seat equally and assign almost no importance to the median of majority-determining seats in each state. In contrast, in electing presidential electoral college electors, *only* the 269th and 270th median seats are important, with marginal seats above or below this threshold being of virtually no substantive value. Elections to state legislatures represent an intermediate case. Here, each state draws the map for the entire legislature, and holding a majority of seats in a legislature is inherently important to substantive outcomes. But having a very narrow majority can also be perilous, and the size of one's delegation, whether in the majority or minority, may be crucial to a party's impact on debate and policy. In the congressional context that is the focus of this book, this may lead to a preference for bias measures that value compositional representation over median representation.

Role of Proportional Representation and Single-Member Districts in Countermajoritarian Outcomes

As shown in Figure 2.2, U.S. congressional elections have consistently displayed a "hypermajoritarian" propensity, common to most single-member district (SMD) systems, in which vote majorities are exaggerated when translated into seat majorities. They have also occasionally led to countermajoritarian outcomes when the national popular vote was extremely close, though these instances are uncommon and might be explained by disproportionate gerrymandering control by one party. Countermajoritarian outcomes can result from SMD systems in districts drawn with no partisan motive, sometimes from a naturally asymmetric distribution of partisans or even from one party getting "lucky" and winning the vast majority of close races. In the 1951 U.K. Parliamentary election, Winston Churchill's Conservative Party won a majority of seats despite losing the popular vote to Labour by 0.8%, and the National Party in New Zealand won legislative majorities in consecutive elections in 1978 and 1981 while losing the popular vote to Labour both times. Countermajoritarian outcomes are even possible in largely proportional systems, based on idiosyncratic factors like representation thresholds, quota calculations, and seat allocation across districts (see, e.g., Miller 2015).[7]

Additionally, we may see SMDs systematically biased for or against minority parties based on the geographic distribution of their voters, with geographically concentrated minorities more consistently successful than dispersed minorities of similar size (e.g., compare the recent electoral success in U.K. elections of the concentrated Scottish National Party with failures of the more dispersed Greens and U.K. Independence Party). This propensity is a major consideration in racial and ethnic gerrymandering in the United States.

In the U.S. partisan context, some of these considerations become much simpler due to the overwhelming dominance of just two parties in virtually every U.S. state. But other considerations become more complicated, in that each state largely chooses its own method of drawing districts. The choice of states to implement a proportionate or more hypermajoritarian system of districts should not lead to systematically countermajoritarian outcomes, as long as each state's plan is individually fair (in the sense of being symmetrical) and each state chooses the same system, even if the distribution of partisans is uneven. Of course, the system may become systematically countermajoritarian if individual states choose biased plans. But additionally, such systematic bias may also occur if states individually choose *different fair plans*.

As an example, consider a hypothetical nation of five states, where each state elects twenty members to a hundred-member national legislature, with only two parties, Democrats and Republicans. States 1 and 2 are heavily Democratic, generally voting 30% and 40% for the Republicans, respectively, while States 4 and 5 are the reverse, voting 60% and 70% Republican, respectively. State 3 is a swing state, and let's say it votes 45% Republican in a given example election, yielding a total national Republican vote of 49%.

First, let's imagine that each state implements a system of proportional representation, in which each party wins the same proportion of seats as the number of votes they won.[8] Table 2.2 shows the election results under that system. In State 1, the Republicans win 30% of the vote, and thus six out of the twenty seats. Nationwide, the overall composition of the legislature perfectly reflects the composition of the voters, with the Democrats winning fifty-one seats based on 51% of the vote, and a majoritarian outcome is achieved.

This result should probably be unsurprising. But next, let's imagine that each state instead draws "fair" SMDs that follow the historically observed pattern of symmetrically exaggerating seat majorities based on a 2:1 seats:votes ratio. Now,

Table 2.2 Toy Example of Legislative Composition under Proportional Representation

State	Electorate	Gerrymander	GOP Vote %	GOP Seats (Out of 20)	GOP Seat %
1	Very Democratic	Proportional Representation	30	6	30
2	Democratic	Proportional Representation	40	8	40
3	Swing	Proportional Representation	45	9	45
4	Republican	Proportional Representation	60	12	60
5	Very Republican	Proportional Representation	70	14	70
Total			49	49	49

Table 2.3 Toy Example of Legislative Composition under Single-Member Districts

State	Electorate	Gerrymander	GOP Vote %	GOP Seats (Out of 20)	GOP Seat %
1	Very Democratic	Typical Fair SMDs	30	2	10
2	Democratic	Typical Fair SMDs	40	6	30
3	Swing	Typical Fair SMDs	45	8	40
4	Republican	Typical Fair SMDs	60	14	70
5	Very Republican	Typical Fair SMDs	70	18	90
Total			49	48	48

in State 1, Republicans only win two of the twenty seats based on the same 30% of the vote. The national results of this system are shown in Table 2.3.

Under fair SMDs, we see almost the same majoritarian composite results as under proportional representation, with Democrats winning 52% of seats based on 51% of the vote, and the exaggerated majorities in the heavily partisan states essentially canceling each other out.

But finally, let's imagine that each state chooses its own districting system. Three states choose "fair" systems, with State 1 choosing proportional representation of our first examples and States 4 and 5 choosing the SMDs of our second example. However, State 2 chooses a gerrymander biased toward the Democrats, in which Republicans receive only four seats despite winning 40% of the vote. (We might analogize this to the Democratic gerrymander in Maryland discussed

Table 2.4 Toy Example of Legislative Composition under Mixed Districting

State	Electorate	Gerrymander	GOP Vote %	GOP Seats (Out of 20)	GOP Seat %
1	Very Democratic	Proportional Representation	30	6	30
2	Democratic	Democratic Gerrymander	40	4	20
3	Swing	Republican Gerrymander	45	11	55
4	Republican	Typical Fair SMDs	60	14	70
5	Very Republican	Typical Fair SMDs	70	18	90
Total			49	53	53

in the *Benisek* case in Chapter 3.) State 3 chooses a gerrymander biased toward Republicans, in which Republicans win 55% of the seats despite winning only 45% of the vote (analogous to the Republican gerrymander of Pennsylvania discussed in *League of Women Voters* in Chapter 3). The national composite of these choices is shown in Table 2.4.

In this example, the choices of the individual states do *not* balance each other out. The Republicans have achieved a countermajoritarian outcome of winning 53% of the national seats despite winning only 49% of the vote. What is responsible for this? It might be natural to first assign most of the blame to State 3's Republican gerrymander, the only state whose delegation itself was countermajoritarian. But this impulse would be misguided. Reversing this gerrymandering alone would *not* reverse the countermajoritarian outcome; Republicans would still win fifty-one seats nationally based on the same voting pattern if State 3 were to adopt proportional representation, and fifty seats were the state to adopt fair SMDs, *despite keeping the Democratic gerrymander in place* in State 2. Instead, "blame" for the countermajoritarian result lies mostly with the individually "fair" choices of States 1, 4, and 5. Were State 1 to adopt fair SMDs as in Example 2, Republicans would now win forty-nine seats based on 49% of the vote, even holding both partisan gerrymanders in place. And if States 4 and 5 were to adopt the proportional representation system of State 1, again retaining partisan gerrymanders in States 2 and 3, Republicans would win just forty-seven seats from their 49% of the vote. Intentional gerrymanders do contribute to a biased outcome in this example, but a much greater factor is the choice of states to implement systems that vary not in their inherent bias but in their sensitivity to voting majorities. Thus, in evaluating a districting system, it is arguably just as important to pay attention to the responsiveness or sensitivity of a map as to its bias at any particular point, particularly in a federal system such as that in the United States, where states make such widely varied choices.

Gerrymandering, Responsiveness, and Electoral Tides: Challenging the Assumptions of an Unchanging Electorate

We have thus far seen how the fairness of a map might vary under different reasonable measurements, and how maps that individually look fair under different perspectives can become unfair when observed collectively. But the examples in Tables 2.2 through 2.4 are still oversimplified in that they deal only with a single, static election result, a snapshot in time of an electorate that is changing and evolving with the ebb and flow of partisan tides. Even during a period of strong political polarization, the partisan composition of the electorate often swings dramatically just between two consecutive election cycles (including an 18-point swing in the national congressional vote margin just between 2008 and 2010). We can account for this by making a fairly elementary change to the Nass toy model first shown in Figure 2.1. Instead of assuming that every citizen votes unerringly for the same party every election, we can allow some small fraction of Independent voters to swing from one party to the other. We can then assess the fairness of the map under different hypothetical elections: one election where Independents evenly split their vote, one election where they vote uniformly Democratic, and one where they vote uniformly Republican. By making this modest adjustment to the toy model, our judgment of what constitutes the "best map" (or, in the words of the Nass model, "Perfect Representation") changes completely. Once we allow the electorate to change over time, we see that the fairness of a map changes not only with *how* we measure it but *when* we measure it.

To see a simple example of how gerrymandering can interact with partisan tides, imagine a toy state with thirty voters, depicted in Figure 2.3. Our toy state is a swing state, evenly balanced between the parties in a neutral election year but also capable of swinging toward either party in a wave election. Forty percent of the population (twelve voters), living on the left-hand side of the state, are Democrats who always vote for the Democratic candidate. Similarly, 40% (twelve voters) on the right-hand side of the state are Republicans who always vote for the Republican. But the 20% of the population (six voters) living in the

Figure 2.3 Toy State of Thirty Voters (Ten Democrats, Ten Republicans, Five Independents)

middle of the state are Independents, who sometimes vote Democratic and sometimes vote Republican. During a "neutral" electoral environment, three of these Independents lean toward the Democrat (denoted "I/D" in the figure), while three Independents lean toward the Republican (denoted "I/R"). However, all Independents will vote Democratic in a Democratic wave election, and they will all swing to the Republicans in a Republican wave election.

Now imagine that we must split our toy state into six districts with five voters each. Let us imagine four ways of gerrymandering our state and see how each gerrymander plays out in a neutral year, a Democratic wave, and a Republican wave.

The Nonpartisan Gerrymander

Perhaps the easiest way to create six districts is simply to draw six horizontal rows of five voters each, as shown in Figure 2.4. Each district will be an approximate microcosm of the state as a whole, with two Democrats, two Republicans, and one Independent. In a neutral year, Democratic candidates win 50% of the vote and three seats (the top three rows with Democratic-leaning Independents), while Republicans also win 50% of votes and three seats (the bottom three rows with Republican-leaning Independents). Thus the map appears unbiased in this condition.[9]

However, in both the Democratic and Republican wave years, we see enormous sensitivity to partisan tides. In the Democratic wave, where all Independents vote Democratic, Democrats win 60% of the vote but win every seat. Conversely, in the Republican wave year, Republicans win 60% of the vote

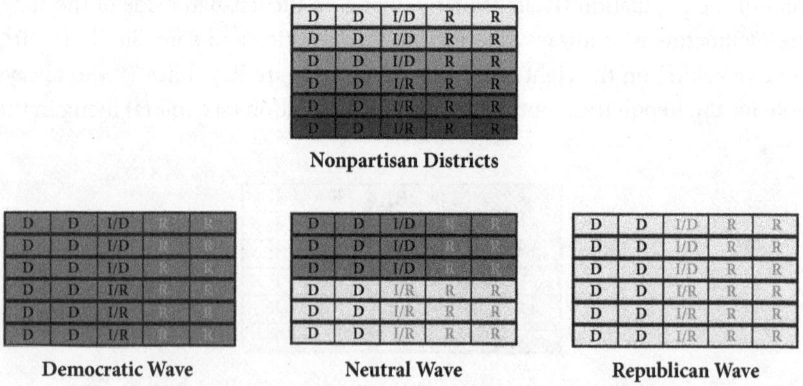

Figure 2.4 Nonpartisan Gerrymander of Toy State

and 100% of the seats. Note that under all three conditions, every seat is won by a close 3–2 margin.

The Bipartisan Gerrymander

Another way of drawing a map that is not obviously biased toward one party might be called the "bipartisan compromise," in which an equal number of safe seats are drawn for each party. An example of the bipartisan gerrymander is shown in Figure 2.5, with three safely Democratic seats on the left side of the state, and three safely Republican seats on the right side of the state. In the neutral year, this map yields the same seat totals as the nonpartisan map, with both parties winning 50% of the vote and three of the six seats. This is roughly analogous to the Perfect Representation example in the Nass toy model.

This map is starkly different from the nonpartisan map under both Democratic and Republican waves. In these wave elections, the Independent voters make no difference to the outcome, as strong partisans on a single side compose 80% of the electorate in every seat. Under all waves, the Democrats and Republicans still win three seats. Moreover, in all scenarios, there is not a single close election in any district, with all races decided by a 4–1 or 5–0 margin.

The Defensive Partisan Gerrymander

Suppose Democrats were given free rein to draw the map in our toy state. One option they might choose would be to "pack" the Republicans into two districts

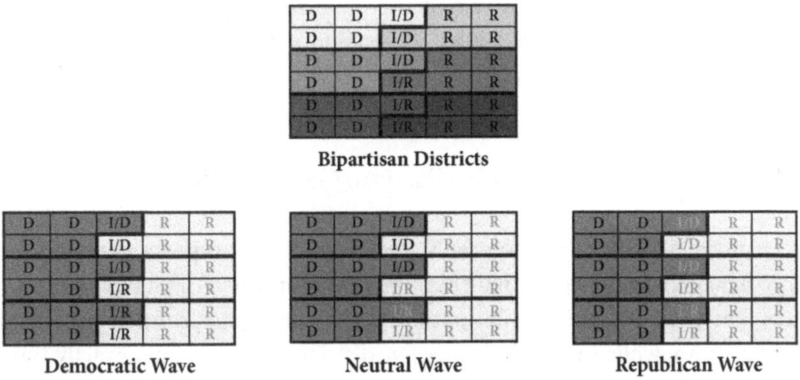

Bipartisan Districts

Democratic Wave   **Neutral Wave**   **Republican Wave**

Figure 2.5 Bipartisan Gerrymander of Toy State

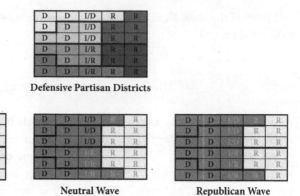

Figure 2.6 Defensive Democratic Gerrymander of Toy State

and make sure that Democrats hold the majority in the remaining districts. Figure 2.6 shows this example, with two right-hand side districts entirely packed with Republicans, while the other four districts each contain three Democrats and two Independents or Republicans. In the neutral election scenario, where each party wins 50% of the vote, the Democrats now win a 4–2 seat majority.

This 4–2 seat majority remains under both the Democratic and Republican wave conditions. In the Democratic wave, the two packed Republican districts stay Republican, as they have no Independent voters. In the Republican wave, all four Democratic districts still contain a controlling majority of Democratic partisans even when all Independents vote against them. In this way, the gerrymander might be called "defensive," as it is created to build a narrow majority for the Democrats that will survive even when tides turn against them and the Republicans win a clear majority of the vote (Kang 2004). Note that in this map, many races are competitive under Republican tides, but all the close races are still won by Democrats. Under other conditions, there are few competitive races.

The Aggressive Partisan Gerrymander

If Democrats were feeling especially ambitious, it is also possible they could draw a map that will likely win them more than four seats. An example is shown in Figure 2.7. Here, five Republicans are packed into a single district in the far right column, while each of the other five districts contains either exactly three Democrats or two Democrats and one Democrat-leaning Independent. Thus, in the neutral year, when the Independents split their vote evenly, Democrats win

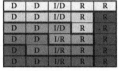

Aggression Partisan Districts

D	D	I/D		
D	D	I/D	R	
D	D	I/D		R
D	D	I/R		R
D	D	I/R		R
D	D	I/R		R

Democratic Wave

D	D	I/D		
D	D	I/D		R
D	D	I/D		R
D	D			R
D	D			R
D	D			R

Neutral Wave

D	D	I/D	R	R
D	D	I/D	R	R
D	D	I/D	R	R
D	D	I/R	R	R
D	D			R
D	D			R

Republican Wave

Figure 2.7 Aggressive Democratic Gerrymander of Toy State

five of the six seats, each by a narrow 3–2 margin, even after winning only 50% of the vote.

In the Democratic wave election, the seat distribution remains the same but with slightly fewer close elections. The big difference comes in the Republican wave, when the three Democratic-leaning Independents swing to the Republicans, and each swings the balance of a district with them. The map that was designed to institute a Democratic supermajority actually elects a Republican majority. In this manner, we might call this gerrymander "aggressive," as it wins a larger majority for the gerrymandering party in neutral years but runs a major risk of "backfire" or "dummymander" when tides turn against them. The defensive map will never win quite as many seats in good conditions but does not carry the same risk of backfire. Obviously, in addition to these two types of Democratic gerrymanders, we could draw aggressive and defensive Republican maps by drawing mirror-image districts to Figures 2.6 and 2.7.

Bias and Competitiveness in the Toy Model

Having defined our four toy gerrymandering models, we can summarize the conditions under which we observe bias, competitiveness, and responsiveness for each. To do so, we must first define each concept in the context of our toy model. With respect to bias, we would certainly intuitively and historically define an unbiased map under neutral tides (when both parties win 50% of the vote) as a map in which Democrats win three of the six seats. The more complicated question is how to define bias under strong partisan tides. Given our historical observation that in congressional elections, parties tend to win an additional 2% of seats for each additional 1% of vote, we will define an unbiased map as the map that gets as close as possible to this trend. In the case of the Democratic wave as we have defined it, where Democrats win 60% of the vote, this would mean Democrats winning four of the six seats (67%); symmetrically, we will define an unbiased map as one where Democrats win two of six seats under Republican tides. We will label a map where a party exceeds these expectations by one seat (e.g., where Democrats win four, five, and three seats, respectively, under neutral, Democratic, and Republican waves) as "biased," and a map where a party exceeds expectations by two seats as "very biased." We might analogize this to a measure of the map's "compositional" representation.

With respect to competitiveness, we define a "close" election as an election won by a vote of 3–2. We will define a map in which no elections are close as having "very low" competitiveness, a map with one to two close elections as "low," three to four close elections as "medium," five close elections as "high," and all six close elections as having "very high" competitiveness. We will define responsiveness according to the number of seats that change hands between the neutral tides condition and each of the two partisan wave conditions. A map where no seats flip under a partisan wave will be described as having "low" responsiveness. One seat flipping is described as "medium" responsiveness, and two or more seats flipping is described as "high" responsiveness. We might analogize this to the map's capacity for "responsive" representation.[10]

Table 2.5 shows the number of seats won by Democrats (out of six total districts) for each map under each condition (out of six total districts, assuming the partisan gerrymanders are drawn by Democrats).

Tables 2.6 through 2.8 evaluate each gerrymander under measures of bias, competitiveness, and responsiveness under each tides' condition. With respect to bias, the first thing to note is that *none* of the maps is unbiased under all conditions. Indeed, every map can be either biased or unbiased depending on the wave. This contrasts with the Nass toy model in Figure 2.1, where one map is definitively described as Perfect Representation and the other two are described

Table 2.5 Democratic Seats under Toy Gerrymandering Models

Gerrymander	Tides		
	Neutral	Democratic	Republican
Nonpartisan	3	6	0
Bipartisan	3	3	3
Defensive Partisan	4	4	4
Aggressive Partisan	5	5	2

Table 2.6 Bias under Toy Gerrymandering Models

Gerrymander	Tides		
	Neutral	Democratic	Republican
Nonpartisan	Unbiased	Very Biased	Very Biased
Bipartisan	Unbiased	Biased	Biased
Defensive Partisan	Biased	Unbiased	Very Biased
Aggressive Partisan	Very Biased	Biased	Unbiased

Table 2.7 Competitiveness under Toy Gerrymandering Models

Gerrymander	Tides		
	Neutral	Democratic	Republican
Nonpartisan	Very High	Very High	Very High
Bipartisan	Very Low	Very Low	Very Low
Defensive Partisan	Low	Very Low	Medium
Aggressive Partisan	High	Low	High

as "unfair." But in our adjusted toy model, the two maps that are unbiased under neutral conditions are biased under both partisan waves, though in opposite directions. Under the nonpartisan maps, every seat is won by the favored party, producing large bias in the direction of the wave. Under the bipartisan map, the delegation is evenly split, even under a 60/40 split of the electorate, resulting in bias *against* the party favored by the wave.

The defensive and aggressive Democratic partisan maps are both biased under neutral conditions, with greater bias seen in the aggressive map. But bias in both maps is reduced under Democratic tides, as we would now expect Democrats to win the majority of seats, and these maps already maximized their Democratic potential in the neutral condition. The greatest difference comes in the Republican wave condition, where the defensive map remains an unchanged Democratic majority, and thus extremely biased, while the aggressive map backfires into an unbiased Republican majority.

Unsurprisingly, the nonpartisan and bipartisan maps exhibit opposite traits with respect to responsiveness and competitiveness, with all elections being closely decided under all conditions in the nonpartisan map, but no close

Table 2.8 Responsiveness under Toy Gerrymandering Models

Gerrymander	Tides	
	Democratic	Republican
Nonpartisan	High	High
Bipartisan	Low	Low
Defensive Partisan	Low	Low
Aggressive Partisan	Low	High

elections occurring under any condition in the bipartisan map. Both the bipartisan and defensive partisan maps create identical delegations regardless of tide, so both score low on responsiveness. The defensive partisan map displays generally lower competitiveness, though at least under adverse tides several elections are close. On the other hand, the aggressive partisan map displays very high but asymmetrical responsiveness to adverse tides, with three districts flipping against the gerrymandering party, and high competitiveness under both the neutral and adverse tides conditions; it is noncompetitive only when tides favor the gerrymandering party. The Nass model in Figure 2.1 does not assess competitiveness, but it is worth noting that the one map described as Perfect Representation would almost certainly be the least competitive and least responsive.

Even in this toy model, we see how the choice of democratic norms and electoral conditions can be pivotal to our evaluation of a gerrymander. Every map is biased under some conditions and unbiased under others, and maps that perform well on one measure will almost invariably perform poorly on others. The notion that any map can be described as Perfect Representation seems almost absurd. The nonpartisan map is competitive and responsive but has the potential to exhibit extreme bias and to completely exclude a party from the delegation under wave conditions. The bipartisan map displays generally low bias but also exhibits very few competitive elections and is entirely unresponsive to tides. The aggressive partisan gerrymander has the potential to result in extremely biased outcomes when the election is close but also creates many competitive elections and has the potential to be very responsive to shifts away from the gerrymandering party. It is actually the defensive partisan gerrymander that has the least obvious upside. This map not only is biased under tied conditions, but it shows generally low competitiveness and responsiveness and has the greatest likelihood of leading to a dramatically countermajoritarian outcome of a Democratic majority during a Republican wave. Yet as we will see in subsequent chapters, it is the aggressive partisan gerrymanders, rather than the defensive or bipartisan gerrymanders, that have been most likely to generate litigation and public controversy.

Despite all these complications, there are several ways in which partisan gerrymandering still seems to violate our sense of fairness at a basic, intuitive level: the notion that voters of different parties are treated differently by our legislators or that one party might consistently hold a controlling majority of the legislature even when winning a minority of the vote seems antithetical to our basic principles of democracy. But is this intuitive unfairness also something we should consider *unlawful*? Given all the considerations and potential complications, is there a simple and practical test that a court could use, and that a mapmaker could follow, to determine when and if the use of partisanship in drawing maps violates the U.S. Constitution? Several parties in recent years have asserted that such a test can be created, which I explore in the next chapter.

3

Legal Developments and Standards in Partisan Gerrymandering

Background

Given the multitude of normative considerations evoked by the process of districting discussed in Chapter 2, it should not be surprising that courts and scholars have struggled to define the legal or constitutional injury caused by partisan gerrymandering, or the threshold about which we might measure this injury. Nevertheless, litigation surrounding partisan gerrymandering has proliferated in the past few years, with each case presenting new facts and proposing new constitutional tests. In this chapter, I explore the tests and evidence presented in each of these cases and ask whether one or any provides a clean and definitive path to resolve this long-standing legal and empirical quandary. Ultimately, I find that no case presents an easy answer, turning instead to potential political solutions that I explore through the rest of the book.

Section 2 of Article I of the Constitution requires, "The House of Representatives . . . shall be apportioned among the several States which may be included within this Union, according to their respective Numbers. . . . The actual Enumeration shall be made . . . within every subsequent Term of ten Years." In conformity with this section, seats in the U.S. Congress have been reapportioned among the states following each decennial national census, with one exception.[1] But it is only within the past sixty years that the federal government and court system have taken on a significant role in regulating the districting decisions within the states, at both the congressional and state legislative levels.

Prior to the 1960s, states often refrained from redrawing districts unless absolutely necessary (i.e., they gained or lost a congressional seat). As populations shifted from rural to urban areas over the course of the late nineteenth and early twentieth centuries, this frequently led to severely malapportioned districts, with primarily rural districts having much smaller populations than urban districts, retaining the balance of political power for the rural minority. Additionally, many state legislative chambers (particularly state senates) were organized around county lines, each county receiving equal representation regardless of population.

Ground War. Nicholas Goedert, Oxford University Press. © Oxford University Press 2022.
DOI: 10.1093/oso/9780197626627.003.0003

But these methods of redistricting were overturned by a series of Supreme Court decisions beginning with *Baker v. Carr* in 1962 (holding that the districting of state legislatures is a justiciable question), leading into *Reynolds v. Sims* (holding that state senate districts must be roughly equal in population) and *Wesberry v. Sanders* (holding that congressional districts must be equal in population) in 1964. Chief Justice Earl Warren famously justified the new standard in his *Reynolds* majority opinion by asserting, "Legislators represent people, not trees or acres. Legislators are elected by voters, not farms or cities or economic interests" (377 U.S. at 562).

With respect to state legislative districts, courts have generally found that minor population deviations (typically assumed to be less than 10% maximum deviation) do not amount to a prima facie Equal Protection claim (see *Gaffney v. Cummings* (1973)). However, the Court has demanded almost exact population equality when it comes to congressional districts, holding that "there are no de minimus population variations, which could be practicably avoided, but which nonetheless meet the standard of Art. 1, § 2, without justification" (*Karcher v. Daggett* (1983), 462 U.S. at 725). Under this demanding standard, the U.S. District Court in *Vieth v. Pennsylvania* (2002) struck down a map in Pennsylvania with a maximum population deviation of nineteen people.[2]

Beyond merely enforcing an equal population standard, the enactment of the Voting Rights Act, particularly as amended in 1982, has led to significant involvement of the federal courts in litigating the racial and ethnic dimensions of gerrymandering. The legal issues involved in this line of jurisprudence are beyond the scope of this chapter, often involving a delicate balancing act of incorporating racial considerations sufficiently to avoid vote dilution under Section 2 of the Voting Rights Act and not allowing racial considerations to predominate to an extent that might violate the Equal Protection Clause of the Fourteenth Amendment.[3]

Prior Legal History (Pre-2015)

In contrast to its active role in correcting perceived constitutional violations with regard to apportionment and racial gerrymandering, the federal courts (and the Supreme Court in particular) have been much more reluctant to police partisan maps. Prior to 2017, the Supreme Court had heard only three cases predominantly related to partisan gerrymandering. In each case, the Court declined to strike down the map at controversy or to set a clear standard for what would constitute a violation, while still holding out the theoretical possibility that a map could be so partisan as to breach this still undefined standard.

The Court arguably first stepped into the issue of partisan gerrymandering in *Gaffney v. Cummings* (1973), a case involving legislative districting in Connecticut. Unlike the subsequent cases discussed here, the maps in *Gaffney* were not drawn to achieve a biased result in favor of one party but rather to create an outcome in which both parties would be represented roughly proportionate to their vote. In doing so, the state drew districts with slightly unequal populations, and Democrats asserted a violation of equal protection. But the Supreme Court upheld the districts, holding it was permissible for the apportionment board to consider partisan interests with the goal of "achiev[ing] a rough approximation of the statewide political strengths of the Democratic and Republican parties . . . by implementing a 'political fairness' plan" (412 U.S. at 752–53). But in doing so, the Court possibly opened the door for states to incorporate partisan considerations into their maps in a more pernicious way going forward.

Davis v. Bandemer (1986) represents the Court's first attempt to tackle partisan gerrymandering head-on. *Bandemer* arose from the state legislative maps drawn by the Republican-controlled legislature in Indiana following the 1980 census. In 1982, in the first election following this census, Democrats won a majority of the popular vote for the Indiana House of Representatives (almost 52%), yet won only forty-three of the one hundred House seats. Some local instances of partisan bias were particularly severe; for example, Democrats won only 14% of the seats in Marion and Allen counties, despite winning 47% of the vote. Based on these data, a federal district court struck down the map as vote dilution in violation of the Equal Protection Clause. But, establishing a pattern repeated several times in the recent past, the plaintiff's victory was short-lived.

In *Bandemer*, the Supreme Court did take the major step of holding that partisan gerrymanders were "properly justiciable" and could potentially represent a denial of equal protection. But the Court failed to agree on a standard under which to evaluate such claims and reversed the district court's decision, holding that "the mere lack of proportional representation will not be sufficient to prove unconstitutional discrimination." Instead, Justice White's majority opinion suggests that "unconstitutional discrimination occurs only when the electoral system is arranged in a manner that will consistently degrade a voter's or a group of voters' influence on the political process as a whole" (478 U.S. at 110). Justice O'Connor went much further in a concurrence joined by Justices Berger and Rehnquist, arguing that political gerrymandering should be an entirely nonjusticiable political question (*id.* at 144).

While upholding the specific Indiana map in *Bandemer*, the Court still left room for optimism for opponents of partisan gerrymandering by clarifying that this issue was justiciable and laying out some principles for attacking it. But the Court's next confrontation on this issue did not occur until two decades later in *Vieth v. Jubelirer* (2004), and its outcome would cause any residual optimism to dissipate almost entirely. *Vieth* involved a map drawn by Republicans of Pennsylvania congressional districts designed to give their party a 14–5 or 13–6 advantage in the delegation by placing several Democratic incumbents in districts with other incumbent Democrats or in heavily Republican districts with an opposed incumbent. Several of the districts in this plan were also noted for their unusual shape; the 6th District in particular was described as a "dragon descending upon Philadelphia" (recalling the namesake "salamander" district drawn by Elbridge Gerry two centuries earlier) (541 U.S. at 340).

Just as in *Bandemer*, the Supreme Court declined to overturn the map, with the five conservative justices voting in the majority, and four liberals dissenting. Justice Scalia, writing the plurality opinion of the Court, struck a tone much closer to *Bandemer*'s concurrence than its majority opinion, arguing, "Eighteen years of essentially pointless litigation have persuaded us that *Bandemer* is incapable of principled application. We would therefore overrule that case, and decline to adjudicate these political gerrymandering claims" (*id.* at 306). Yet Scalia could not quite assemble a majority for such an extreme position. Rather, Justice Kennedy, casting the deciding vote, concurred that no justiciable standard for judging partisan maps existed, but did not completely foreclose the possibility that such a standard could arise in the future. But while Kennedy acquiesced, writing "[that] no such standard has emerged in this case should not be taken to prove that none will emerge in the future" (*id.* at 311), he was still skeptical, concluding, "[T]he failings of the many proposed standards for measuring the burden a gerrymander imposes on representational rights make our intervention improper" (*id.* at 317). Although the liberal justices, across three separate dissents, proposed several different potential tests, Kennedy found all of them unsatisfactory, though he did suggest that the First Amendment may be a fruitful argument in the future: "First Amendment concerns arise where an apportionment has the purpose and effect of burdening a group of voters' representational rights" (*id.* at 314).

Two years later, in *LULAC v. Perry* (2006), Democrats challenged a congressional map in Texas drawn by Republicans in the middle of the decade, abruptly replacing a court-drawn map that had nonetheless favored Democrats. The Supreme Court's final disposition in *LULAC* struck down a single district on racial vote dilution grounds but rejected the argument that partisan gerrymanders were unconstitutional merely by virtue of being done mid-decade. Justice Kennedy, this time writing the majority opinion, reiterated his skepticism about a manageable standard, explicitly rebuffing the partisan symmetry test and stating more generally, "[W]e are wary of adopting a constitutional standard that invalidates a map based on unfair results that would occur in a hypothetical state of affairs" (548 U.S. at 420). With no justiciable standard suggested by the Court, parties appeared largely unfettered in their efforts to draw district lines to suit their own partisan purposes for the foreseeable future, constrained mainly by state law, the equal population requirement, and the Voting Rights Act.

Recent Partisan Gerrymandering Litigation

In the wake of *Vieth* and *LULAC*, federal litigation into partisan gerrymanders was largely dormant for several years. But a combination of factors led to several lawsuits filed in state and federal courts in the mid-2010s. The 2010 elections produced a Republican wave that, when accompanied by strategic targeting of state legislative seats, yielded Republican control of state governments in many important or swing states immediately before the national census (see Daley 2016 for a narrative of the national "REDMAP" Republican strategy in this election cycle). This allowed Republicans to draw the subsequent congressional and state legislative maps for the next decade in many more, larger, and closely contested states than Democrats going into 2012. Especially in swing states, these maps in many cases were more severe and more aggressive than previously seen partisan gerrymanders (which this book explores in Chapters 5 and 6). McGann et al. (2016) argue that it was Scalia's opinion in *Vieth* that gave Republicans the freedom to gerrymander in this cycle without the looming fear of court interventions. And 2012 saw a very closely contested congressional election at the national level, which yielded the rare outcome of Republicans winning a clear majority of congressional seats despite Democrats winning a narrow majority of the national vote. This put the effects of partisan gerrymanders into much starker relief in the minds of practitioners, officials, and the interested public.

The discussion that follows summarizes the facts and arguments presented in four recent cases alleging unconstitutional partisan gerrymandering under a wide range of contexts. In each case, the map was indeed struck down by at least one court. Table 3.1 summarizes the legal context and argument of each example. For each case, I highlight both the standard suggested by the plaintiff for measuring gerrymandering and the standard adopted by the highest court that struck down the map. While each case is complex and subtle in the arguments and evidence it presents, I also try to distill one or two key tests or principles employed that distinguish the decision from those used in other contemporary cases. Because I am exploring the various standards proposed or employed to strike down partisan gerrymandering, I give much less attention in my overview of each case to arguments made by the defendants and court decisions *upholding* partisan maps. Finally, I attempt to cross-apply the principles in each case to the facts of the other cases to see if there is one principle that could decide each case in a consistent fashion. I conclude that none of the standards adopted in these cases (particularly the three cases that privilege one or two measurable standards) would find a constitutional partisan

Table 3.1 Summary of Recent Partisan Gerrymandering Cases

Case	State	Legislative Body	Party in Control	Court	Primary Claim	Stylized Test(s)
Whitford v. Gill	WI	State Assembly	GOP	Federal District Court	Equal Protection Clause	Efficiency Gap & Durability of Bias
LWV v. Pennsylvania	PA	U.S. Congress	GOP	PA Supreme Court	PA Constitution Free & Equal Clause	Compactness & Existing Subdivisions
Benisek v. Lamone	MD	U.S. Congress	Dem	Federal District Court	First Amendment	Population Movement & Chilling
Common Cause v. Rucho	NC	U.S. Congress	GOP	Federal District Court	Equal Protection Clause, First Amendment, Elections Clause	Simulation, District specific, All of above

gerrymander across all other contexts. Moreover, only one of the four maps would be found to be an unconstitutional partisan gerrymandering under each of the tests; curiously, this is the only one of the four cases that was *not* brought in federal court alleging a federal constitutional question.

Gill v. Whitford

Factual Background
At the state level, one of the clearest antimajoritarian outcomes in 2012 occurred in Wisconsin, where Republicans won 61% of the seats in the state General Assembly despite winning only 49% of the vote, the result of the "Act 43" maps enacted by a Republican-controlled legislature in 2011. In June 2015, litigation was filed against the map premised on "efficiency gap," a new principle for measuring the bias in the balance between votes and seats originally suggested by McGhee (2014). Efficiency gap is explored much further in Chapter 5, but at its heart is a "fair" seats-votes curve with zero bias and a slope of 2. In other words, when a party wins 50% of the vote, it should win 50% of the seats in a fair map, and for every additional 1% of the vote the party wins, they should win an additional 2% of seats, in line with the historic responsiveness observed in Chapter 2. Stephanopoulos and McGhee (2015) expand on efficiency gap, measured in the first election cycle following redistricting, as one essential prong in a new proposed test for unconstitutional partisan gerrymandering. A litigation team including Stephanopoulos challenged the State Assembly map in Wisconsin in the case *Whitford v. Nichol* (which would reach the Supreme Court as *Gill v. Whitford*), proposing the efficiency gap test as a solution to Kennedy's impasse over the lack of a judicially manageable standard.

Plaintiff's Arguments
In the initial complaint, the plaintiff in *Whitford v. Gill* (2016) propose a two-prong test for the constitutionality of a partisan gerrymander:

> The first step in the analysis is whether a plan's efficiency gap exceeds a certain numerical threshold. If so, the plan is presumptively unconstitutional, and if not, it is presumptively valid. The second step, which is reached only if the efficiency gap is sufficiently large, is whether the plan's severe partisan unfairness is the necessary result of a legitimate state policy, or inevitable given the state's underlying political geography. (*Whitford* 1st Complaint, 25)

The plaintiff's proposed threshold in the original complaint is both strict and flexible, simultaneously claiming "even a 7% efficiency gap should be presumptively unconstitutional," but also that "this Court need not decide at what point an efficiency gap is large enough to trigger a presumption of unconstitutionality" (*id.* at 26). Note that in this initial proposal, there is no requirement to prove a discriminatory process or intent, suggesting that a measurement of high efficiency gap bias is alone enough to show presumed unconstitutionality. However, in the first of many instances gradually reducing the role of efficiency gap in the case, the next plaintiff's reply brief clarified this as a three-prong test, summarized by the district court as follows:

- First, plaintiffs would have to establish that a state had an intent to gerrymander for partisan advantage. (Intent prong)
- Second, the plaintiffs would need to prove a partisan effect, by proving that the efficiency gap for a plan exceeds a certain numerical threshold (which the plaintiffs proposed, based on historical analysis, to be 7%). If a plan exceeds that threshold, the plaintiffs asserted that it should be presumptively unconstitutional. (Effect prong)
- Third, and finally, the burden is shifted to the defendants to rebut the presumption by showing that the plan "is the necessary result of a legitimate state policy, or inevitable given the state's underlying political geography." If the state is unable to rebut the presumption, then the plan is unconstitutional. (Justification prong) (*Whitford v. Gill* (2016), 218 F. Supp. 3d at 855)

The plaintiff then moves on to providing evidence of each prong. First, with respect to the intent prong, the plaintiff emphasizes the secrecy of the process. They describe how "the Current Plan was drafted via a secret process run solely by Republicans in the State Assembly and their agents, entirely excluding from participation all Democratic members of the Assembly as well as the public" (Whitford 1st Complaint, 10). This is bolstered by evidence that "even Republican state legislators were prevented from receiving any information that would allow public discussion or deliberation about the plan existing districts" (*id.* at 11). The evidence presented that Republicans intended to gain a partisan advantage through the map is sufficiently convincing that the brief notes a previous court called efforts to refute it "almost laughable" (*id.* at 9).

With respect to the second prong, the plaintiff emphasizes the historically high bias of 13% and 10% observed after the 2012 and 2014 elections, respectively, noting that "between 1972 and 2010, not a *single* plan anywhere in the United States had an efficiency gap as high as the Current Plan in the first two elections after redistricting" (*id.* at 4, emphasis in original). This is bolstered by expert testimony with respect to the durability of this level of bias, as well as likely bias observed under plausible swings in electoral conditions in addition to

several specific examples of "packing and cracking" employed in the Act 43 map
(*id.* at 18–23).

Finally, with respect to the justification prong, the plaintiff argues that the
plan's "poor performance [on efficiency gap metrics] was entirely unnecessary
and served no legitimate purpose" (*id.* at 23–24), supported by an alternate dem-
onstration plan developed by a plaintiff's expert that "would have had an efficiency gap of just 2% in 2012" and "performs at least as well as the Current Plan
on every other relevant metric" (*id.* at 24).

The plaintiff's brief concludes by asserting two constitutional grounds on
which the Court should find the Act 43 map unconstitutional. The first, rooted
in the Equal Protection Clause, is "The Current Plan is a partisan gerrymander
so extreme that it violates Plaintiffs' Fourteenth Amendment right to equal protection of the laws" (*id.* at 25). The second, rooted in the right to freedom of
speech and freedom of association, is "Wisconsin Act 43 violates the First and
Fourteenth Amendments because it intentionally uses voters' partisan affiliation
to affect the weight of their votes" (*id.* at 28). The plaintiff, however, does not suggest any sort of different test or standard that would differentiate between these
claims. Moreover, the plaintiff's proposed test is based on explicit comparisons to
similar tests developed for malapportionment claims rooted in Equal Protection
jurisprudence, suggesting the first claim as central to their argument and the
First Amendment claim as more of an afterthought, a disparity that the Supreme
Court would highlight further down the line.

District Court Judgment

A three-judge panel of the federal district court in Wisconsin heard oral
arguments in the case in May 2016 but waited until November 21, 2016, shortly
after the federal elections, to issue their judgment. In a 2–1 decision, the court
struck down the State Assembly map in Wisconsin and ordered a new map to
be drawn.

A few broad elements of Judge Ripple's majority opinion stand out. First, the
court does not cleanly distinguish the plaintiff's two claims as requiring separate
analysis, and in fact explicitly links them. Second, the court adopts the broad
contours of the plaintiff's suggested three-prong test, though without incorporating its specific metrics, as applicable to both counts:

> We conclude, therefore, that the First Amendment and the Equal Protection
> clause prohibit a redistricting scheme which (1) is intended to place a severe
> impediment on the effectiveness of the votes of individual citizens on the basis
> of their political affiliation, (2) has that effect, and (3) cannot be justified on
> other, legitimate legislative grounds. (*Whitford v. Gill* (2016), 218 F. Supp. 3d
> at 884)

And finally, it is important to note that one of the several ways in which *Whitford* differentiates itself from the litigation in Pennsylvania and Maryland is that the shape of the districts and other "traditional" principles are not at issue. Indeed, the district court acknowledged that "the drafters were attentive to traditional districting criteria like population equality, compactness, and municipal splits throughout the drafting process" (*id.* at 849). Indeed, the court explicitly rejects a claim from the state that "a redistricting plan that 'is consistent with, and not a radical departure from, prior plans with respect to traditional districting principles' cannot, as a matter of law, evince an unconstitutional intent" (*id.* at 888).

While the court weighs the evidence on each of the three prongs, it is striking how much emphasis is given to the first "intent" prong. The opinion especially emphasizes the views of the drafters toward durability of the map, also repeating quotes of one of the drafter's notes stating, "The maps we pass *will determine who's here 10 years from now*," and "We have an *opportunity* and an obligation to draw these maps that Republicans haven't had in decades" (*id.* at 853, emphasis in original). Curiously, the court largely ignores evidence of the secrecy of the process, or the exclusion of input from Democrats or the public, that was central in the plaintiff's complaint on this prong.

The court next finds that the second "effect" prong of the plaintiff's proposed test is satisfied, though the court does not rely predominantly on the plaintiff's proposed efficiency gap test. Instead, the court leans heavily on "swing analysis" done by both experts advising the Wisconsin state legislature and the plaintiff. The court finds that this analysis "makes a firm case on the question of discriminatory effect, [and] that evidence is further bolstered by the plaintiffs' use of the 'efficiency gap' " (*id.* at 903). But the court is also careful to "further emphasize that we have not determined that a particular measure of EG [efficiency gap] establishes presumptive unconstitutionality. . . . Instead, we acknowledge that . . . EG is corroborative evidence of an aggressive partisan gerrymander" (*id.* at 910). Similar to their emphasis on the first prong, the swing analysis the court relies on stresses the probable durability of Republican control, suggesting that "under any *likely* electoral scenario, the Republicans would maintain a legislative majority" (*id.* at 899). This contrasts with a pure efficiency gap test, which might show extreme bias, but only under a single actual observed election outcome.[4] In doing so, the court appears to be valuing the importance placed by the *Bandemer* plurality on showing a map "consistently degrades" a group's influence over Justice Kennedy's concern in *LULAC* over employing measures that simulate a "hypothetical state of affairs."

The court finally moves on to the justification prong, finding that "benign factors cannot explain this substantial increase in Republican advantage between the Current Map and the plan that would become Act 43" (*id.* at 922). After reviewing various measurements of the geographic dispersion of partisans, the court finds that "Wisconsin's political geography affords Republicans a modest natural advantage in districting" (*id.* at 101), but that this alone cannot explain the bias in the Act 43 map. Instead, the court leans on the record showing that the Republican legislature themselves developed various alternative maps with a wide range of expected partisan outcomes and chose among them the one most favorable to Republicans. Therefore, the court concludes, "although Wisconsin's natural political geography plays some role in the apportionment process, it simply does not explain adequately the sizeable disparate effect seen in 2012 and 2014 under Act 43" (*id.* at 91), and thus the final prong of the three-prong test is satisfied. In January 2017, the district court issued their opinion with respect to a remedy, ordering Wisconsin to draw new maps to be in place prior to holding any additional elections.

Supreme Court Action

Given that the district court's decision in *Whitford* demonstrated a clear deviation from recent federal court precedent (being the first map struck down for purely partisan reasons since *Bandemer*), the Supreme Court unsurprisingly both granted cert to the Wisconsin defendants' appeal and stayed the lower court's order to redraw the map. Many were surprised by the emphasis placed on various issues during the oral arguments held on October 3, 2017, with the proposed efficiency gap standard barely mentioned, and Justice Kennedy in particular focused on the potential First Amendment claim.

The Supreme Court issued their decision on June 18, 2018, a unanimous ruling reversing the lower court's decision and remanding the case due to lack of standing, a decision that many interpreted as "punting" on the merits of the case. However, a close reading of the decision reveals that the Court's opinion made a significant statement with respect to the substance of how partisan gerrymandering should be measured. The majority opinion holds that "to the extent the plaintiffs' alleged harm is the dilution of their votes, that injury is district specific" (*Gill v. Whitford* (2018), 138 S. Ct. at 1930) and does *not* derive from the statewide composition of the legislature. However, "the plaintiffs before us alleged that they had such a personal stake in this case, but never followed up with the requisite proof" (*id.* at 1923). The Court finds:

> The plaintiffs did not seek to show such requisite harm since, on this record, it appears that not a single plaintiff sought to prove that he or she lives in a cracked or packed district. They instead rested their case at trial—and their arguments before this Court—on their theory of statewide injury to Wisconsin Democrats. (*Id.* at 1932)

In particular, the plaintiff's employment of statewide measures of bias does not establish individual injury. Instead, "[p]artisan-asymmetry metrics such as the efficiency gap measure something else entirely: the effect that a gerrymander has on the fortunes of political parties" (*id.* at 1933).

The four liberal justices filed a concurrence written by Justice Kagan in which they agreed to remanding the lower court's judgment but disagreed on the use of statewide evidence. Kagan argues that statewide measures such as efficiency gap could potentially still be useful in two contexts: to establish *intent* to dilute votes in a specific district, and in a First Amendment claim, where "the valued association and the injury to it are statewide" (*id.* at 1939). However, Kagan's concurrence acknowledges that although they alleged a First Amendment injury in their complaint, the plaintiff "did not advance it with sufficient clarity or concreteness to make it a real part of the case" (*id.* at 1934).

As a result, though the majority opinion does not completely exclude partisan gerrymandering claims, it does seem to foreclose on the possibility of using statewide measurements as evidence that an individual's vote has been diluted. The results can clearly be seen in the arguments developed in subsequent cases (discussed later), including the centrality of the First Amendment claim in *Benisek* and the focus on district-specific evidence in *Rucho*.

Summary and Stylized Test

Though reversed by the U.S. Supreme Court, the evidence relied on by the district court in *Whitford* is still worth considering as a potential avenue to establish an unconstitutional partisan gerrymander. In ruling that the map of Wisconsin Assembly districts violated the Equal Protection Clause of the U.S. Constitution, the district court relied on evidence that the voting power of certain voters was consistently degraded. This is most directly measured by (a) evidence of extreme "efficiency gap" bias in elections immediately following redistricting and (b) evidence of the likely durability of that bias through simulated elections or historical trends. The efficiency gap, measured over the life of the plan, will therefore be employed as the "stylized test" drawn from the *Whitford* district court case.

League of Women Voters v. Commonwealth of Pennsylvania

Factual Background

As discussed in Chapter 1, the Pennsylvania congressional map during the 2000s decade was the result of a controversial Republican gerrymander which backfired in the 2006 and 2008 election cycles, a period in which Democrats took control of the Pennsylvania state government. This made Pennsylvania ground zero for the REDMAP strategy in 2010, described as a "project that would solidify conservative policymaking at the state level and maintain a Republican stronghold in the U.S. House of Representatives for the next decade" (*League of Women Voters v. Commonwealth of Pennsylvania* [2018; hereinafter *LWV*] Opinion, 16, quoting from REDMAP Summary Report). This project was a success, yielding Republican control of all branches of state government. Though Republicans also won a 12–7 majority in the state's congressional delegation, the legislature in 2011 "set to work to redraw the congressional map in a way that would entrench the Republican Party's dominance in Pennsylvania's delegation to the U.S. House for the next decade" (*id.* at 17).

The result was a map described by experts as the "the Gerrymander of the Decade" (*LWV* Complaint, 20) and "[t]he most gerrymandered map seen in the modern history of our state" (*id.* at 19–20), a collection of bizarre twists and turns that would yield a 13–5 Republican majority in 2012 (as well as 2014 and 2016), despite Republicans winning only 49% of the statewide congressional vote.

Unlike other cases discussed in this chapter, the plaintiffs filed suit against the Pennsylvania map in Pennsylvania *state court* in June 2017 (in the wake of the temporary success of the *Gill* case).[5] The Pennsylvania Supreme Court acted quickly to take jurisdiction over the case. A trial was held in the lower Commonwealth Court in December, with the Supreme Court collecting briefs, hearing oral argument, and reaching a final decision barely a month later, on January 22, 2018.

Plaintiff's Arguments

The plaintiff's petition in *LWV* makes two broad claims against the constitutionality of the map under the Pennsylvania constitution. First, they claim it violates the rights to free expression and free association guaranteed in Article I, Section 7 ("The free communication of thoughts and opinions is one of the invaluable rights of man, and every citizen may freely speak, write and print on any subject, being responsible for the abuse of that liberty") and Section 20 ("The citizens have a right in a peaceable manner to assemble together for their common good") (*LWV* Complaint at 44) of the state constitution, because "[t]he Plan has had the effect of burdening and disfavoring Democratic voters in Pennsylvania, including Petitioners, by reason of their constitutionally-protected conduct" (*id.*). The claim here is closely analogous to the federal First Amendment claim in *Benisek v. Lamone*, discussed later.

Secondarily, the plaintiff claims the map violated the Equal Protection guarantees in Article 1, Sections 1 and 26, and the Free and Equal Elections Clause in Article 1, Section 5. The plaintiff groups these provisions together, with specific reference to the Equal Protection claim in *Whitford*.[6] While the plaintiff mentions the Free and Equal clause, which has no federal equivalent, they do not attempt to separately analyze what enforcement of this clause might entail. Although the plaintiff relies on provisions of the state constitution, they mostly leverage its similarities to the federal document rather than its difference, an important contrast to the ultimate court opinion in this case.

Along these lines, the plaintiff provides qualitative and quantitative evidence to support these claims with respect to discriminatory intent and effect, similar to the structured tests in *Whitford* and *Benisek*. They argue that intent can be shown through both the strange shape of several districts ("the districts are so bizarrely engineered that the only fair inference is that the Republican mapmakers made them so for partisan advantage" (*id.* at 6)) and through statistical simulation. Further, they offer qualitative evidence of the secrecy of the process. Most incriminating, "[a]s introduced, Bill 1249 was simply an empty shell. . . . [O]n the morning of December 14, 2011—the day of the vote on the bill—the Republicans suddenly amended the bill to add for the first time the actual descriptions of the congressional districts" (*id.* at 19). To demonstrate partisan effect, the plaintiff's complaint does not suggest a single empirical test but relies on several statistical techniques as persuasive evidence, including computer simulations, efficiency gap, and mean-median gap. Thus, although the legal avenue pursued by the plaintiff was unique among cases of this era, neither the legal nor the empirical arguments are particularly distinctive, recalling arguments and evidence from an assortment of recent federal litigation. There is little in the plaintiff's original filings to suggest the innovation of the Pennsylvania Supreme Court's opinion, which would instead lean heavily on alternative theories from amicus briefs.

Court Judgment

In a 5–2 decision (with one partial concurrence with the majority), the Pennsylvania Supreme Court struck down the state's congressional map and ordered a new map to be drawn prior to the 2018 elections. Ultimately the majority opinion in *LWV* ignores the Free Speech, Free Association, and Equal Protection clause claims made by the plaintiff and strikes down the map based solely on its interpretation of the Free and Equal Elections Clause in the state constitution, a clause without any equivalent in the U.S. Constitution.

Curiously, the plaintiff does not make a claim in their own petition that the Free and Equal clause should be given independent effect from the state Equal Protection Clause, and they largely argue that this equal protection claim should be analyzed similarly to federal Equal Protection claims like the lower court did in *Whitford*. Thus, in their opinion, the court leans heavily on amicus briefs to make the initial argument for the Free and Equal clause. In particular, the court highlights the arguments of the amicus brief submitted by Common Cause. The opinion overviews several such briefs, but discusses Common Cause first and in the most detail. Common Cause "assert[s] that this [Free and Equal] clause provides greater protections to the right to vote than the federal Equal Protection Clause" (178 A. 3d at 792). They note that, because the clause was enacted in 1790, many decades before Reconstruction, "[i]t is incoherent to assume that Pennsylvania's jurisprudence under the [Free and Equal Elections Clause] disappeared into the Fourteenth Amendment" (*id.* at 793). In order to analyze this clause, "Common Cause submits that the three criteria long used for drawing voting districts in Pennsylvania—compactness, contiguity, and integrity of political subdivisions—provide a sufficient standard by which to assess whether an electoral map violates the Free and Equal Elections Clause . . . because these criteria are specifically written into the Pennsylvania Constitution" (*id.* at 794). This interpretation and analysis would indeed be close to the framework the court adopts in their opinion. In addition to the Common Cause brief, amicus briefs filed by the AFL-CIO and ACLU also emphasize the distinct nature and history of the state's Free and Equal clause.

In latching on to the Free and Equal clause as the basis for its decision, the *LWV* opinion avoids any reliance on provisions of the state constitution that have a federal equivalent. Indeed, the opinion outlines the clause's extensive history, arguing that it is both expansive and entirely independent from the U.S. Constitution, being intertwined with the unique history of the state. Emphasizing its independence, the court notes that "[t]his clause first appeared, albeit in different form, in our Commonwealth's first organic charter of governance adopted in 1776, *11 years before the United States Constitution was adopted*" (*id.* at 804, emphasis mine), and "when properly presented with the argument, our Court entertains as distinct claims brought under the Free and Equal Elections Clause of our Constitution and the federal Equal Protection Clause, and we adjudicate them separately" (*id.* at 812). And emphasizing the potential scope of the clause, they state, "The broad text . . . of this provision mandates clearly and unambiguously, and in the broadest possible terms, that all elections conducted in this Commonwealth must be 'free and equal'" (*id.* at 804).

Once the court has settled on the Free and Equal Elections Clause as the relevant source of injury, they proceed to examine how a possible violation of this clause might be measured. While relying on different parts of the U.S. Constitution to reach their decisions, the district courts in *Whitford* and *Benisek* (discussed later) both applied the provision to the question of partisan gerrymandering using a similarly structured three-part test (with intent, effect, and justification prongs). The Pennsylvania Supreme Court uses a much different analysis, eschewing a multiprong test or sophisticated election analysis in lieu of "traditional redistricting criteria" written in the state constitution with respect to state legislative districts.[7] Those criteria are:

(1) the population of such districts must be equal, to the extent possible;
(2) the district that is created must be comprised of compact and contiguous geographical territory; and
(3) the district respects the boundaries of existing political subdivisions contained therein, such that the district divides as few of those subdivisions as possible. (*Id.* at 835)

The court does "recognize that other factors have historically played a role in the drawing of legislative districts, such as . . . the political balance which existed after the prior reapportionment" (*id.* at 817). But they also "view these factors to be *wholly subordinate* to the neutral criteria of compactness, contiguity, minimization of the division of political subdivisions, and maintenance of population equality" (*id.*, emphasis mine).

The first benchmark, population equality, is not at issue in this case. But with respect to the other two (compactness and existing boundaries), the court finds the map is a clear outlier. Here, the court relies on the expert witness Jowie Chen's simulated districts, describing:

> Dr. Chen's Simulated plans achieved population equality and contiguity . . . and had a range of Popper-Polsby Compactness Scores from approximately .29 to .35, *which was significantly more compact than the 2011 Plan's score of .164.*[8] Further, his simulated plans generally split between 12–14 counties and 40–58 municipalities, *in sharp contrast to the 2011 Plan's far greater 28 county splits and 68 municipality splits. (Id.* at 818, emphasis mine)[9]

Under the court's reasoning, failure to comply with traditional criteria is enough to invalidate the map under the Free and Equal clause, irrespective of any analysis of intent, justification, or actual or projected election outcomes.

Two weeks prior to releasing the full opinion striking down the map, the court set forth a process giving the state government the first opportunity to implement a remedial map, but with the court as a backstop. With control of the Pennsylvania state government now split with a Democratic governor, the state was unable to ratify a new plan, and the court released a new map drawn by appointed special master Nathaniel Persily on February 19.

Supreme Court Action and a Redrawn Map

Given that the Pennsylvania court's decision hinged on provisions of the state constitution without federal equivalents, the prospect of raising a federal question was dim. Nevertheless, Pennsylvania legislative leaders appealed to the U.S. Supreme Court. As expected, the Court declined to get involved, denying cert in October 2018 without any substantive comment or opinion, finally concluding the litigation and ensuring that the November elections would take place under redrawn maps. The new maps drew districts much more compactly, yielding two new, heavily Democratic seats around Philadelphia and reducing the partisan advantage in a few additional seats held by Republicans. Under the new map, Democrats gained three seats (in addition to one gained in a special election earlier in the year), to yield a 9–9 split of the statewide delegation.

Summary and Stylized Test

In ruling that the Pennsylvania congressional map violated the Free and Equal Elections Clause of the state constitution, the Pennsylvania Supreme Court relied on the measurement of "traditional districting principles." As equal population is not an issue in this or any of these cases, this can be summarized as (a) compactness of districts and (b) splits in existing political boundaries, especially counties and municipalities. The average Polsby-Popper compactness score and the total number of county splits are thus employed as the "stylized tests" drawn from the *LWV* Pennsylvania Supreme Court case.

Benisek v. Lamone

Factual Background

Litigation over partisan gerrymandering during the 2010s has not been entirely confined to Republican-drawn maps. *Benisek v. Lamone*, originally filed in 2013 (and thus actually the first of the cases from this decade considered in this chapter), challenged "the 'cracking' of Maryland's 6th Congressional District, which was purposefully and successfully flipped from Republican to Democratic control by strategically moving the district's lines by reason of citizens' voting records and known party affiliations" (*Benisek* 2nd Complaint, 3). For most of the 2000s, Maryland's congressional delegation was represented by six Democrats and two Republicans, with the 6th District encompassing the westernmost, and generally most heavily Republican, counties in the state (as it had for several decades). But in 2011, the Democrats in control of state government ratified a new map that moved several Republican areas of the 6th District in Frederick and Carroll counties into other safely Democratic districts and replaced this with territory from Montgomery County in liberal suburban DC.[10] A Democratic challenger defeated longtime 6th District incumbent Roscoe Bartlett in a landslide in 2012, and Maryland's delegation has held firm at 7–1 Democratic–Republican in each election since.

Plaintiff's Arguments

Benisek differs most obviously from *Whitford* and *LWV* in challenging a Democratic map. But more important, it also differs in specifically challenging only one district rather than relying on statewide evidence, and also making the First Amendment to the U.S. Constitution the heart of its claim.

The plaintiff first alleges that while Maryland lawmakers were very open about their intent to crack the 6th District, the process behind the map was extremely secretive. This begins when "Governor O'Malley, a Democrat, appointed the five members of the [Redistricting Advisory Committee], stacking it with reliably partisan confidantes" (*Benisek* 2nd Complaint, 14) and continues to how "the Plan was drafted in secret, and Democratic lawmakers and committee members rushed it through the legislature hastily and with no input from their Republican colleagues" (*id.* at 6).

The complaint then details that the Democrats achieved their partisan goals by altering the boundaries of districts much more than necessary to equalize the population. In particular, "[t]he redistricting cracked the 6th District by removing over 360,000 residents from the mostly-Republican northern counties of the district and adding nearly 350,000 residents from predominantly Democratic and urban Montgomery County . . . a net transfer of over 65,000 Republican voters out of the district and over 30,000 Democratic voters into the district" (*id.* at 26). The 6th District saw almost half of its population replaced despite only 10,000 voters needing to be moved to balance it, and the percentage of registered Republicans in the district fell from 47% to 33%.

In addition to asserting that the plaintiff's rights were curtailed by a reduced ability to elect a representative of their choice, the complaint also asserts an indirect effect on their speech and association rights. In several ways, it argues that the "dilution of Republicans' votes in Maryland has chilled and manipulated political participation since 2011 in precisely the ways that the Supreme Court had warned against" (*id.* at 34). Specifically, "some Maryland voters who would otherwise register as Republicans have been chilled from doing so" (*id.*), and some "[v]oters . . . feel that the outcomes of elections are preordained by the legislature's map-drawing and discouraged from casting their votes or engaging in the political process at all" (*id.* at 35). In their opinion, the district court quotes testimony from several plaintiffs who felt the gerrymander impeded overall political engagement. These include the statements "[E]very time we were out [campaigning], we met somebody who said, it's not worth voting anymore. . . . [T]hey just [felt] disenfranchised that . . . they don't have somebody that represents them anymore . . . [a]fter the redistricting" (348 F. Supp. 3d at 508), as well as a plaintiff who "described personally feeling 'disoriented' by and 'disconnected' from his new congressional district" (*id.*).

The final element of the complaint argues against the possibility of a benign justification for their contours of the map, such as geography or traditional districting criteria. This is evidenced by the fact that members of the governor's redistricting committee themselves considered many alternative plans that would have avoided cracking the 6th District while better respecting traditional districting principles. Thus, the *only* motivation for the district's shape was to reduce the power of residents of the old 6th District to elect a (Republican) representative of their choice.

Beyond asserting their core First Amendment claim, the *Benisek* complaint also advances a claim that the gerrymander violates Article I, Sections 2 and 4 of the U.S. Constitution, also known as the Elections Clause. This claim largely seems like an afterthought, as its brief mention in the complaint invokes the same three-prong test as the First Amendment claim.

Court Judgment

The district court first ruled on the merits in November 2018, overturning the map as a violation of "the First Amendment by burdening both the plaintiffs' representational rights and associational rights based on their party affiliation and voting history" (348 F. Supp. 3d at 497). Judge Niemeyer's majority opinion is completely based in the First Amendment, with no mention of the plaintiff's additional Article I claims, though it separates out claims of "representation" and "associational" harms.

In articulating the fundamental principle of their analysis, the court stated, "To be sure, citizens have no constitutional right to be assigned to a district that is likely to elect a representative that shares their views. But they do have a right under the First Amendment not to have the value of their vote diminished *because of* the political views they have expressed through their party affiliation and voting history" (*id.* at 514). The court then advanced a three-prong test for stating such a First Amendment claim to "representational harm":

(1) that those responsible for [a redistricting] map redrew the lines of his district with the *specific intent* to impose a burden on [the plaintiff] and similarly situated citizens because of how they voted or the political party with which they were affiliated;

(2) that the challenged map diluted the votes of the targeted citizens to such a degree that it resulted in a tangible and concrete adverse effect; and

(3) that "the mapmakers' intent to burden a particular group of voters by reason of their views" was a but-for cause of the "adverse impact. (*Id.* at 515)

Note that while its exact expression is different, this test follows the same basic intent/effects/justification structure as the test employed by the district court in *Whitford*. However, immediately after articulating this test, the court is careful to distinguish this case from that unsuccessful effort, stating, "The plaintiffs in this case, unlike the plaintiffs in *Whitford*, have brought and pursued the kind of single-district challenge that *Whitford* recognized as providing such plaintiffs with standing" (*id.* at 517).

Having delineated this test, the court finds each prong fairly easy to adjudicate. The court finds the first prong of this test, related to intent, particularly obvious. Relying on evidence of both the drafters' meticulous use of partisan voting statistics in crafting the maps and statements made by Democratic Party leaders about the specific goals for the 6th District, the court finds "there can be no doubt that at every stage of the process, the State's Democratic officials . . . specifically intended to flip control of the 6th District from Republicans to Democrats" (*id.* at 519). The court next addresses what is framed as a "burden prong" but essentially asks about the effect of the gerrymander. Compared to the district court opinion in *Whitford*, the analysis in this section is relatively brief. It relies on changes to the balance of registered partisans in the 6th District, as well as changes to the Cook "Partisan Voting Index" and expert ratings of race competitiveness to conclude that "Republican voters in the new Sixth District were, in *relative* terms, much less likely to elect their preferred candidate than before the 2011 redistricting, and, in *absolute* terms, they had no real chance of doing so" (*id.*).[11]

The court also dispenses with the final "but-for" prong fairly swiftly. This is somewhat parallel to *Whitford*'s justification prong, showing that there is no other benign explanation for the burden on the rights of the plaintiff. Here, the court leans on both the unnecessarily large change in the 6th District's population and the historically anomalous nature of it. Earlier in the opinion, Niemeyer notes, "Since 1966, the Sixth District had always been configured to include all of Maryland's five most northwestern counties" (*id.* at 6), and significantly, "in creating the 2011 redistricting plan, the Democratic officials responsible for the plan redrew the Sixth District's boundaries far more dramatically than was necessary" (*id.* at 498–99). The court also dismisses arguments by the state that the new 6th District actually did represent a coherent community, and holds "the plaintiffs have established that, without the State's retaliatory intent, the Sixth District's boundaries would not have been drawn to dilute the electoral power of Republican voters nearly to the same extent" (*id.* at 520).

In addition to violating the plaintiff's "representational rights," Judge Niemeyer's opinion also finds the Maryland plan to be a violation of their "associational rights," specifically their right to associate with their chosen political party. Niemeyer advances a similar three-prong test to analyze this claim, with only the second prong relying on different evidence. In lieu of evidence of partisan voting patterns and movement of partisans from one district to another, here the count refers to the evidence of "chilling" political participation. Specifically, this includes evidence that "Republican participation in Republican primaries in the counties that remained entirely in the Sixth District fell significantly" (*id.* at 523), and "testimony provided by several of the plaintiffs revealed a lack of enthusiasm, indifference to voting, a sense of disenfranchisement, a sense of disconnection, and confusion after the 2011 redistricting by voters" (*id.*).

This aspect of the opinion may be especially important because it does not rely at all on *election results* data, which a majority of Supreme Court justices in *Whitford* seemed averse to considering. In fact, this aversion prompted one of the judges on the three-judge panel to issue a separate concurrence in judgment. Judge Bredar states, "I cannot join because Judge Niemeyer's opinion leans on the results of elections in assessing the lawfulness of the Maryland gerrymander" (*id.* at 526). Instead, Bredar finds Maryland's plan to violate *only* the plaintiff's associational rights, not their representation rights. Here, Bredar is even more explicit that "the State *retaliated* against voters for those associations [with a disfavored party]" (*id.* at 528, emphasis in original). To Bredar, it is important that the harms manifested on the plaintiff were both wide in scope and enduring, as they included "building roadblocks to fundraising, registering voters, attracting volunteers, generating support from independents, and recruiting candidates to run for office" and that "this harm occurs before Election Day and persists long after" (*id.* at 528). The two-prong test expressed here seems almost the exact opposite of the effect prong advocated by the *Whitford* plaintiff. While the efficiency gap test had the appeal of being simply applied to one election result, the "associational rights" test leans on everything except the results of a single election.

Judge Niemeyer's opinion concludes with the remedy of enjoining the State of Maryland from conducting further elections under the current map and "directing the State to adopt promptly a new congressional districting plan" (*id.* at 525).

Supreme Court Action

In response to the district court's decision overturning the Maryland congressional map, the *Benisek* defendant appealed to the Supreme Court, which granted cert in January 2019 and heard oral arguments on March 26. In a joint opinion with *Rucho v. Common Cause* on June 27, 2019, the Supreme Court vacated the district court's ruling and held the partisan gerrymandering was a nonjusticiable political question. This decision is discussed in greater detail in the next section, detailing the *Rucho* litigation.

Summary and Stylized Test

In ruling that the map of Maryland congressional districts violated the First Amendment to the U.S. Constitution, the district court relied on evidence that the representation and associational rights of individuals were intentionally burdened. This is less amenable to direct quantitative analysis than the previous case, but to the extent this is used, it is measured by (a) the movement of sufficient people into and out of the district to swing the election results and (b) "chilling" factors such as changes in voter registration, turnout, and party fundraising. Since the chilling factors used by the court are largely anecdotal, they are difficult to measure in reference to other cases. Therefore, the "stylized test" drawn from the *Benisek* case for use later in the chapter will be movement of an unnecessarily large population to transform the partisanship of a district and crack opposing partisans.

Rucho v. Common Cause

Factual Background

The last major redistricting case considered here challenged a Republican gerrymander of North Carolina congressional districts, *Rucho v. Common Cause*. Like the other federal cases, *Rucho* involves a map struck down by the district court but later upheld in a reversal by the U.S. Supreme Court. In contrast to the other three cases, *Rucho* revolves much less around a single claim or distinguishing standard. Instead, the lower court decision especially takes a much more "kitchen sink" approach of incorporating all possible evidence as potentially persuasive toward all possible claims.

As with Wisconsin and Pennsylvania, Republicans won large majorities in both houses of the North Carolina state legislature in 2010, and because the Democratic governor has no veto over redistricting, they set out to draw a congressional map that would yield a 10–3 Republican majority in the state's congressional delegation. Though Republicans achieved this result in 2014, the congressional districts were overturned in 2016 as an unconstitutional *racial* gerrymander in *Cooper v. Harris*. The still-Republican legislature responded by drawing new districts that were more compact and involved slightly less packing of Black voters, but still explicitly sought to maintain the existing Republican balance according to the legislature's "2016 Adopted Criteria." In the 2016 elections, Republicans achieved this goal of a 10–3 supermajority in the delegation.

The new congressional map was again challenged in federal court, this time as an unconstitutional *partisan* gerrymander, with plaintiffs alleging violations of the Equal Protection Clause, the First Amendment, and the Elections Clause of Article I. The district court struck down the North Carolina districts under all the plaintiff's theories in January 2018. But the maps were never redrawn, as the Supreme Court first stayed the verdict and then vacated it in June 2018, to be reheard in light of their decision in *Whitford*. The new trial at the district court was held quickly, the verdict once again striking down the North Carolina map being issued on August 27, 2018.

Plaintiff's Argument

Common Cause's amended complaint filed in September 2016 (before the district court's opinion in *Gill*) makes four separate federal constitutional claims against the 2016 North Carolina congressional map: (a) an Equal Protection claim similar to the claim emphasized in *Gill*; (b) a First Amendment claim similar to that emphasized in *Benisek*; (c) an Article I, Section 2 claim related to the direct election of House members by the people; and (d) an Article I, Section 4 claim related to the delegation of federal election administration to state governments. The complaint also specifies that the set of plaintiffs includes at least one registered Democratic voter from each congressional district in the state.

Key to the plaintiff's overall argument is the legislature's explicit use of "political data" to gain a partisan advantage for Republicans. They note the "Adopted Criteria" that the redistricting joint committee voted to use in drawing districts, including the requirement that "[t]he only data other than population data to be used to construct congressional districts shall be election results in statewide contests since January 1, 2008, not including the last two presidential contests. Data identifying the race of individuals or voters shall not be used" (*Rucho Complaint*, 19). One could argue this was adopted in response to the decision striking down the state's 2011 map due to the use of racial data. However, the plaintiff also highlights another Adopted Criteria: "The Committee shall make reasonable efforts to construct districts in the 2016 Contingent Congressional Plan to maintain the current partisan makeup of North Carolina's congressional delegation" (*id.*), thus maintaining the 10–3 Republican advantage. And plaintiff argues that the use of these two criteria together constitutes a constitutional violation on each claim.

Lower Court Decision

The district court's second opinion in *Rucho* is superficially remarkable, first for its length, consisting of over 90,000 words (slightly longer than the length of this book). But it is also remarkable for its breadth, striving to make use of all available evidence on several prongs of each count, and separately analyzing these data both at a statewide level and with respect to each individual district. In the end, Judge Wynn's majority opinion strikes down all but one of North Carolina's thirteen congressional districts as individual violations of the Equal Protection

Clause, while also finding the map in violation of the First Amendment and the Elections Clause of Article I of the Constitution.

The first task of the court is to distinguish their decision from the very recent Supreme Court holding in *Whitford* denying the potential for statewide challenges to partisan gerrymanders. On this point, the court states, "[T]here can be no question that Common Cause Plaintiffs have 'meaningfully pursued' a district-by-district vote dilution claim under the Equal Protection Clause" (318 F. Supp. 3d at 817), and concludes that "at least one of the named Plaintiffs residing in each of the State's thirteen congressional districts has standing to lodge a partisan vote dilution challenge under the Equal Protection Clause to each district . . . and further hold that Gill does not call into question our earlier conclusions that Plaintiffs have standing" (*id.* at 814).

To establish a structure to consider these claims, the court is resolute that there is no one particular test that must be employed or one universal standard that must be surpassed. Instead, they state, "[I]n none of these cases did the Supreme Court hold that the particular statistical or social science analyses upon which it relied had—or had to have—constitutional pedigree, or that the plaintiff had to identify a specific empirical threshold, across which the relevant constitutional provision would be violated" (*id.* at 854). Moreover, the court explicitly welcomes the development of new methods and standards that were not presented or not available in previous cases, arguing, "The Constitution does not require the federal courts to act like Galileo's Inquisition and enjoin consideration of new academic research, and the knowledge gained therefrom, simply because such research provides a new understanding of how to give effect to our long-established governing principles" (*id.* at 858). These principles set the tone for the opinion's analysis, in which many dimensions of evidence are considered at every step. The Equal Protection analysis follows a three-prong structure similar to that in *Whitford* (intent/effect/justification), though with the addition of district-specific consideration. But distinct from *Whitford,* the court uses quantitative evidence, and especially simulation studies, to establish not just partisan effects but also partisan intent. This is on top of the qualitative evidence typical on this prong of analysis, including the exclusionary process and overtly partisan "adopted criteria."

With respect to the effect prong, the court uses a multitude of methods:

[W]e rely on the following categories of evidence: (i) the results of North Carolina's 2016 congressional election conducted using the 2016 Plan; (ii) expert analyses of those results revealing that the 2016 Plan exhibits "extreme" partisan asymmetry; (iii) Dr. Mattingly's and Dr. Chen's simulation analyses; and (iv) the results of North Carolina's 2012 and 2014 elections using the 2011

Plan—the partisan effects of which the General Assembly expressly sought to carry forward when it drew the 2016 Plan. (*id*. at 884)

One curious aspect of this part of the opinion is the court's skeptical treatment of the efficiency gap test, a test so crucial to the plaintiff's claim in *Whitford*. Though the court considers all available data, they find that efficiency gap has several drawbacks, agreeing with the defendant that "the error rate [in efficiency gap durability] weighs against relying on Dr. Jackman's proposed thresholds as the sole basis for holding unconstitutional a districting plan" (*id*. at 890) and "the efficiency gap does not provide redistricting bodies with an incentive to draw districting plans with more competitive districts" (*id*. at 891).

After quickly dismissing several of the state's counterarguments on the topic of justification, the court analyzes each district separately, here largely relying on the sort of compactness and subdivision data important to the Pennsylvania court in *LWV*. The opinion finds that "a lack of 'respect for political subdivisions' may indicate an improper motive predominated" (*id*. at 899) and "the shape or appearance of a district also may speak to whether an improper motive predominated" (*id*. at 900).

On top of finding an Equal Protection violation, the court strikes down the North Carolina districts on First Amendment grounds. On this claim, the opinion recalls the arguments in *Benisek*, with the court not only employing a similar three-prong analysis (intent/burden/but-for causation) but also relying on similar evidence of a "chilling" effect of political speech, finding that "the 2016 Plan has had a constitutionally cognizable chilling effect on reasonable North Carolinians' First Amendment activities" (*id*. at 931), such as fundraising.

The final claim made by the *Rucho* plaintiff is a more novel one, that partisan gerrymanders violate the powers delegated to state governments under Article I of the Constitution. Recalling past precedent related not to partisan gerrymandering but to apportionment and term limits, the court agrees, arguing that this delegation "did not empower State legislatures to disfavor the interests of supporters of a particular candidate or party" (*id*. at 937).

As a remedy, the court gave the North Carolina General Assembly another chance to draw a constitutional map. As the case was decided only two months before the 2018 federal general election, the court asked the parties to submit further arguments about the feasibility of changing the map prior to the elections but ultimately conceded to leaving the old map in place for the time being and staying enforcement pending review by the Supreme Court.

Intervening Decisions
On the back of the district court ruling in *Rucho* but prior to the Supreme Court's decision, federal district courts also struck down legislative maps in Michigan

(*League of Women Voters v. Benson*) and Ohio (*Ohio A. Philip Randolph Inst. v. Householder*) in early 2019. In both decisions, the court adopted an approach similar to the North Carolina district court, using a broad range of evidence and a three-prong test applied to challenges to specific districts, with particular emphasis on computer-simulated districts as counterfactuals. The *Benson* case in Michigan challenged thirty-four districts across the congressional, state senate, and state house maps. In this case, the lower court struck down all thirty-four districts on First Amendment grounds, and twenty-seven of the thirty-four districts on vote dilution grounds, relying almost exclusively on simulation evidence. The Court struck down individual districts where most or all iterations of a simulation placed residents of that district in a more competitive district, but not those districts where the simulation usually placed those residents in a similarly or less competitive district.

In the *Householder* case in Ohio, the lower court embraced the use of multiple standards and methods, including simulations, compactness scores, subdivision split data, and four measures of bias, favorably citing the *Rucho district* court's attitude toward this. In their district-by-district analysis, the Ohio court relies largely on qualitative testimony about specific boundary choice, reinforced with simulation data. But the court does not specifically strike down or uphold individual districts, instead finding the whole of Ohio's congressional map to be unconstitutional on Equal Protection, First Amendment, and Article I grounds.

The district court ordered new maps to be drawn in each case, but both orders were stayed by the Supreme Court. Since these decisions would seem to only incrementally build on the evaluation metrics used in *Rucho,* and ultimately received no further consideration beyond summary dismissal following the Supreme Court's *Rucho* decision, it is not necessary to discuss them in greater detail or develop a stylized test derived from them.

Supreme Court Action
When the U.S. Supreme Court handed down their opinion in *Gill v. Whitford* in 2018, many interpreted the decision as "punting" on the substantive issue and ruling only narrowly on standing grounds. But while evidence for a broader interpretation was present in that decision, the Court's next effort at tackling partisan gerrymandering left no room for doubt about the breadth of its ruling. On June 27, 2019, the U.S. Supreme Court ruled partisan gerrymandering entirely nonjusticiable, at least for the time being completely closing the door opened in *Bandemer* and left just barely ajar in *Vieth.* The Court had granted cert to the state's appeal of the district court's ruling in *Rucho* on January 4 and heard oral arguments on March 26, the same day as *Benisek v. Lamone.*

In a 5–4 opinion covering appeals from both the *Benisek* and *Rucho* cases, Chief Justice John Roberts held that "partisan gerrymandering claims present political questions beyond the reach of the federal courts" (139 S. Ct. at 2506). In doing so, the Court reversed the lower court decisions striking down partisan gerrymanders in Maryland and North Carolina, instead allowing those partisan maps to remain in place. But more significant, in instructing the lower courts to dismiss these cases for lack of jurisdiction, it held that the federal court system should not be involved in the issue of partisan gerrymandering in any way, and also effectively reversed recent lower court decisions in Ohio and Michigan and dismissed ongoing litigation in Wisconsin.

The Court has generally applied the political question doctrine to areas where the Constitution has expressly assigned authority to another branch of government or in which the Court believes there are no "judicially manageable standards" for them to evaluate when the Constitution has been violated without first taking an inherently partisan or political position. Roberts's opinion in *Rucho* leverages both of these concerns. Referencing the Elections Clause, Roberts describes how districting authority was expressly assigned to state legislatures and Congress:

> The Framers were aware of electoral districting problems and considered what to do about them. They settled on a characteristic approach, assigning the issue to the state legislatures, expressly checked and balanced by the Federal Congress. . . . At no point was there a suggestion that the federal courts had a role to play. (*Id.* at 2495)

But more important, Roberts holds that on the question of partisan gerrymandering, "[t]here are no legal standards discernible in the Constitution for making such judgments, let alone limited and precise standards that are clear, manageable, and politically neutral" (*id.* at 2500). He points to the complexity of the North Carolina court's ruling, relying on simulated maps and hypothetical elections:

> [T]he test adopted by the *Common Cause* court requires a far more nuanced prediction than simply who would prevail in future political contests. Judges must forecast with unspecified certainty whether a prospective winner will have a margin of victory sufficient to permit him to ignore the supporters of his defeated opponent (whoever that may turn out to be). Judges not only have to pick the winner—they have to beat the point spread. (*Id.* at 2503)

Justice Elena Kagan filed a strong dissent from Roberts's opinion in *Rucho* and *Benisek*, joined by the other three liberals on the Court, beginning, "For the first time ever, this Court refuses to remedy a constitutional violation because it thinks the task beyond judicial capabilities" (*id.* at 2509). She charges, "If left un-checked, gerrymanders like the ones here may irreparably damage our system of government. And checking them is *not* beyond the courts" (*id.*). Instead, Kagan believes that "courts across the country, including those below, have coalesced around manageable judicial standards to resolve partisan gerrymandering claims" (*id.*), specifically the three-prong test employed with some variation in both cases. Like the *Rucho* district court, Kagan is willing to embrace compli-cated standards and innovative methods, arguing that "the same technologies and data that today facilitate extreme partisan gerrymanders also enable courts to discover them" (*id.* at 2517). But while Kagan suggests that the three-prong approach in *Rucho* and *Benisek* does represent a judicially manageable standard, she acknowledges that different evidence of partisan effect (and thus a different test) was used by the two lower courts across the two cases. She describes how the North Carolina plaintiff used "advanced computing technology to randomly generate a large collection of districting plans that incorporate the State's phys-ical and political geography and meet its declared districting criteria" (*id.* at 2518), while "because the Maryland gerrymander involved just one district, the evidence in that case was far simpler" (*id.*), going on to detail the population movement evidence pivotal to the *Benisek* decision.

Roberts's majority opinion does acknowledge, "Excessive partisanship in districting leads to results that reasonably seem unjust" (*id.* at 2506). But he concludes his opinion by pointing out that partisan gerrymandering could be, and in many cases *is being*, addressed by the political branches of government, be they state legislatures, state constitutions through the state courts, citizen initiatives, or even federal legislation passed by Congress. As I detail in the last two chapters of this book, such efforts have indeed been ongoing and effective. And after the *Rucho* decision, this is where future reform attempts will need to concentrate.

Summary and Stylized Test
The district court's opinion in *Rucho* is by far the most expansive of the four examined here with respect to both the constitutional grounds on which it strikes down the map and the quantitative evidence it employs at each stage of its analysis. Yet it is also in some sense among the most narrow in its examina-tion of the boundary decision made on a district-by-district basis. Because the court explicitly declines to give more weight to one test than others among the many it employs, I do not attempt to distill a single "stylized test" from this case that could be applied to other cases. If one were to try to distill one test the court places more weight on than others, it would likely be the counterfactual com-puter simulations, and this is certainly what courts have latched onto most in

later federal decisions in Ohio and Michigan, as well as state court decisions in North Carolina (described in the next section). However, these simulations do not fit the profile of an easily applicable universal standard, as their algorithms are highly specific to the expert witness supplying the opinion in each individual case. I discuss in greater detail the strengths and weaknesses of simulations in this context in my concluding Chapter 8.

Subsequent Action to *Rucho*: *Common Cause v. Lewis*

Following their decision on nonjusticiability in *Rucho*, it was inevitable that the Supreme Court would also reverse the lower court decisions striking down gerrymanders in Ohio and Michigan. And the Court formally overturned both these rulings in October 2019, sending them back to the lower court with instructions to dismiss, effectively ending all remaining federal litigation on the issue. Nevertheless, once the Supreme Court's decision closed the door on federal litigation related to partisan gerrymanders, plaintiffs quickly embraced the more successful strategy from *LWV* of claims rooted in state constitutions. And North Carolina, fresh off seeing their maps upheld in federal court, would immediately become the focus of this new strategy.

On September 3, 2019, the Wake County Superior Court in *Common Cause v. Lewis* struck down the state legislative maps in North Carolina as in violation of the state's constitution. Noting Justice Roberts's comment in his *Rucho* opinion that "state constitutions can provide standards and guidance for state courts to apply" in an area that Roberts had ruled nonjusticiable in federal court, the Wake County court relied on Article I, Section 10 of the North Carolina Constitution, stating "all elections shall be free" to be "of particular significance" (*Common Cause v. Lewis* (2019) at 8). The Wake County court's use of the Free Elections Clause clearly parallels the reliance by the Pennsylvania Supreme Court on their state's Free and Equal Clause in *LWV*, though the lack of an "equal" requirement in North Carolina makes the application to partisan gerrymandering slightly less straightforward. Nevertheless, as *LWV* was the only one of the 2018 partisan gerrymandering cases to ultimately produce a redrawn map, it is perhaps unsurprising that its legal justification became a model for future cases.

But while *Lewis* draws heavily from *LWV* in its state constitutional grounding, it borrows much less in its use of empirical evidence. In finding partisan intent, the court relies largely on files found on the hard drive of a recently deceased Republican consultant charged with drawing the map, clearly demonstrating the primacy that partisan data held in how the lines were drawn. In showing partisan effect, the court placed great reliance on quantitative analysis done by three expert witnesses, using a variety of techniques. A small fraction of this evidence (data on county split and compactness in simulated maps) overlaps with the evidence the *LWV* court found decisive. But much greater weight is placed on the finding that the state's map was an outlier in terms of partisan balance and results under three different methodologies, all analyzed at both the statewide and regional levels. Thus, while the *Lewis* court's legal grounding was most similar to *LWV*, its empirical methodology was much closer to the kitchen-sink approach of *Rucho*.

In drawing their legal conclusion, the Wake County court ultimately goes further than the *LWV* court, who confined their holding to Pennsylvania's Free and Equal Elections Clause. The *Lewis* court first finds the map in violation of the North Carolina Free Elections Clause, stating that "the North Carolina Supreme Court has enforced the Free Elections Clause to invalidate laws that interfere with voters' ability to choose their representative" (*id.* at 304) and adding, "Extreme partisan gerrymandering does not fairly and truthfully ascertain the will of the people. Voters are not freely choosing their representatives. Rather, representatives are choosing their voters" (*id.* at 302). But the court *also* finds the map in violation of the state's Equal Protection Clause and the state's guarantee of Freedom of Speech and Freedom of Assembly, holding that these state constitutional clauses "provide greater protection for voting rights than their federal counterparts" (*id.* at 307). While the *LWV* court was careful to steer clear of constitutional clauses with federal equivalents (despite claims by the plaintiff related to such clauses), the Wake County court was willing to steer straight into them. Additionally, the court here refused to embrace a simple test rooted in traditional principles like that used in *LWV*, instead relying on diverse tests employing multiple simulation methodologies.

As a remedy, the court ordered the state General Assembly to redraw fifty-eight state house and twenty-one state senate districts, and remedial maps were approved on October 28. And following the success of *Lewis v. Common Cause*, plaintiffs quickly filed suit against North Carolina's *congressional districts* in September 2019, and the Wake County court granted an injunction against the use of the existing congressional map a month later. Given their grim prospects of success in light of the outcome of the previous *Lewis* case and the partisan makeup of the North Carolina Supreme Court, the Republican-controlled legislature declined to appeal the injunction and instead redrew the congressional map to create two additional, heavily Democratic districts. The court approved the new map in December 2019, and as expected, Democrats gained two seats to bring the balance of the state's delegation to 8–5 in the 2020 elections, a rare bright spot on a generally disappointing night for congressional Democrats.

Use of Proposed Standards across Case Facts

We have now seen how four different courts in four different contexts and fact patterns each applied different legal standards and evidentiary inquiries to arrive at the same conclusion striking down a partisan gerrymander. None of the cases employs one test exclusive of any other evidence, and in each case there is also considerable variation between the test proposed by the plaintiff and employed by the court. But in three of these four cases, I have highlighted one or two particular pieces of quantifiable evidence that seemed particularly important to the outcome, and distilled it into a highly simplified "stylized test" that might be both generalizable to multiple situations and easily understood by legislators and the public. (See Table 3.1 earlier in the chapter for a summary of these tests.) For the purposes of a thought exercise, I apply each of these "stylized tests" to the facts of the other cases, to explore whether one test or evidentiary outlook performs better at arriving at a universally consistent conclusion.

Whitford Efficiency Gap Standard

Probably the most straightforward of the standards proposed to evaluate partisan gerrymandering is the efficiency gap threshold, originally broached in the plaintiff's complaint in *Gill v. Whitford*. While the plaintiff does not demand that the Court establish a bright line for when an extreme efficiency gap should imply presumptive unconstitutionality, and the district court did not adopt any such line, other writings by efficiency gap advocates (mainly Stephanopoulos and McGhee) suggest thresholds. Beyond any initial measurement threshold, additional questions arise over such issues as when efficiency gap should be measured, how uncontested elections should be treated, and what, if any, "sensitivity testing" should be included to improve the robustness of the measurement. Setting aside the minutiae of these issues, I evaluate how the Pennsylvania, Maryland, and North Carolina cases might be analyzed were the Court to adopt an efficiency-gap-centric standard.

League of Women Voters v. PA under the Efficiency Gap Standard
While the state supreme court in Pennsylvania primarily used quantitative evidence related to compactness and cohesion of existing political boundaries to rule the state's congressional map in violation of the state constitution, they also mention (*LWV* opinion, 124) that the map performs poorly under various

Table 3.2 Efficiency Gap in Pennsylvania Congressional Elections, 2012–2018

Year	GOP Vote Share	GOP Seat Share	GOP Expected Seat Share	Efficiency Gap %	GOP Expected Seats	GOP Seat Gap
2012	49.2	72.2	48.4	23.8	8.7	4.3
2014	55.5	72.2	61.0	11.2	11.0	2.0
2016	54.1	72.2	58.2	14.0	10.5	2.5

measures of partisan outcomes, including the efficiency gap standard promoted in *Whitford*.

In each election in which the map was in effect (2012–16), Pennsylvania elected a delegation of thirteen Republicans (72.2%) and five Democrats (27.8%), with statewide Republican vote share ranging from 49.2% to 55.5%. As shown in Table 3.2, this yields a pro-Republican efficiency gap ranging from 4.3 seats in 2012 to 2.0 seats in 2014. In their article broaching efficiency gap as a constitutional standard, Stephanopoulos and McGhee advocate that the efficiency gap threshold for presumed unconstitutionality of congressional maps should be set at two *seats* rather than a percentage of the total seats. Thus, the map easily exceeds the recommended threshold in the first election after redistricting, and at least meets the threshold in the other two elections conducted under the map.[12] So it appears likely that a court adopting an efficiency-gap-based standard as recommended by Stephanopoulos and McGhee would also be likely to strike down Pennsylvania's congressional districts as an unconstitutional partisan gerrymander.

Benisek v. Lamone under the Efficiency Gap Standard

We can also consider the Democratic gerrymander of Maryland evaluated under the efficiency gap standard advocated by the plaintiffs in *Whitford*. Note that as efficiency gap is a statewide measure, we must consider the Maryland map as a whole rather than confining our analysis to the 6th District. Here, we see the importance of choosing the election benchmark(s) by which to measure efficiency gap. In each of the four congressional elections this decade, Republicans have won just one of the state's eight congressional seats (12.5%), while their two-party statewide congressional vote share has varied from 33.7% to 41.9%. The resultant efficiency gaps are shown in Table 3.3.

The pro-Democratic efficiency gap ranges from 4.8% to 21.3%, translating to between 0.4 and 1.7 seats more than expected given the vote share. Thus, the

Table 3.3 Efficiency Gap in Maryland Congressional Elections, 2012–2018

Year	GOP Vote Share	GOP Seat Share	GOP Expected Seat Share	Efficiency Gap %	GOP Expected Seats	GOP Seat Gap
2012	34.5	12.5	19.0	−6.5	1.5	−0.5
2014	41.9	12.5	33.8	−21.3	2.7	−1.7
2016	37.0	12.5	24.0	−11.5	1.9	−0.9
2018	33.7	12.5	17.3	−4.8	1.4	−0.4

Table 3.4 Efficiency Gap in North Carolina Congressional Elections, 2016–2018

Year	GOP Vote Share	GOP Seat Share	GOP Expected Seat Share	Efficiency Gap %	GOP Expected Seats	GOP Seat Gap
2016	53.3	76.9	56.6	20.3	7.4	2.6
2018	51.1	75.0	52.2	22.8	6.3	2.7

Maryland map never exceeds the two-seat threshold for presumptive uncon-stitutionality of a congressional map. And even if the stricter recommended 8% threshold for state legislative seats is used, Maryland exceeds this threshold in only two of the four elections and does not exceed it in the first election following redistricting, where efficiency gap is most frequently measured. Thus, it is *unlikely* that a court adopting a largely efficiency-gap-based test would invalidate the Maryland map as an unconstitutionally egregious par-tisan gerrymander.

Common Cause v. Rucho under the Efficiency Gap Standard

Finally, we can measure the efficiency gap observed in the congressional map at issue in *Rucho*. As this map was adopted in 2016 as a result of litigation, we have only two elections' worth of observations in this case, as shown in Table 3.4.[13]

The pro-Republican efficiency gap in both elections is about 20%, corre-sponding to between two and three seats. Thus, in this case, the threshold suggested by efficiency gap proponents would be cleanly met in both elections, though it is possible that the result would be more ambiguous in a different en-vironment. Nevertheless, it does seem likely that a court employing an efficiency gap test would find the North Carolina map unconstitutional.

League of Women Voters v. PA Compactness and Subdivision Splits Standard

While the Pennsylvania court in *LWV* did weigh a wide range of statistical evidence in reaching its decision (see Grofman and Cervas 2018 for a discussion), it ultimately evaluates all such data as "wholly subordinate" to the "traditional districting principles" of compactness and preserving existing subdivisions. This is most easily evaluated across cases by measuring the average Polsby-Popper or Reock compactness score across districts, and the proportion of counties split across district lines, especially compared to previous maps or suggested alternatives.

Gill v. Whitford under Compactness and Subdivision Splits Standard

As mentioned in the summary, the compactness and subdivision splits were not an issue in the Wisconsin litigation, with all parties and the court acknowledging that the legislature weighed these traditional principles in drawing the Act 43 map. Because this litigation involves a state assembly map with much smaller districts than a congressional district, we cannot make a direct comparison of compactness and splits with maps from other cases. But Figure 3.1, drawn from plaintiff's filings, gives a visual representation of the Act 43 map in contrast to both the previous bipartisan map and the proposed Democratic alternative, with little difference in compactness apparent. One of the plaintiff's experts submitted a possible alternative "fair" map that improves on the compactness of the Act 43 map but involves a very similar number of subdivision splits (with the Act 43 map including three more county splits but two fewer city or township splits). Thus, it is unlikely that a court adopting a compactness or subdivision

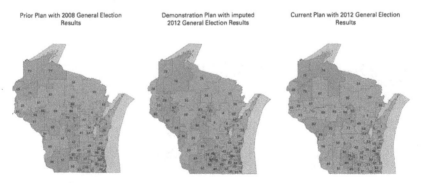

Figure 3.1 Compactness of Alternative Wisconsin Assembly Districts
Source: Whitford 1st Complaint, at 31.

splits-centric standard would strike down the Act 43 map at issue in the *Gill v. Whitford* litigation.[14]

Benisek v. Lamone under Compactness and Subdivision Splits Standard

Evaluating the claim against the Maryland 6th District under a compactness standard yields an ambiguous conclusion. When taken as a whole, the congressional districts in Maryland are almost absurdly not compact. Multiple districts in the state (especially the 2nd, 3rd, and 4th) are frequently cited as facially extreme examples of partisan gerrymandering based on shape alone, and, on average, Maryland's congressional districts consistently score either worst or second worst among all states on a wide range of compactness score (with Pennsylvania's 2012 districts averaging in the tenth-worst range) (Azavea 2012).

But *Benisek* did not challenge Maryland's entire congressional map, only the 6th District. Being long and thin in shape with several bulges, the 6th District performs poorly on some measures of compactness (Azavea 2012). But the boundaries of the district have for several decades mostly coincided with the boundaries of a very noncompact portion of a noncompact state and, as shown in Figure 3.2, did not significantly change in its overall compactness compared to the previous decade, or even several decades earlier.[15] The

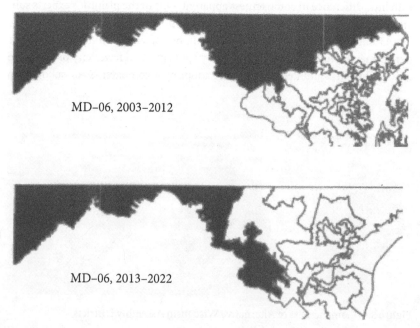

MD–06, 2003–2012

MD–06, 2013–2022

Figure 3.2 Maryland 6th District in 2000s and 2010s

lack of compactness of Maryland's districts is largely attributable to idiosyncratic changes in the middle part of the state accommodating the desires of specific incumbents, but in which the partisan balance of the delegation was unchanged. The average Polsby-Popper compactness of the Maryland congressional districts under the 2011 map was 0.112. While this is a very bad score relative to most other states,[16] it is notable that this is actually *better* than the average compactness of 0.071 of the same congressional districts under the previous map. Thus, it seems likely that a court adopting a purely compactness-based test for partisan gerrymandering would have strong evidence to invalidate several of Maryland's congressional districts in a vacuum, but not if compared to the previously drawn map, and perhaps not the 6th District when considered alone.

Additionally, the Maryland map actually performs fairly well under the other empirical measure relied on by the *LWV* court, county splits. The 2011 map splits nine of Maryland's twenty-four counties (including Baltimore City). In contrast, the previous Maryland map split eighteen of twenty-four counties. The map splits a smaller percentage of counties than the Pennsylvania map from *LWV*, a state with significantly less populous counties on average. Moreover, it is virtually certain that five specific counties would be split in almost any map: three counties (Montgomery, Prince George's, Baltimore County) have a larger population than a congressional district; two additional counties have populations almost as large as a congressional district (Baltimore City, Anne Arundel); and all five lie adjacent in a region of the state mandating the creation of two Black VRA influence districts. While the Maryland map includes absurd-looking boundaries drawn within the safely Democratic highly populated areas of the state, the map actually does a good job of respecting existing boundaries in splitting only four of the state's remaining nineteen counties. Thus, a court would be unlikely to strike down the map of Maryland under a standard focused on splits of existing subdivisions.

Rucho v. Common Cause under Compactness and Subdivision Splits Standard

Although subdivision splits are used as persuasive evidence in the *Rucho* court's analysis of some specific districts, the overall compactness and respect for existing subdivisions of the 2016 North Carolina map substantially improved upon both the 2011 map and the map drawn by Democrats in the previous decade. While the "Adopted Criteria" of the redistricting committee explicitly advocated using partisan data to achieve a Republican advantage, it also recommended that "the Committee shall make reasonable efforts to construct districts in the 2016 Contingent Congressional Plan that improve the compactness of the current districts and keep more counties and voting districts whole as compared to the

current enacted plan" (318 F. Supp. 3d at 807). The average Polsby-Popper compactness score of districting under the 2016 plan was 0.242, far greater than both
the 0.117 average under the 2011 plan and the 0.137 under the plan used in the
2000s.[17] Additionally, the 2016 map splits only thirteen of North Carolina's one
hundred counties (including two counties larger than a congressional district),
compared with forty county splits under the 2011 map and twenty-eight county
splits under the 2000 map. This improved compactness is facially apparent when
visually comparing the maps, shown in Figure 3.3. Thus, it seems unlikely that
a court using a statewide compactness or subdivision-centric standard would
strike down the 2016 *Rucho* map as unconstitutional (though they may have
struck down the 2011 map).

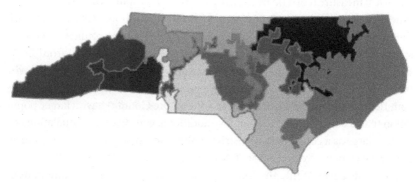

North Carolina Congressional Map, Adopted 2011

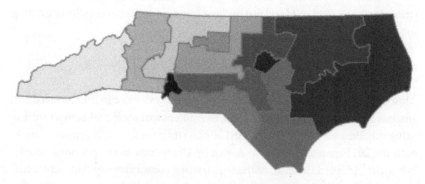

North Carolina Congressional Map, Adopted 2016

Figure 3.3 2011 versus 2016 Congressional Map of North Carolina

Benisek Retaliation/Population Movement Standard

The court in *Benisek*, in adjudicating a First Amendment claim confined to one district, relies on much less quantitative evidence than the courts in *Gill* or *LWV*. But one element that is crucial to their decision (and emphasized most in the plaintiff's complaint) is the unnecessary degree of change in the 6th District. The complaint details the number of people moved into and out of each district (specifically as retaliation for their political affiliation), showing that almost half of the 6th District were moved out, at the same time as population changes necessitated moving only about 10,000 voters. In doing so, the partisanship of the district (measured by Cook's PVI) was transformed from a solidly Republican district to a likely Democratic one. The equivalent figures for each Maryland district are shown in Table 3.5.

Population movement and shifts in partisanship would certainly not be the *only* evidence employed by a court using *Benisek* as a partisan gerrymandering standard. (In particular, the court also heavily relies on both quantitative and qualitative evidence of "chilled" political participation.) But we might use unnecessary population movement across districts, accompanied by significant changes in the partisanship of the district, as an indicator of presumptive unconstitutionality.

Table 3.5 Change in Population of Maryland District in 2011 Redistricting

District	Moved In	Remain	Moved Out	% New in District	Partisanship	
					Old	New
1	114,161	608,489	135,786	15.8	R+13	R+14
2	149,128	574,319	126,574	20.6	D+7	D+11
3	236,128	483,966	235,890	32.8	D+6	D+13
4	305,393	414,672	299,647	42.4	D+31	D+28
5	26,359	694,113	73,256	3.7	D+11	D+16
6	**349,937**	**378,511**	**360,429**	**48.0**	R+13	D+6
7	111,788	605,074	54,702	15.6	D+25	D+26
8	284,991	436,523	291,601	39.5	D+21	D+14
Average	197,236	524,458	197,236	27.3		

League of Women Voters v. PA under Population Movement Standard

Unlike in Maryland, the 2011 Pennsylvania legislature could not merely move a few voters around among the existing congressional districts to equalize population. Because the state was losing a congressional district, at the very least one district would have to be dismantled and its voters spread out among other underpopulated districts. Thus, if a single Democratic district were cracked under the new plan, the legislature could possibly claim this was done merely because it was constitutionally required. However, a *second* cracked Democratic district might lead to a more convincing claim under a population-movement standard.

Table 3.6 shows the movement and partisan changes between the 2002 and 2011 Pennsylvania districts.[18] And this shows evidence of at least two Democratic-held districts that were dismantled. The 12th District population in southwest Pennsylvania was distributed across five districts, with incumbent Democrat Mark Critz forced to run a hopeless campaign against an incumbent Republican in a new R + 9 district. The previously compact Harrisburg-based

Table 3.6 Change in Population of Pennsylvania District in 2011 Redistricting

District		Moved Out	Remain	Moved In	% New in District	Partisanship	
Old	New					Old	New
1	1	215,105	440,041	265,647	37.6	D+35	D+28
2	2	106,876	523,401	182,287	25.8	D+38	D+38
3	3	148,323	492,033	213,655	30.3	R+3	R+8
4	12	193,705	453,713	251,975	35.7	R+6	R+9
5	5	135,747	516,015	189,673	26.9	R+9	R+8
6	6	383,950	342,515	363,173	51.5	D+4	R+2
7	7	277,034	396,589	309,099	43.8	D+3	R+2
8	8	47,436	625,249	80,439	11.4	D+2	R+1
9	9	172,917	493,893	211,795	30.0	R+17	R+14
10	10	206,468	462,789	242,898	34.4	R+8	R+12
11	17	504,996	377,415	328,272	46.5	D+4	D+4
12	N/A	612,384	0	0	N/A	R+1	N/A
13	13	272,337	401,851	303,836	43.1	D+7	D+13
14	14	5,984	578,509	127,179	18.0	D+19	D+15
15	15	217,413	504,415	201,272	28.5	D+2	R+2
16	16	118,505	605,472	100,216	14.2	R+8	R+4
17	11	310,445	162,743	542,945	76.9	R+6	R+6
18	18	94,666	558,719	146,969	20.8	R+6	R+10
19	4	71,752	656,878	48,809	6.9	R+12	R+9
Average		193,537	477,347	228,341	32.4		

17th District was split among eight districts. Incumbent Democrat Tim Holden would lose his primary in 2012 running in an almost entirely new district, while Harrisburg itself would largely move to the safely Republican 10th District.

The population movement in the *LWV* map was significantly more complicated than the *Benisek* map. And the legislature could plausibly argue that some of this movement was necessitated by the loss of a district and the associated underpopulation of most existing districts. But the fact that at least *two* districts held by Democrats were completely cracked in the 2011 map would likely create a strong argument that the map would be ruled unconstitutional under a population-movement-based standard.

Rucho v. Common Cause under Population Movement Standard

The North Carolina map at issue in *Rucho* differs from the other three maps in several ways that might be relevant to a population movement standard. First, it is a middecade redistricting prompted by a court decision striking down two districts as racially gerrymandered. Thus, it was constitutionally required for the North Carolina legislature to make more changes to their districts than simply to equalize population. Second, the map was not redrawn to create a delegation *more* biased toward the Republicans but merely to preserve the existing (im)balance of ten Republicans and three Democrats. So in contrasting the 2011 and 2016 maps, the legislature on the one hand needed to make fewer changes to achieve their partisan goals, but on the other hand needed to make more changes to satisfy other constitutional considerations.

Table 3.7 shows the population and partisanship changes in the *Rucho* map. Unlike the other maps examined here, we see significant shifts in population in many districts, but almost no significant changes in partisanship. There are no previously Democratic districts that are either packed or cracked. Instead, the three already overwhelmingly Democratic districts (including the 1st and 12th districts at issue in *Cooper v. Harris*) actually become slightly less packed while still being solidly Democratic, thus slightly more efficiently distributing Democratic voters. Several previously Republican districts dramatically changed their geography without significantly changing their partisanship.

As it is difficult to isolate a specific district that was further packed or cracked in the map compared to the 2011 map, it might be a stretch for the court to strike down this map under a population-movement-based standard. It is worth noting that if such a claim were brought against the 2011 map in comparison to the 2001 map, the case would be much stronger. In particular, the previously Democratic and reasonably compact 13th District from the 2001 map was completely dismantled by the 2011 plan, with no district containing more than one-third of the 13th District's population. Under this standard, a map preserving an existing gerrymander would be much more likely to be upheld than a map drawing a new one, even if only one seat is disrupted.

Table 3.7 Change in Population of North Carolina District in 2016 Redistricting

District				% New	Partisanship	
Old	New	Moved Out	Remain	in District	Old	New
1	1	224,064	509,435	30.5	D+19	D+17
2	N/A	502,207	231,292	68.5	R+10	(R+7)
3	3	142,042	591,457	19.4	R+11	R+12
4	4	278,020	455,478	37.9	D+20	D+17
5	5	197,241	536,258	26.9	R+11	R+10
6	6	366,277	367,222	49.9	R+10	R+9
7	7	206,036	527,462	28.1	R+12	R+9
8	8	422,448	311,051	57.6	R+11	R+8
9	9	445,283	288,215	60.7	R+8	R+8
10	10	32,039	701,460	4.4	R+11	R+12
11	11	25,931	707,568	3.5	R+13	R+14
12	12	351,120	382,379	47.9	D+26	D+18
13	2	318,058	415,440	43.4	R+8	R+7
Average		270,059	463,440	36.8		

Whitford v. Gill under Population Movement Standards

Applying the population movement stylized test to the Wisconsin case is also tricky, as with ninety-nine state assembly districts, there is much more opportunity for change in single districts than among the eight congressional districts in Maryland. The plaintiff's expert reports in Whitford do detail several examples of specific existing Democratic districts being cracked as a result of the Act 43 map, especially in the Madison and Sheboygan regions. Moreover, we might draw some conclusions from comparing average population movement. Appendix Table 3.1 shows the total percentage of population that was retained in each district from its parent district under the Act 43 map, by incumbent party. Overall, the mean district in Wisconsin retained only 62% of its parent population (standard deviation of 24%), compared with 73% in Maryland. So it is certainly true that district lines were changed in most districts far more than necessary to simply balance population. More important, we see a significant partisan distinction. Districts with Republican incumbents retained an average of 66% of their population, while districts with Democratic incumbents retained only 55% of their population, a difference significant at $p<0.05$. Thus, while the "population movement in a single district" test would likely need to be modified in a map with one hundred districts, a reasonable reinterpretation of such a test would likely find the Act 43 map presumptively unconstitutional.

Summary

Applying several simplified tests drawn from prominent redistricting cases to the facts of other cases reveals that none of these tests is entirely satisfying, in the sense that none would strike down all of the alleged gerrymanders. The test drawn from *LWV* (the only case that did ultimately result in a redrawn map), based on "traditional redistricting criteria," perhaps performs the worst. Despite the apparent bias in their resulting elections, the districts drawn in Wisconsin and North Carolina do appear mostly compact and reasonably shaped. And while several districts drawn in Maryland indeed look absurd, the worst of these are not the ones at issue in the *Benisek* case. Moreover, as *Benisek* alleges partisan gerrymandering in only one Maryland district, the election results do not come close to exceeding the statewide standard for efficiency gap bias suggested in *Whitford*. And while *Benisek* alleges that a specific population change in one district could be grounds for unconstitutionality, such a test would likely not satisfy a case like *Rucho*, where mapmakers sought merely to preserve the composition of an existing delegation. It is possible that a multifaceted and amorphous test such as that employed in *Rucho* may be shaped to apply to all these cases, but such a test would likely strain the criterion of being "judicially manageable" inherent in the analysis of "political questions."

But this points to another factor shared by these cases: the covert and exclusionary nature of the map-drawing process. Perhaps a court adopting a purely process-based standard would not just remove the "outliers" that each plaintiff in these cases claimed their situation represented, but incentivize states to dramatically reform their redistricting body toward a more public and fundamentally less political institution. As the next several chapters will explore, this political movement toward nonpartisan commissions is indeed gaining momentum even without court intervention, and when it has succeeded, it has produced positive results on several normatively desirable dimensions.

Despite the very disparate empirical evidence employed across these cases, they do all share common aspects, particularly with respect to partisan intent and process. In each case, the plaintiffs and the lower courts highlight evidence that legislators actively sought to draw a map that would crack opposing partisans. In many cases, particularly evident in the records in *Benisek* and *Rucho*, elected officials were very open about their desire to implement a map that would yield optimal election results for their party. Of course, were a court to adopt a standard striking down only maps where officials were public about their partisan intent, this would likely create further incentives for public officials to be more secretive and disingenuous.

4

Gerrymandering and
Competitive Elections

The previous two chapters emphasized that measuring the effects of districting on the quality of representation is a very difficult task involving several interlocking pieces and many often conflicting factors.[1] So our empirical investigation going forward will follow several different tracks. Throughout most of this chapter, I examine the effects of gerrymandering on a very narrow but easily understood and commonly used measure of competition: close elections. But I test these effects on a large data set of congressional elections nationwide across several decades. At the end of this chapter, I shift the dependent variable to seat turnover in the context of case studies of several specific wave elections. In the next three chapters, I develop a more comprehensive and nuanced measure of bias and competitiveness, which I use to more closely study individual maps drawn in the most recent period.

While the application of the specific dependent variable used throughout most of this chapter (close elections) may seem quite limited, the findings of this chapter will demonstrate two important principles. First, that districting institutions have a statistically and substantively significant impact on at least one measure of representation, spanning elections across the nation over a long period of time. But second, that this impact can be fully understood only in interaction with the national partisan environment in a particular election cycle.

The opening vignette of Chapter 1 shows that it is possible for partisan gerrymanders to backfire spectacularly on the party that drew them in the face of either unexpected long-term demographic changes or short-term partisan tides. Pennsylvania Republicans in 2001 failed to foresee either the local shift away from the Republican Party by voters in the Philadelphia suburbs or the national unpopularity of the Bush administration that swept Democrats into power in 2006 and 2008. The result was not only a shift in the balance of Pennsylvania's delegation but an unusually high number of close and competitive congressional elections across the state in 2006, 2008, and 2010, while the safe districts drawn through bipartisan compromise like those in California remained largely immune to those waves. We've also seen through our toy model in Chapter 2 both how backfires might result from overly aggressive decisions coupled with

Ground War. Nicholas Goedert, Oxford University Press. © Oxford University Press 2022.
DOI: 10.1093/oso/9780197626627.003.0004

adverse tides and how such tides might also create more electoral competition across partisan maps.

But although both anecdotes and models provide obvious examples of waves creating backfires and electoral competitions, it remains unproven how common such "dummymanders" are and how much these maps systematically diverge from those drawn by bipartisan compromises and nonpartisan commissions. This chapter provides empirical evidence for the effects of gerrymandering and wave elections on competition and partisan balance across the past half-century of congressional elections.

I first show that not only are "wave elections" (in which one party wins a substantial majority of the national vote) more common than close congressional election cycles, but that overall levels of district-level competition are heightened during these waves. I then demonstrate that backfiring partisan gerrymanders are systematically responsible for this increase in competition during waves. These dummymanders stand in contrast to bipartisan maps, which experience consistently low levels of competition, and to nonpartisan maps, where competitiveness appears uniformly high. Finally, I show that this difference in competitiveness during national waves has a real impact on the partisan balance of congressional delegations. I establish this first through a series of analyses of all congressional elections from 1972 to 2010, and then through short case studies of four notable wave elections across this period.

Thus, this chapter develops the anecdotal evidence from Grofman and Brunell's (2005) dummymanders into a more general hypothesis about the interaction of tides and partisan gerrymandering on congressional competition. In doing so, I demonstrate that backfires of partisan gerrymanders are both historically common and largely responsible for national variations in the competitiveness of congressional elections across election cycles. Thus, a fair measure of bias and responsiveness must incorporate this likelihood of wave elections and backfires. Chapters 5 through 7 develop and apply just such a measure.

Previous Research on Districting and Competition

While scholarship related to the effects of gerrymandering has honed its focus toward partisan bias just in the past few years, the influence of districts on electoral competition has been a foremost concern for at least the past half-century. Declining competition in U.S. congressional elections has worried scholars since David Mayhew's (1974) seminal article "Congressional Elections: The Case of the Vanishing Marginals." Mayhew does not arrive at an explanation for the paucity of close elections and districts that he observes, but the role of redistricting in fostering or suppressing such competition has been controversial throughout subsequent work. Tufte (1973) argues that redistricting was the cause of a reduction in marginal seats during the 1960s. However, later studies concluded that redistricting, whether partisan or bipartisan, has had little effect on the competitiveness of seats or the advantages of incumbency (Glazer, Grofman, and Robbins 1987; Ferejohn 1977). Moreover, Gelman and King (1994) find that temporally proximate redistricting, both partisan and bipartisan, leads to an *increase* in electoral responsiveness in state elections, measured by the slope of the seats/votes curve. And Gopoian and West (1984), analyzing vote margins in two electoral cycles, suggest that many partisan maps in the 1980s appear to have reduced the security of their incumbents.

Scholars took up this topic in perhaps the greatest force in the mid-2000s, when competitive elections were at their lowest ebb. Cox and Katz (2002) argue that the reapportionment revolution in the 1960s itself has led to decreased competition by reducing the frequency of quality challengers. Research also commonly points to bipartisan legislative agreements as reducing competition and nonpartisan commissions as encouraging it. Carson Crespin, and Williamson (2014, see also Carson and Crespin (2004)) find evidence that courts and commissions increase competition in years immediately following redistricting (using data from 1992 and 2002 in their original article, and from 1972–2012 in the 2014 update). Lindgren and Southwell (2013) also argue that independent commissions did reduce the average margin of victory in U.S. House elections from 2002 to 2010. But neither of these articles distinguishes between bipartisan and partisan legislative maps. More generally, Cain, MacDonald, and McDonald (2005) find that an overall decline in competitive elections has tracked with an increase in the number of districts drawn by bipartisan agreement. And McDonald (2006) concludes that legislative districting was responsible for decreased competition in the 2000s, while nonpartisan commissions facilitated more competitive districts.

Yet other recent works claim much less of a role for districting in contributing to this trend. In an examination of state legislative elections in 2000–2008 (and using the same definition of competitive elections as this chapter), Masket, Winburn, and Wright (2012) find little impact of redistricting institutions on the likelihood of a close election. And Abramowitz, Alexander, and Gunning (2006) find that while much of the decline in competition since the 1970s can be attributed to the increased partisan polarization of districts, this is explained much more by population sorting than intentional districting.

And the specific role of partisan districting in inducing or suppressing competition is perhaps even more ambiguous. Hirsch (2003) focuses on Republican-drawn maps as causing historically low competitiveness in the 2002 elections. But employing data from the same election cycle, Yoshinaka and Murphy (2009, 2011) find that partisan maps increase competition and the recruitment of quality challengers, particularly in years immediately following redistricting. But Yoshinaka and Murphy constrain their explanation to the deliberately increased difficulty that out-party members face rather than unanticipated close races faced by in-party members during unexpected waves. And as part of a series of articles showing the effects of moving voters to unfamiliar districts, Hood and McKee (2008) found that a mid-decade partisan gerrymander in Georgia made two districts in the state more competitive.

Yet the fact that partisan gerrymanders do not always turn out as planned for the controlling party has not gone unnoticed by scholars. Grofman and Brunell (2005), in a series of short case studies they refer to as "dummymanders," show that many maps drawn by southern Democrats in the 1990s failed to anticipate trends favoring the Republican Party. Conversely, Seabrook (2010, 2017) argues that the effects of Republican partisan maps were largely washed out by mid-decade partisan trends in the 2000s. However, the global effect of dummymanders on competition, and the frequency of their occurrence, is largely still unexamined beyond anecdotal evidence and narrow case studies. This chapter tests the global effect of whether unexpected electoral environments indeed make partisan gerrymanders more competitive.

Wave Elections and National Tides

As this chapter argues that short-term shifts or "tides" in national public opinion are crucial to understanding how gerrymandering impacts electoral competition, we first must be able to measure the concept of electoral tides. And as we are primarily concerned with the closeness of electoral competition while caring less about the partisanship of the winner, it is mostly important to measure how strongly the leading party is favored rather than *which* party is favored. Throughout the analysis, this is done through the variable *National Tides*, defined as the national popular vote margin for the winning party. In contrast, the terms "waves" and "wave elections" are used casually and without formal definition to refer to election cycles in which one party wins a large majority of the congressional popular vote. However, these concepts are closely connected: what we commonly refer to as "wave elections" will be those cycles in which *National Tides* is highest (e.g., 1974 or 2008 on the Democratic side; 1994 or 2010 on the Republican side). And as *National Tides* increase, we might also expect district-level election results to deviate more from their "normal vote" of the baseline partisanship of the district.

Specifically, *National Tides* is the absolute value of *National GOP Vote Margin*, the aggregated Republican margin in the nationwide congressional popular vote in a given cycle. Our key independent variables of interest are the interactions of

National Tides with redistricting institutions. For example, because Democrats won the 2006 national congressional popular vote by 7.9%, *National GOP Vote Margin* takes a value of –7.9, and *National Tides* takes a value of 7.9 for all 2006 data points. In a very closely divided election like 2000, *National Tides* takes a value 0.3. Thus the more informal notion of wave elections is operationalized as the absolute margin for the winning party in the national congressional popular vote throughout the analysis.

Hypotheses

Building upon the theory and examples from Chapter 2, I hypothesize that a typical strategy employed by partisan mapmakers will be to draw seats that will be largely safe for their own incumbents under neutral electoral conditions (when the national popular vote is close to even), but which will become increasingly competitive as national tides adverse to the gerrymandering party increase. Thus, the overall effect of partisan gerrymanders on competition can be considered only in interaction with national competition.

Individual partisan gerrymanders will make varied choices as to how to balance the competing considerations of maximizing expected seats under neutral conditions and protecting incumbents against adverse tides, as noted in the contrast between "aggressive" and "defensive" maps in Chapter 2. But despite these diverse choices, all partisan maps will have the potential to become a dummymander when tides reach a certain magnitude. As adverse tides grow, the number of partisan maps that backfire should increase, leading to more competitive elections where mapmakers expected safe sailing for their own party's incumbents. In contrast, we should not observe this interaction of tides and competition when it comes to bipartisan and nonpartisan maps.

Therefore, we would expect to see the following interactions between national tides and redistricting institutions:

- We expect *low* competitiveness in districts drawn by *bipartisan* agreement regardless of electoral environment.
- We expect *high* competitiveness among districts drawn by *nonpartisan* commissions when the national electoral environment is close.[2] As national tides increase, competitiveness in these districts may decline or stay steady.
- When the national electoral environment is close, we expect *low* competitiveness among districts drawn by legislatures controlled by *one party*. As national tides *increase*, we expect competitiveness to *increase*, particularly when tides run adverse to the gerrymandering party.

- In cases where we observe high competition during wave elections under partisan gerrymanders, we expect a *greater* proportion of competitive races to occur in *districts held by the party adverse to tides*, relative to both other redistricting regimes and other electoral environments.

Figure 4.1a depicts a schematic of these hypotheses, showing low competition under bipartisan maps, high competition under nonpartisan maps, and competition under partisan maps increasing with adverse tides.[3] Figure 4.1b depicts 1a folded in on itself at the middle, so that the x-axis represents the magnitude of a wave without regard to direction, and combines the two partisan lines into one.

The analysis will first test the theory as presented in Figure 4.1b (leveraging the size of tides irrespective of direction), as this allows us to test the entire data set of congressional elections using a straightforward two-way interaction. The analysis will then move on to testing the asymmetric prediction for the partisan maps in 4.1a, examining the subsets of the elections data for Democratic and Republican gerrymanders. Next I will test the specific piece of the hypothesis that increased competitiveness under partisan gerrymanders during adverse tides

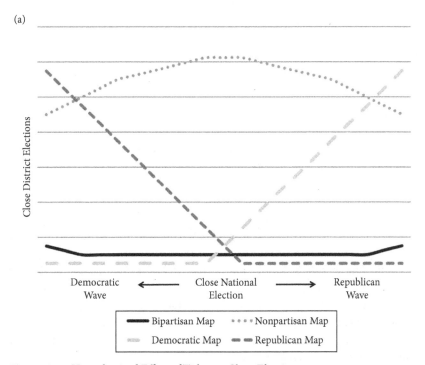

Figure 4.1a Hypothesized Effect of Tides on Close Elections

(b)

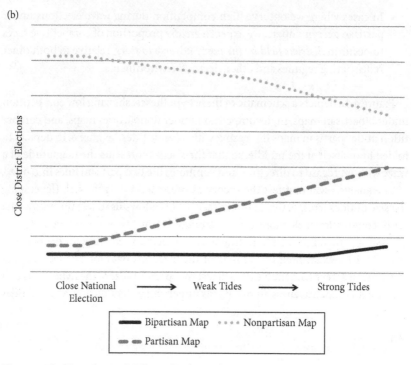

Figure 4.1b Hypothesized Effect of Tides without Regard to Direction on Close Elections

will be found in seats drawn to be held by the gerrymandering party. Building on its findings on close elections, I demonstrate how differences in competition also lead to differences in the partisan makeup of delegations. Finally, I describe how both these differences in competitions and turnover across gerrymandering regimes played out in specific wave elections.

Measures and Controls

My main data set consists of all congressional elections from 1972 through 2010 (excluding special elections).[4] The process by which each state was redistricted at the start of the decade was coded as Democratic-controlled, Republican-controlled, bipartisan, nonpartisan, or court.[5] Throughout the analysis, the bipartisan maps, under which we hypothesize low levels of competition regardless of tides, serve as the reference group.[6]

This analysis attempts to isolate the effects of the redistricting *institution* and not the effects of the specific districts drawn. Therefore, any controls that might be endogenous and causally posterior to the actual districts have been deliberately omitted. This of course includes district-specific demographics and partisanship, but also candidate-specific data like campaign spending and incumbency. Although all of these factors are of course important to the outcome of a congressional race, the variables that are included (statewide presidential vote, regional and statewide demographics, and redistricting institution) are causally prior, and thus the exclusion of district-specific factors should not contaminate the coefficients testing the theory.[7] This requirement is necessarily suspended in the final segment of the analysis, which tests the portion of the hypothesis related to the incumbent party holding the seat.

As examples, two district-level variables in particular may come to mind as strongly affecting electoral competition: incumbency and district partisan balance. Yet both are also clearly endogenous to our independent variables of interest. In the case of district partisan balance, we would expect more closely divided districts to generate close elections more frequently. However, the number of closely divided districts is typically a deliberate choice of the gerrymander, with some institutions consistently drawing more competitive districts than others (as shown in Appendix Table 4.2). Controlling balance at the district level may actually remove some of the genuine effects of a gerrymandering regime. Similarly, we would expect more close races in the case of open seats. But open seats themselves may partially be a function of both gerrymandering and tides, as members may choose to retire because their district has been drawn to be much more difficult to run in or because the overall political climate is such that they expect adverse partisan tides. On the other hand, we should be much less concerned that these variables are causing, or are otherwise correlated in a causally prior way with, the gerrymandering institution or national-level tides. Nevertheless, the inclusion of these two factors, both of which strongly correlate with competitiveness, ultimately has little effect on the influence of partisan tides, gerrymandering institutions, or their interactions; results including both of these variables are shown in Appendix Table 4.14.

To get a complete picture of the effects of redistricting on competition, I employ two measures of competitiveness as independent variables: *National Tides* (described earlier) and *Statewide Competition*, a control for the competitiveness of the state as a whole. *Statewide Competition* is a measure of the overall partisan balance of the state, with lower values indicating swing states and higher values indicating solidly partisan states. Unlike the partisan balance of a district, *Statewide Competition* is causally prior to gerrymandering. It is used as an important control in the analysis, as it is a measure of competitiveness that is not affected by the shape of congressional districts. It is defined as the absolute value of the difference between the average statewide GOP presidential vote margin and the average national GOP vote margin over the previous two elections for a given district in a given year, that is, a rough measure of a state's partisan extremism in a given period. For example, for all California districts in 2006, this variable takes a value of 13, because California voted 13% more Democratic than the nation in the 2000 and 2004 presidential elections.

The dependent variable in the analysis is *Close Race*, a dummy variable coded as 1 for each individual congressional race in a specific year if the election was won by less than 10 percentage points.[8] As we are mainly interested in how often congressional elections are competitive, this is the dependent variable throughout most of the analysis. Overall, 14% of congressional elections are *Close Races* under this definition.

While we do not want to control out district-level variables whose correlation to gerrymandering is causally posterior, we do need to be wary of selection effects from statewide variables that may correlate with gerrymandering institutions in a causally prior way. If states with a particular redistricting regime also share some other quality, it is possible that this other quality may be causing what appears to be an effect of that regime. Specifically, three such effects are anticipated, with specific controls employed in various configurations to account for plausible alternative causal stories. First, states that lean heavily in one partisan direction are more likely to have a gerrymandering process controlled by that party, so the *Statewide Competition* control is employed in all specifications. Second, because small states may be simultaneously less amenable to drastic gerrymanders and more likely to establish nonpartisan commissions, results are run both with and without a control for state size. Finally, because the partisanship of southern states during much of this period tended to be much more Democratic at the state legislative level than the presidential level, results are run both including and excluding the southern region (defined as the former Confederacy).[9]

Results

The Pseudoparadox of Competition

Looking at the partisan balance of a district assuming a neutral environment, as is common in the scholarship, tells us little about what will occur when tides swing distinctly in one direction. Yet it is apparent that national tides have a dramatic and surprising impact on district-level competition. As discussed, many of the recent claims about declining congressional competition, in both the media and the literature, occurred in the wake of an era of parity at the national level. Between 1996 and 2004, no party won a majority of the national popular vote in congressional elections, nor did any party win that popular vote by more than 5 points, or win more than 54% of congressional seats.

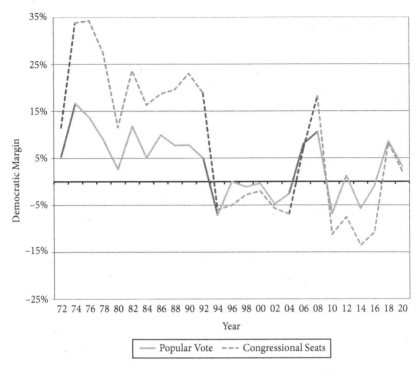

Figure 4.2 National Popular Vote vs. Seats Won in Congressional Elections

But this is actually something of a historical anomaly. Figure 4.2 shows the national popular vote advantage and seat advantage achieved by Democrats in congressional elections from 1972 to 2020, revealing the frequency of large swings in both votes and seats in both directions. Of the twenty-five election cycles from 1972 to 2020, one party failed to win by at least 5 points in the popular vote only ten times, including those five consecutive cycles beginning in 1996. During a time when the country appeared so evenly divided, it would be intuitive to expect that many individual races would also be close, but less than 11% of races during this era were decided by 10 points or less (our definition of *Close Races*).

But this era of parity was immediately followed by three consecutive wave elections, from 2006 through 2010. And despite the national electorate clearly favoring one party in these three cycles, the number of races that were closely contested paradoxically rose to 15%. Recently, it seems that close national competition has led to less competitiveness at the local level, and this phenomenon is borne out by looking further into the past, at least as far back as the equal-population standard has been applied to congressional districts. The top left quadrant of Figure 4.3 shows the correlation of the proportions of *Close Races* in each

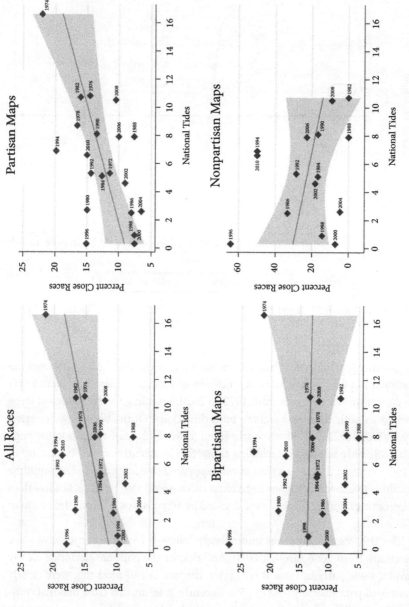

Figure 4.3 Close Races by Year and Gerrymandering Institution

Table 4.1 Probability of Close Race Controlling for Statewide and National Competitiveness

Pr(Close Race)	(1)	No South (2)	(3)	No 1974 (4)
Statewide Competition	−0.003	0.000	−0.001	−0.003
	(0.003)	(0.003)	(0.003)	(0.003)
National Tides	*0.019****	*0.017****	*0.017****	*0.013***
	(0.005)	*(0.005)*	*(0.005)*	*(0.006)*
Year	–	–	−0.002	–
			(0.002)	
Redistricting Year	–	–	0.004	–
			(0.041)	
Constant	−1.18	−1.16	3.32	−1.15
	(0.048)	(0.055)	(4.37)	(0.050)
Observations	8,700	6,300	8,700	8,265

Notes: Entries are probit coefficients. Standard errors clustered by district interacted with decade.
* = $p<0.10$, ** = $p<0.05$, *** = $p<0.01$

cycle 1972–2010 with *National Tides*; as the national popular vote gets closer, the number of competitive races tends to decline.

As a more rigorous test, Table 4.1 shows the effect of *National Tides* on the percentage of *Close Races* (each data point is an individual race, with races clustered by state crossed with decade) from 1972 to 2010, when we control for the competitiveness of individual states by including *Statewide Competition*. In the first column, we see that the competitiveness of a *state* has very little effect on its propensity toward competitive congressional elections.[10] However, the positive coefficient on *National Tides* (significant at $p<0.01$) indicates that more extreme wave elections do tend to create more close races. The second column excludes races in the South, with no effect on the *National Tides* coefficient, indicating the phenomenon cannot be explained merely by increased competitiveness of the Republican Party in the South in the most recent decades, or the creation of majority-minority districts in those states. The third column addresses the argument that competition has steadily declined over time by including a *Year* variable, as well as the argument that competition increases in years immediately following redistricting (e.g., Yoshinaka and Murphy 2011; Hetherington, Larson, and Globetti 2003); the *Gerrymander Year* dummy variable takes a value of 1 for election years ending in 2. Neither of these variables is statistically significant, and neither mediates the strong effect of *National Tides*. Finally, we see in Figure 4.3 that 1974 appears to be an outlier both in terms of wave strength and number of close races. The fourth column of Table 4.1 shows that the effect of *National Tides* on *Close Races* is still significant at p < 0.05 even when this cycle is excluded.[11]

Effects of Gerrymandering

So what explains this "pseudoparadox" that less national competitiveness correlates with greater local competition in congressional races? The answer appears to lie in the partisan gerrymanders. When we isolate only the partisan maps (shown in the top-right quadrant of Figure 4.3), the negative effect of national competitiveness on local competitiveness is strengthened (and significant at p < 0.02). In contrast, the magnitude of *National Tides* has no effect on competitive elections under bipartisan maps (shown in the bottom left of Figure 4.3), which follows if these maps drew districts safe enough for both parties to withstand strong tides in either direction.[12] Moreover, the coefficient for the nonpartisan maps is in the opposite direction of partisan maps, although not significant due to the high variance from the small sample size; this would also follow if such maps tended to draw many "naturally" competitive districts. This conforms exactly to the schematic in Figure 4.1b: an upward slope in the case of partisan gerrymanders, a flat line with respect to bipartisan maps, and a downward (though nonsignificant) slope in the case of nonpartisan maps.

Yet it is also possible that these observed differences are merely the result of the types of states that tend to adopt these varying institutions. That is, perhaps swing states tend to adopt nonpartisan regimes or extreme states adopt bipartisan regimes. So I also run a probit analysis of *Close Race* on *National Tides* and the various gerrymander dummies including the *Statewide Competition* control, and assess the slope of the effect of tides by interacting *National Tides* with the gerrymander dummies. As before, the unit of analysis in Table 4.2 is individual congressional races from 1972 to 2010, clustered by year crossed with decade; the excluded category is bipartisan maps. The key analyses are shown with and without a control for state size (expressed as number of districts).

Figure 4.4 shows the number of close races predicted under each redistricting regime in a tied national election, with estimates drawn for a swing state from column 1 of Table 4.2. In every analysis, we see that nonpartisan commissions create more close elections than bipartisan maps or partisan maps (controlling for state ideology and national tides), with the effect of nonpartisan maps large enough to be significant despite the small sample size. From the figure, we estimate that while only 11% of elections overall will be close races with neutral electoral and tides conditions under partisan and bipartisan maps, almost 20% of races will be close under nonpartisan commission maps.[13]

Table 4.2 Probability of Close Race Controlling for Redistricting Institution and State and National Electoral Trend (Congressional Races 1972–2010)

Pr(Close Race)	(1)	No South (2)	w/CDs control (3)	(4)	No South (5)	w/CDs control (6)
Statewide Competition	-0.0030 (0.0031)	-.00023 (0.0034)	-0.0047 (0.0031)	-0.0027 (0.0032)	0.00017 (0.0034)	-0.0045 (0.0031)
National Tides	0.020*** (0.0045)	0.019*** (0.0053)	0.020*** (0.0045)	0.015* (0.0083)	0.012 (0.009)	0.016** (0.0080)
Democratic Gerrymander	-0.10** (0.052)	-0.085 (0.077)	-0.14*** (0.052)	-0.12 (0.090)	-0.122 (0.147)	-0.17* (0.088)
Republican Gerrymander	-0.016 (0.059)	0.036 (0.066)	-0.015 (0.058)	-0.20* (0.11)	-0.195 (0.118)	-0.21** (0.10)
Court Gerrymander	0.065 (0.050)	0.083 (0.062)	0.091* (0.050)	0.068 (0.083)	0.090 (0.101)	0.13 (0.081)
Nonpartisan Gerrymander	*0.33*** (0.098)*	*0.32*** (0.099)*	*0.21** (0.10)*	*0.41** (0.17)*	*0.382** (0.172)*	*0.29* (0.17)*
Democratic Gerrymander* Tides	–	–	–	0.0035 (0.011)	0.0065 (0.017)	0.0045 (0.011)
Republican Gerrymander* Tides	–	–	–	*0.025** (0.012)*	*0.032** (0.013)*	*0.028** (0.012)*

(continued)

Table 4.2 *Continued*

Pr(Close Race)	(1)	No South (2)	w/CDs control (3)	(4)	No South (5)	w/CDs control (6)
Court Gerrymander* Tides	–	–	–	-0.00040 (0.0099)	-0.0008 (0.0118)	-0.0057 (0.0098)
Nonpartisan Gerrymander* Tides	–	–	–	-0.013 (0.021)	-0.011 (0.021)	-0.014 (0.021)
CDs	–	–	-.0094*** (0.0018)	–	–	-.0096*** (0.0018)
Constant	-1.20*** (0.058)	-1.21*** (0.065)	-1.00*** (0.067)	-1.17*** (0.074)	-1.17*** (0.081)	-0.98*** (0.079)
Observations	8,700	6,300	8,700	8,700	6,300	8,700

Notes: Entries are probit coefficients. Standard errors clustered by district interacted with decade.

* = p < 0.10, ** = p < 0.05, *** = p < 0.01

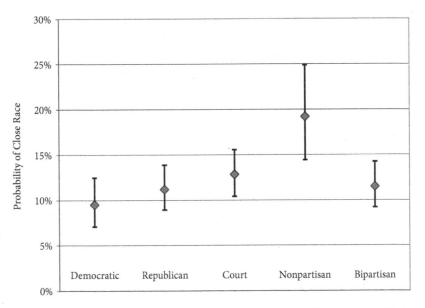

Figure 4.4 Estimated Close Races by Redistricting Institution (Swing State in Tied Popular Vote Election)

Notes: Entries represent the estimated probability of a race being won by less than 10% under various redistricting institutions, taken from model 1 in Table 4.2, if *Statewide Competition* and *National Tides* are set to 0. Error bars represent the 95% confidence interval of the probit coefficient.

But note that in all these specifications, the effect of *National Tides* is positive and significant, consistent with earlier nationally aggregated results. We can test how this effect varies under different gerrymanders in two ways. First, we can include interaction terms nested into the model run on the entire data set. This is shown in columns 4 through 6 of Table 4.2, which adds the interactions of each regime with tides. Matching the aggregated data in Figure 4.3, we see that the pseudoparadox effect of tides is again largely explained by gerrymandering institutions. The positive effect of *National Tides* is even larger when applied to Republican-drawn gerrymanders, but not significant when applied to nonpartisan maps.[14]

A second way of analyzing this interaction effect would be to measure the influence of tides on the data subsetted by redistricting regime. We do this by estimating the effect of *National Tides* when the first model in Table 4.1 is run only on subsets of districts drawn under a particular institution. Again, the results conform to our predictions, with full results in Appendix Table 4.4. *National Tides* are significantly and positively correlated with close elections under Republican and Democratic gerrymanders, suggesting that partisan maps suffer a backlash when tides go against them, leading to many close races as national tides

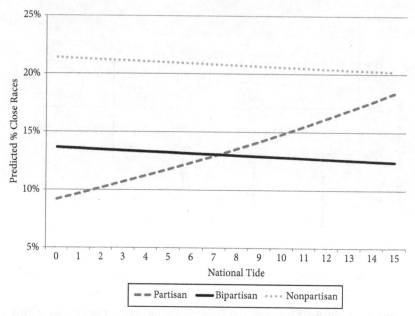

Figure 4.5 Estimated Close Races by National Tide and Redistricting Institution
Notes: Estimated proportions from slope estimates in Table 4.3 for nationally average state.

increase. But there is no significant effect of tides under bipartisan gerrymanders, with robustly safe districts drawn, or nonpartisan gerrymanders, where competition is high even in closely balanced elections. The difference between these coefficients for partisan and bipartisan maps is significant at p < 0.02. In support of our hypotheses, competition at the district level increases as tides increase under partisan maps, but not bipartisan or nonpartisan maps.

This analysis estimates that as *National Tides* rise from 0 to 10 (where 10 represents a wave similar to 2008), the proportion of close races in an average state will rise from 9% to 15% under partisan gerrymanders, remain stable at 13% under bipartisan gerrymanders, and fall from 22% to 19% under nonpartisan maps. This change in estimated proportions is shown in Figure 4.5, almost perfectly matching the predictions in the schematic Figure 4.1b. And both techniques confirm at the district level the effect of partisan gerrymanders on competition observed at the national level in Figure 4.3.

Differences by Party of Wave and Gerrymander

The analysis thus far has shown that electoral competition conforms to the schematic in Figure 4.1b, showing interaction with tides without regard to direction. But we have yet to test the asymmetric expectations from partisan gerrymanders depicted in Figure 4.1a, to actually show that increasing competition under them is generated largely from backfires or dummymanders. I hypothesize that we should observe greater competition only under waves *adverse* to the map-drawing party (i.e., Republican maps under Democratic waves such as 1974 and 2008, and Democratic maps under Republican waves like 1994). Our findings support this hypothesis for Democratic maps, with the difference in responsiveness to tides under Democratic and Republican waves for Democratic gerrymanders significant at $p < 0.01$ (and results in Appendix Table 4.5). Unfortunately, performing the same analysis for Republican maps would involve drawing conclusions based on a very small number of elections;[15] the difference in responsiveness by wave direction for Republican maps is not significant.

Although the sample size of elections, particularly Republican-wave elections, limits our ability to demonstrate the different responses to waves under Democratic and Republican regimes in a statistically robust way, we can at least observe these differences anecdotally. Table 4.3 depicts the percentage of close races in states with Democratic maps in the 1990s and 2000s and in states with Republican maps in the 1970s and 2000s.[16] Elections with strong opposing tides, where we would hypothesize a greater number of close races, are shown in italics.

With one exception, the results conform to our expectations. In both the 1990s and the 2000s, Democratic maps saw more close races in the two Republican-wave elections (1994 and 2010) than in other years during their respective decades. Republican maps also saw the greatest number of close elections in the post-Watergate cycle of 1974, and many more close elections in the Democratic waves of 2006 and 2008 than the previous two cycles. Contrary to Yoshinaka and Murphy (2011), partisan gerrymanders do not seem to increase competition in years immediately following redistricting, but do so in years when tides turn against the party in control.

The table also reveals that one cycle in particular deviates from our predictions: 2010, which saw many close races under both Democratic and Republican maps. That was a very unusual election in that it involved a strong Republican wave immediately succeeding a strong Democratic wave; the difference in popular vote between 2008 and 2010 is by far the largest between any two consecutive elections in the data set, and it unsurprisingly resulted in the largest seat turnover.[17] This resulted in many Democratic incumbents facing a Republican wave in Republican-leaning districts drawn by Republican gerrymanders, and these situations tended to generate close elections. So we must be mindful that the factors measured in this chapter are of course not the only factors that contribute to competitiveness. For example, 2010 shows an effect of incumbency, though perhaps in the opposite direction we would typically

Table 4.3 Percentage of Close Races by Year and
Gerrymandering Party Close Races in Seats Drawn
by Democrats

Year	National GOP Vote Margin	Seats	% Close
1992	−5.3	122	16
1994	*6.9*	*122*	*20*
1996	−0.3	122	14
1998	0.9	122	8
2000	0.3	122	7
2002	4.6	111	11
2004	2.6	79	8
2006	−7.9	66	5
2008	−10.5	66	6
2010	*6.6*	*66*	*15*

Close Races in Seats Drawn by Republicans

Year	National GOP Vote Margin	Seats	% Close
1972	−5.3	119	18
1974	*−16.6*	*119*	*28*
1976	−10.8	119	17
1978	−8.7	119	17
1980	−2.7	119	12
2002	4.6	98	7
2004	2.6	130	5
2006	*−7.9*	*143*	*13*
2008	*−10.5*	*143*	*13*
2010	6.6	143	15

expect: Democratic incumbents were able to keep many races close under tides
conditions that would have resulted in easy Republican wins if the seat were
open or held by a Republican. Despite this outlier, the asymmetric effects of
tides on competition shown in Figure 4.1a are strongly supported through both

statistical and anecdotal evidence in the case of Democratic gerrymanders, and more weakly supported through anecdotal evidence in the case of Republican gerrymanders.

Differences by Party Holding Seats

Crucial to a generalized theory of dummymanders is that gerrymandering parties will see increased competitiveness under adverse tides in the *seats that they already hold* as opposed to seats they have ceded to the opposing party. Testing this proposition requires testing a somewhat complicated three-way interaction involving the size of the wave, the party drawing the lines, and the party controlling the seat prior to the election. We have already shown that the number of competitive elections increases in states with partisan gerrymanders as tides adverse to the gerrymandering party increase. And it should be obvious that under strong partisan tides, most of the vulnerable seats will be those held by the adverse party, regardless of gerrymandering regime, and thus we should see more competitive elections under Democratic tides in seats held by Republicans (and vice versa).

What the generalization of the dummymander hypothesis predicts is that, as Democratic tides increase (for example), the share of competitive elections that are contested in Republican-held seats should *increase more* in states with Republican gerrymanders than in states with other redistricting regimes. Specifically, the interaction of (1) Republican-held seats with (2) Republican gerrymanders *and* (3) Republican national vote share should be *negative* (since Republican vote share *decreases* during Democratic waves). As an example of this interaction: under a Democratic tide, competitive races will be more likely in Republican-held seats (those targeted by Democrats during the wave) than in Democrat-held seats across the board. However, I hypothesize that this disparity will be greater in Republican-gerrymandered maps (i.e., dummymanders) than in other maps. And we should see a similar effect of Republican waves on Democratic seats in Democratic gerrymanders.

Indeed, our data show exactly this phenomenon. Where Republicans drew the lines, competition becomes significantly more concentrated on Republican-held seats under Democratic-wave elections compared to neutral elections (excluding Republican waves). And conversely, where Democrats drew the lines, competition becomes more concentrated on seats held by Democrats as Republican tides increase (excluding Democratic waves). Complete regression results are shown in Appendix Table 4.6. Overall, this three-way interaction suggests that backfires under adverse tides occur predominantly in seats held by the gerrymandering party.

Competition and Partisan Turnover

As discussed in Chapter 2, many may consider electoral competitiveness a political good to be valued on its own; for example, it may enhance citizen engagement with the electoral process. But others may argue that competition is instrumental to public responsiveness only in the form of seat change. And indeed, essential to the idea of the dummymander is that failure to anticipate future political trends causes not just increased competition but ultimately the loss of seats for the gerrymandering party, potentially also leading to the loss of partisan control of Congress. Grofman and Brunell's (2005) original example of the dummymander concerned Democratic seat losses under southern Democratic gerrymanders in the 1994 Republican-wave election, while Seabrook (2010, 2017) argues that Republicans lost a disproportionate number of seats in states they gerrymandered in the consecutive Democratic waves in 2006 and 2008.

The impact of dummymanders on partisan election outcomes can indeed be tested through the four-decade data set of congressional elections. I estimate the probability of a Republican victory (rather than the probability of a close election) as a function of tides interacted with gerrymandering regime. In this case, our controls for national tides and statewide presidential partisanship are directional, with positive values indicating Republican tides, and the dependent variable is the proportion of seats won by Republicans. The key outcome is a positive and significant slope for the interaction of national vote and Republican gerrymanders, especially when Republican-wave elections are excluded. This shows that Republican gerrymanders are significantly more sensitive to Democratic tides than bipartisan or other gerrymanders. (We would also expect Democratic gerrymanders to be more sensitive to Republican tides, but as with much of the previous analysis, the very limited number of Republican waves in our data set do not allow us to draw conclusions beyond the anecdotal sort similar to Grofman and Brunell.)

While a table showing the full results of this model is included in Appendix Table 4.7, Figure 4.6 summarizes the result in graphic form, when estimated for a swing state (nationally average at the presidential level). Tides in this figure range from –15 (15% national Democratic advantage) to 6 (6% GOP advantage), as that is the range of the actual popular vote from my data set.[18] When national tides are even, partisan maps lead to about 58% seat share for the map-drawing party in the case of both Democrats and Republicans. As expected, bipartisan gerrymanders show no particular partisan bias.[19]

In this graph, the bipartisan maps have the lowest slope, while nonpartisan commissions show the highest slope. As predicted in our toy model in Chapter 2, delegations from bipartisan maps are least sensitive to tides, while delegations from nonpartisan maps are most sensitive. But most importantly, the figure

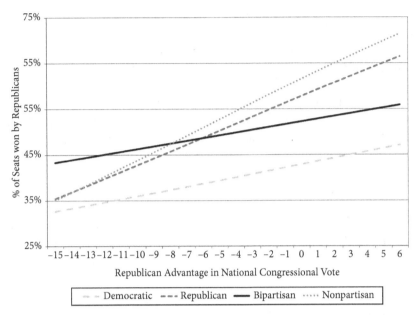

Figure 4.6 Estimated Effect of Partisan Tides and Redistricting Institution on Partisan Composition of Congressional Delegation

Notes: Entries represent the estimated probability of a race being won by a Republican under various redistricting institutions and national popular vote conditions taken from Appendix Table 4.7, if Statewide Presidential Vote is set to 0.

depicts a very high slope for Republican maps and a low slope for Democratic maps. Because almost all of our data lie in conditions of either fairly neutral tides or tides favorable to Democrats, it is also consistent with the model that the Democratic maps have a low slope and the Republican maps have a higher slope (though only significantly different from bipartisan maps at p<0.10), indicating backfires in the partisan gerrymander during Democratic tides. This analysis estimates that for a swing state, moving from neutral tides to a strong, 15-point Democratic tide (a slightly bigger wave than 2008 but smaller than 1974) would reduce Republican seats won under Republican gerrymanders by 22% (from 58% to 36%) but would reduce Republican seats under bipartisan maps by only 9% (from 52% to 43%) and Democratic maps by 10% (from 42% to 32%). The difference in this slope between Republican and bipartisan maps is significant at p<0.05. And note that the number of Republican seats remaining after a 15-point Democratic wave is actually fewer in absolute terms under a Republican gerrymander than under a bipartisan map. So backfiring of Republican gerrymanders under Democratic waves leads not only to more close races but ultimately to more responsiveness to voters in the form of partisan seat turnover.

Evidence from Wave Elections

To gather one last piece of evidence about the propensity of partisan maps to backfire, the final question we might ask is: In years when one party flips *a lot* of seats, *where* are they winning the most?

To do this, I highlight the effect of waves on different redistricting regimes by homing in on specific "wave" elections where the electorate shifts from a fairly neutral electoral environment to an environment clearly favoring one party. In such elections, our model would predict the following:

- We should see *high* volatility where maps are drawn by:
  - Nonpartisan commissions.
  - Legislatures controlled by the party *disfavored* by the current partisan tides.
- We might or might not expect high volatility where maps are drawn by:
  - Courts, depending on the issues considered by the court and the partisan character of the judiciary.
  - Very small states where gerrymandering is not feasible, depending on the overall partisan balance of the state.
- We expect *low* volatility when maps are drawn by:
  - Bipartisan committees.
  - Legislatures under split control.
  - Legislatures controlled by the party *favored* by the current partisan tides.

To look for empirical support, I have examined three periods of dramatic mid-decade shifts in partisan tides in national congressional voting since the first round of post-*Wesberry* reapportionment in 1970. Recall Figure 4.2, depicting the swings in congressional vote and seats in each election cycle. Three periods with shifts of greater than 10% in the popular vote are highlighted in this figure, each resulting in turnover of approximately fifty seats:

- 1974: The "Watergate babies" election; Democrats gained forty-nine seats.
- 1994: Newt Gingrich's "Republican Revolution"; Republicans gained fifty-four seats.
- 2006 and 2008: I have combined these two cycles where Democrats were restored to power in Congress, gaining fifty-five seats between them.[20]

The 2010 election would certainly be considered a Republican-wave election but is not included here because our predictions cannot be cleanly tested in the same way in the case of back-to-back opposing wave elections. I analyze each wave in three ways:

1. An "eyeball" test looking at how many seats switched to the favored party for each gerrymandering regime.
2. A probit analysis of the probability of a member of a given party holding a seat before and after each wave, controlling for statewide partisanship.
3. A probit analysis of the probability of a seat flipping toward the favored party under each regime, controlling for statewide partisanship.

As in the earlier analysis in this chapter, the unit of analysis is again the congressional district, and I have omitted any controls that would be endogenous to the districts themselves.

2006 and 2008

The 2006 midterm election saw an interruption to a relatively stable period of narrow Republican control of the House of Representatives. In gaining thirty-one seats, Democrats exactly flipped this control from a 202–233 deficit to a 233–202 majority. With Barack Obama on the ballot and the incumbent president, Republican George W. Bush, deeply unpopular, Democrats built on this majority in 2008 by adding an additional twenty-one seats and winning the national House popular vote by over 10%, the largest margin for either party since 1982. Including a few special election wins during that period, Democrats entered the Obama era with a 257–178 majority.

These back-to-back waves occurred during a decade that saw Republican or split control of the redistricting process in many states, providing a good test of the partisan gerrymandering "backfire." Additionally, three states (Arizona, Iowa, and Washington) were districted by nonpartisan committees or bureaucracies, and three states saw their maps drawn by courts. At first glance, our prediction that we should see more turnover in states redistricted by Republican or nonpartisan committees than those drawn by legislatures with Democratic or split control appears to be true; Table 4.4 shows the number of seats that shifted from Republican to Democrat at some point during the 2005–2009 period by redistricting institution.[21]

The 2006 wave cycle in particular created significant turnover in commission states, with two seats flipping to Democrats in each state of Iowa and Arizona, and the most aggressive of the partisan gerrymanders in Pennsylvania, where four incumbent Republicans were defeated. The slightly stronger 2008 wave wore down the more fortified Republican gerrymanders, with three Republican seats flipping in each state of Florida, Ohio, and Virginia, along with one additional seat each in Arizona and Pennsylvania.

Table 4.4 Congressional Seat Flips by Redistricting
Institution, 2005–2009

Redistricting Institution	States	CDs	Flips R to D	Flip %
Bipartisan	12	169	18	10.6
Republican	7	124	20	16.1
Democratic	8	69	4	5.8
Nonpartisan	3	22	5	22.7
Court	3	19	4	21.1
Small States	17	32	7	21.8

In addition to the raw turnover numbers, I estimate the probability of Republicans holding each seat following the 2004 election and following the 2008 election, and of flipping from Republican to Democrat at some point during this period (including special elections), with controls for statewide presidential vote, change in presidential margin, region, and statewide percentage Black and Latino. Results of this probit analysis, including confidence intervals, are shown in Figure 4.7, interpreted for a state that voted with the national mean

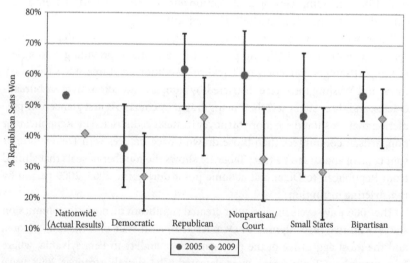

Figure 4.7 Estimated Republican Congressional Delegation (2005 vs. 2009) in State with National Mean Presidential Vote

Notes: Entries represent the estimated probability of a Republican win in each election cycle under various redistricting institutions, taken from the first model in Appendix Table 4.8 if Statewide Presidential Vote is set to 0. Error bars represent the 95% confidence interval of the probit coefficient of the redistricting institution variables.

in each presidential election (with full results in Appendix Table 4.8). As shown in the graph, while in 2005 such a state with a Democratic-controlled gerrymander would be predicted to have a congressional delegation that was only 36% Republicans, the same state with a Republican or nonpartisan gerrymander would have a 62% or 60% Republican delegation. However, in 2009, the estimated Republican delegations drop 16% and 27% under Republican and nonpartisan gerrymanders, respectively, while dropping only 9% and 8% for the Democratic and bipartisan gerrymanders, respectively.

Finally, we can also isolate the probability that a seat will change parties, where the dependent variable takes a value of 1 if the seat switched from Republican to Democrat at some point during the four years in question.[22] With full results shown in Appendix Table 4.9, Republican and nonpartisan/court-drawn seats were significantly more likely to flip than Democratic maps (used as the control).

1974

The 1974 midterm election, held just a few months after President Richard Nixon's resignation following the Watergate scandal, represents the largest wave in the past fifty years measured from the standpoint of the congressional popular vote. In this cycle, Democrats won by a nearly 17-point margin, and gained forty-nine seats to take a more than two-to-one seat majority in the House. Although the Democrats had controlled a sizable majority in the first Congress following the 1970 apportionment, this was largely due to holding approximately 70% of the seats in the South, which in this era was still dominated at the congressional level by conservative Democrats. Outside of the South, Congress was closely balanced until the post-Watergate election in 1974; in this election, Democrats went from holding 51% of non-southern seats to holding 64% of these seats. So this election should also provide a good example of moving from a relatively neutral partisan environment to one with strong partisan tides.

Democrats in the 1970s controlled the redistricting process in many more states than Republicans, but this was also due largely to their dominance in the South. Thus, in the probit analysis, it becomes particularly important to isolate the South from the rest of the country. Once this is done, we see a much more balanced variety of redistricting regimes, although there were no nonpartisan commissions during this period. As with the 2006 and 2008 waves, we predict higher turnover among states where Republicans controlled the process than those under Democratic or split control.[23] In line with these predictions we see results very similar to the 2000s wave at first glance in

Table 4.5 Congressional Seat Flips by Redistricting
Institution, 1973–1975 (California Excluded)

Redistricting Institution	States	CDs	Flips R to D	Flip %
Bipartisan	8	75	9	12.0
Republican	5	65	13	20.0
Democratic	14	144	11	7.6
Court	6	81	13	16.0
Small States	16	27	3	11.1

Table 4.5, with the exception of the small states where we expect gerry-mandering to have little effect.

Here, we again see dramatic turnover, especially in a handful of large states mapped by Republicans, including five flips each in New York and Indiana (with Indiana going from 7–3 Republican to 8–2 Democrat). While no states during the period were drawn by commissions, Illinois and New Jersey were both mapped by a process that could be categorized as either Republican or court-drawn and saw seven flips between them.

Figure 4.8 models the likelihood of Republican seat control before and after this election, assuming a swing state specifically outside the South (with full results in Appendix Table 4.10).[24] As with the data from thirty years later, we see that again Republican gerrymanders were much more effective for their party prior to the anti-Republican wave in 1974. Under a Democratic ger-rymander, such a state would be estimated to elect a congressional delega-tion that was 44% Republican in 1972 and 40% Republican in 1974. But under a Republican gerrymander, the same state would elect 47% Republicans in 1972 but only 29% Republicans in 1974. We see greater volatility in the bi-partisan maps in this decade than in the 2000s, but still less than those under Republican maps in both cases.

Republican maps are also shown to be significantly more likely to pro-duce turnover in this cycle than Democratic maps, with the full model shown in Appendix Table 4.11. Overall, the trends in this election seem sim-ilar to those in 2006–2008, with the obvious exception of the Democratic dominance in southern states and the lack of maps drawn by nonpartisan commissions.

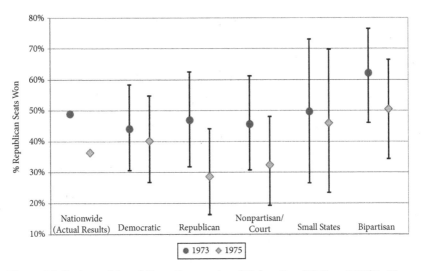

Figure 4.8 Estimated Republican Congressional Delegation (1973 vs. 1975) in Non-Southern State with National Mean Presidential Vote

Notes: Entries represent the estimated probability of a Republican win in each election cycle under various redistricting institutions, taken from the second model in Appendix Table 4.10, if Statewide Presidential Vote and South are set to 0. Error bars represent the 95% confidence interval of the probit coefficient of the redistricting institution variables.

1994

The theory presented in this chapter should predict not only greater turn-over in Republican maps during Democratic waves but symmetrically greater turnover in Democratic maps during Republican waves. There have been two significant Republican waves in the House of Representatives during the past fifty years: 1994, when Newt Gingrich led his party to a fifty-four-seat gain and the first Republican House majority in forty years; and 2010, when Republicans gained sixty-three seats to retake the House after just four years of Democratic control. In terms of total turnover, the 2010 wave appears to be the larger one. However, as most of the Republican gains in 2010 were simply winning back seats lost in the two immediately previous Democratic waves, 1994 provides a better test of contrasting a wave to a relatively neutral prior environment.

In this election, we predict that Democratic and nonpartisan maps would show higher turnover than Republican or bipartisan maps. This seems partially true, shown in Table 4.6, with a number of caveats. First, no state with more than three CDs had a Republican-controlled state government in 1991, so we cannot

Table 4.6 Congressional Seat Flips by Redistricting
Institution, 1993–1995

Redistricting Institution	States	CDs	Flips D to R	Flip %
Bipartisan	9	81	10	12.3
Democratic	12	119	24	20.2
Court	10	192	14	7.3
Nonpartisan	2	14	7	50.0
Small States	17	31	6	19.4

directly compare maps drawn by favored and disfavored parties. Second, most states with Democratic control of state government in 1991 were southern states; as many analysts attributed Republican gains in 1994 to partisan trends in the South, we must take care not to confuse these effects. And finally, an unusually large number of maps in this decade were drawn by courts, often deciding on matters related to majority-minority districting requirements, which might tend to make districts less competitive rather than more. So even any guess that court-drawn maps will look similar to those drawn by bipartisan commissions may be particularly inaccurate during this decade.

Only two states in the 1990s had maps drawn by nonpartisan commission, but one in particular experienced massive turnover: six seats in Washington flipped to Republicans, including the defeat of sitting House Speaker Tom Foley. Democratic maps in the South were also targeted, with four seats falling to Republicans in North Carolina and another three in Georgia. But even Democratic maps outside the South were vulnerable, as three seats each also flipped in Indiana and Oklahoma.

However, court-drawn maps and bipartisan seats are predicted to be slightly less likely to flip in this election than Democratic maps, but the results of a model of seat turnover (shown in Appendix Tables 4.12 and 4.13) are not statistically significant. There are a number of possible reasons why this wave looks different from the others studied. One remarkable result is that Statewide Presidential Vote has no significant effect on the probability that a Republican held a seat in 1993, but it does have a significant effect on this probability in 1995 and the probability of partisan turnover (which was not true in the other waves). It thus appears that at least some of the Republican gains in the 1994 election were the result of geographical party sorting rather than national trends. In 1993, a state's congressional delegation bore little resemblance to its partisan character at the presidential level, but in 1995, perhaps due to a large number of incumbent retirements, the partisan trends in congressional elections finally caught up to those at the presidential level.

Along the same lines, it might be inaccurate to describe the 1994 election as involving a strong Republican tide. As shown in Figure 4.2, both 1974 and 2006 involved voters moving from essentially a neutral partisan electorate to a strongly pro-Democratic one. It might thus be appropriate to look to the neutral and strong Democratic tides conditions in the simulation Figure 4.1 for comparison. But the 1994 tide moved the electorate from being slightly pro-Democratic (+5% in the national popular vote) to slightly pro-Republican (–6%), so we should be looking at weaker tides conditions in the model for comparison, and these tend to show less difference by gerrymandering regime. And finally, the new issues involving implementation of amendments to the Voting Rights Act to strengthen minority representation that dominated the redistricting debate during this decade might confuse our predictions about what maps coming from the various institutions should look like at a fundamental level. So while there is some weak evidence of partisan gerrymander backfires by the Democrats in this period, there is little evidence of volatility differences between split-controlled legislatures and courts. Moreover, the trends we saw in other decades seem overwhelmed by other factors, including regional party sorting and majority-minority districting concerns.

Discussion and Conclusion

The results in this chapter provide evidence of the limitations of partisan gerrymanders and at least one benefit of nonpartisan commissions, results derived even in the absence of information about what lines were actually drawn and how those lines specifically affected the resulting campaigns. As hypothesized, seats gerrymandered by nonpartisan commissions appear significantly more competitive than those drawn by bipartisan legislatures, whether competitiveness is measured by district partisan demographics or by vote margins in congressional elections. Additionally, while partisan maps draw many districts that appear noncompetitive at the demographic level, they generate greater competition in actual elections as national tides increase. Further, the pseudoparadox of greater national competition inducing less local competition, specifically under partisan maps, suggests that partisan mapmakers are drawing lines to create safe seats, particularly in anticipation of close national conditions, discounting the possibility of uncertain future tides. It is only after accounting for this pseudoparadox that previous conflicts in the literature can be resolved; works such as Hirsch (2003) and McDonald (2006) find that partisan gerrymandering reduces competition but draw from elections where tides were low and the national partisan environment evenly balanced, while works drawing from cycles with larger and less stable tides (e.g., Gopoian and West 1984; Hood and McKee 2008) show the opposite. And while Carson and Crespin (2004) and Yoshinaka and Murphy (2011) find increased competition immediately following a redistricting cycle, the effects of gerrymandering are here shown to persist through the decade.

Moreover, this evidence clarifies how we should measure competition and bias. One of the primary arguments that reform advocates advance for nonpartisan commissions is the lack of competitive districts under legislative districting. And indeed, both partisan maps and bipartisan maps draw districts that are less closely balanced ideologically than nonpartisan commissions (see Appendix Table 4.2). But closely balanced districts are not the same as competitive elections. When speaking of the impact of legislative districting on actual election results, some partisan maps foster competition and responsiveness to changes in voter preferences. As Grofman and Brunell implied in coining the term "dummymander," much of the increased competition may be unintended by the mapmakers, but it is observable not just as anecdote but also as a statistically and substantively significant result across the nationwide election data over the past fifty years.

Additionally, these results emphasize that not all reform plans will have a similar impact on competitiveness. While real nonpartisan commissions that explicitly strive to create more closely contested districts (such as exists in Arizona) may indeed enhance the probability of close elections, bipartisan commissions appointed equally of legislators from both parties (such as exists in New Jersey) may ossify noncompetitive districts to an even greater degree than even the most egregious partisan gerrymander. Chapter 7 delves into the differences seen across commission types in much greater detail.

Taken together, these results emphasize that in order to judge the fairness or normative value of a map or a reform proposal, one should not merely look at the underlying partisanship of districts in a neutral environment or the outcome of a map following a single election. Instead, it would be more appropriate to consider the diversity of possible outcomes over a plausible range of election results. Over the next several chapters, I employ a new measure of bias and responsiveness that does consider this full range and describe how this measure leads to different judgments than other proposed alternatives.

5

Measuring Historical Bias

Historically Weighted Efficiency Gap

Having reached the halfway point of our expedition, it is worth pausing to recap where we have been and where we are headed. In Chapter 2, we explored the theory of gerrymandering with several toy examples, in particular showing the importance of accounting for *responsiveness to different electoral conditions* when evaluating a map. In Chapter 3, we surveyed legal standards proposed in recent gerrymandering litigation and found that no single standard or test lends itself to easy application in all situations. And in Chapter 4, we examined the bias and competitiveness of different redistricting systems in the United States since the 1970s, showing that important differences across regimes reveal themselves only when examined across a range of electoral contexts.

This leads us to the central empirical enterprise of this book: the development and use of a measurement that will allow us to fully understand the impact of a map on both partisan bias and competitiveness under the complete range of possible electoral environments.

In this chapter, I advance a new measure for evaluating the bias of a legislative map, which I will refer to as "historically weighted efficiency gap" (HWEG), contrasting it to several other existing measures. This measure is designed to capitalize on many of the advantages of the efficiency gap (EG) measure proposed by Stephanopoulos and McGhee (2015), while also addressing what is often perceived as its greatest weakness. From this bias measure, we can additionally derive a measure of the map's competitiveness or responsiveness, "historically weighted slope" (HW Slope).

The HWEG measure uses new estimates of both the normal vote and district-specific variance for congressional districts in thirty-one states, evaluated over a wide range of national electoral conditions. In doing so, I explore several advantages of using a bias measure weighted across a long-term average over measures anchored to either a statewide 50/50 vote point or a single observed election outcome. Use of the HWEG measure uncovers several patterns in both the apparent strategies used by mapmakers under different regimes and the divergent conclusions drawn about these regimes under different standards.

Although this chapter explores a new measure for evaluating the bias and responsiveness of congressional maps, it is *not* intended to propose a new

Ground War. Nicholas Goedert, Oxford University Press. © Oxford University Press 2022.
DOI: 10.1093/oso/9780197626627.003.0005

standard to evaluate the constitutionality of partisan gerrymanders, unlike the efficiency gap as originally proposed by Stephanopoulos and McGhee. Rather, it is intended as a tool to evaluate the likely outcomes of both specific maps and overall redistricting institutions through the lens of varying electoral conditions. Chapters 6 and 7 make use of this tool to draw conclusions about consistent patterns seen in recent partisan and nonpartisan redistricting systems.

The exploration in the chapter proceeds as follows. First I give an overview of some of the strengths and weaknesses of several prominent proposals to measure bias in legislative maps, with emphasis on their treatment of partisan swings and noncompetitive states. Next I summarize the biggest benefits and drawbacks of my proposed HWEG measure in contrast. I then describe the methodology of HWEG, detailing how it estimates these quantities at any split in the two-party vote (generating an "EG curve"), and then averages over this curve based on historical weights. I demonstrate how these estimates and EG curves work in detailed examples from three states, and I delineate which congressional maps in the 2010s decade show the highest and lowest levels of bias and responsiveness under HWEG, contrasting these with other methods of estimating bias. I describe the overall bias and responsiveness of the nation as a whole using the HWEG measure, finding a national Republican bias of around 5 percentage points. The next two chapters then break down the sources of this bias in depth by redistricting institution, with Chapter 6 describing several patterns in the efficiency gap and slope curves in states with partisan gerrymanders, and Chapter 7 examining several cases of commissions or nonpartisan systems as an alternative.

Proposals for Measuring Bias

Proposed Standards for Gerrymandering

Recent scholarship has proposed a variety of ways to evaluate the bias of a map at either an observed or a hypothetical point along the seats/votes curve or over a range centered on such a point (see Nagle 2015, Best et al. 2018, Tapp 2019, and Grofman 2019 for an overview of methods). One method in particular, "efficiency gap," became the central proposed standard for measuring partisan effect in the *Whitford* case discussed in Chapter 3. As I leverage efficiency gap extensively in my own measure employed throughout the rest of the book, this section first provides a broad overview of several competing methods and standards before discussing efficiency gap in much greater detail.

Perhaps the most accessible of these other standards evaluates the map at the point at which both parties in a two-party system win 50% of the vote. There is an intuitive sense that a party that wins more than 50% of the vote should win more than 50% of the seats, and thus a fair seats/votes curve must pass through this 50/50 point. Some scholars propose measuring bias at the 50/50 point, across a range centered around this point (King and Browning 1987), or both (McGann et al. 2016). The notion of "partisan symmetry" expands on this by requiring that if Party A wins x seats given y share of the vote, Party B should also win x seats given y share of the vote, for any y, regardless of what x is. Recently, Katz, King, and Rosenblatt (2020) formally defined and developed this partisan symmetry measure, contrasting its properties to other prominent measures.

Alternate suggestions (including efficiency gap) observe the seats/votes relationship under real elections, with a range of variations. One common method, "mean/median difference," involves taking the difference between a party's mean vote share across all districts in a state (in one election or an average of multiple elections) and that party's vote share in the state's median district (e.g., Wang 2016). A large difference would indicate a gerrymander against the party in question, as they would likely perform much worse in a majority of districts than in the state as a whole. A group of scholars from Binghamton University propose a multiprong test for "packing" gerrymanders combining the mean/median difference under observed elections with the bias at the hypothetical 50/50 point, while very recent scholarship from this school appends a separate standard using vote share variance to test for "cracking" gerrymanders (McDonald and Best 2015; McDonald et al. 2018).

Another class of proposals that have gained recent traction does not evaluate maps in comparison to some universal standard of fairness. Instead, these proposals compare existing or proposed maps to simulated random or algorithmic maps that can account for the underlying geography of a state (e.g., Chen and Rodden 2015; Tam Cho and Liu 2016). In some cases, these comparisons might be used as rebuttals to claims that a map is biased under the universal standard (Stephanopoulos and McGhee 2015). The Binghamton school has also suggested using simulations in conjunction with their packing and cracking bias measures. (e.g., Best et al. 2018). Simulations as "counterfactuals" became essential tools in several of the gerrymandering cases discussed in Chapter 3, with one simulation expert, Jowei Chen, extensively cited in the Pennsylvania Supreme Court decision in *LWV* and in the district court opinions in North Carolina and Michigan. Of course, the exact domain of possible simulated maps will depend heavily on the exact algorithm used to draw them, and no actual commission or legislative body has used random simulation to draw actual maps, leading several judges and scholars to question the appropriateness of such measures as counterfactuals.[1]

Of particular interest is the way in which these various methods handle maps drawn in noncompetitive states, in which the balance of voting heavily favors one party in a typical election. In these states, reliance on a bias at the 50/50 point, or a majoritarian principle, may be especially problematic or inapplicable. McGann et al. (2016) use a modified version of the partisan symmetry test to evaluate gerrymanders in competitive states but essentially ignore the possibility of gerrymandering in noncompetitive states. They claim that no "motive" for partisan bias exists in noncompetitive states, as these states could easily draw all districts to favor their party, confining their analysis to competitive states with "motive" (148). Yet most noncompetitive states with more than a handful of districts do not elect delegations entirely of one party. Maryland is an example of a state with no motive for bias in McGann et al.'s analysis, yet its choice to draw one Republican district instead of two (or even none) has been highly controversial and subject to the *Benisek* lawsuit detailed in Chapter 3.

The line of research led by scholars at Binghamton University (e.g., McDonald and Best 2015; McDonald et al. 2018) has advocated for the use of a mean/median difference standard combined with "violation of majority rule" to evaluate packing gerrymanders, where out-party members are packed into a small number of noncompetitive districts. But while earlier articles in this line focus on these packing gerrymanders, the most recent work also recognizes that some gerrymanders, particularly in noncompetitive states, might not require packing. Instead, they propose that cracking gerrymanders, in which out-party members are spread thinly across the state, would be analyzed by looking for unusually low variance in party vote patterns. Thus, competitive and noncompetitive states would be analyzed under a completely different theory and statistical test.

Methods for Imputing Votes and Swings

Where hypothetical election conditions must be imputed, scholars have additionally proposed a similarly broad range of methods for what data should be used in this imputation. First, the underlying partisanship of a district must be estimated. Most often, this involves using past observed congressional elections, supplemented by presidential election data in the case of unopposed congressional races (e.g., McGann et al. 2016; Stephanopoulos and McGhee 2015). Another method, often called Cook's PVI and most popular among media and practitioners, characterizes the underlying partisanship of a district by comparing the average of the past two presidential votes in a district to the national average (e.g., Cook and Wasserman 2014). Statewide election data are drawn from less frequently; in this case, scholars have deliberately selected races that were closely balanced (Gronke and Wilson 1999) or had a low profile (Backstrom, Robins, and Eller 1990).

There is also variance in the methods used to resolve uncertainty over electoral swings. The most simple is the "uniform swing assumption" that all districts will swing equally when a universal swing is observed (see Royden, Li, and Rudensky 2018). A more accepted method among scholars is to supplement a uniform swing with an independent random term to simulate some uncertainty and variance in district-specific conditions across election cycles (e.g., McGann et al. 2016; Gelman and King 1994). But most typically, the variance in this random term is equal across districts, often a faulty or oversimplified assumption (see Converse 1966).

Efficiency Gap

Among all the recently proposed metrics, Stephanopoulos and McGhee (2015) have attracted the most attention among legal scholars and practitioners with their efficiency gap proposal, a measurement used by opponents of partisan gerrymandering in recent legal challenges as a standard to evaluate the partisan outcome of the delegation produced by a given election, most prominently in *Whitford v. Gill* (2018). This proposed standard suggests that the bias in a map should be measured by the balance of "wasted votes" for each party under a real observed election, most often the first election following redistricting (see McGhee 2014; Stephanopoulos and McGhee 2015). In single-member, majority-rule districts, all votes for a losing candidate are wasted, and votes for a winning candidate in excess of the 50% threshold needed for victory are also wasted. Thus in all individual-seat elections with two candidates, exactly half of the votes are counted as wasted, with the losing candidate accounting for a greater share of wasted votes the closer the election is. When turnout in every district is equal, EG simplifies into the difference from a seats/votes curve with no bias and a slope of 2. For example, if Republicans won 60% of the vote, a "fair" map would imply winning 70% of the seats; if they instead won 75% of the seats, this outcome would have a pro-Republican EG of 5%. The most common applications of EG, including in this book, employ this shortcut version.

The writings of Stephanopoulos, McGhee, and other EG proponents have advanced many arguments for its adoption and use, which I will consolidate into three broad categories: the normative argument, the practical argument, and the historical argument.

The *normative argument* is that by grounding EG in the concept of *wasted votes*, the measure seeks to treat the weight of the voting of each party equally. Stephanopoulos and McGhee (2015, 16) claim, "[N]ormatively, the efficiency gap identifies a concrete harm worthy of judicial intervention. A gap in a party's favor enables the party to claim more seats, relative to a zero-gap plan, without claiming more votes. After voters have decided which party they support . . . the votes cast by supporters of the gerrymandering party translate more effectively into representation and policy than do those cast by the opposing party's supporters." In this sense, EG is deeply linked to the notions well-developed in constitutional jurisprudence on apportionment and gerrymandering related to vote dilution and the effective power of a citizen to elect a representative of their choice. Given their definition, McGhee (2017, 2) argues, "While wasted votes are inevitable in SMD [single-member district] elections, there is no reason why some parties must have more wasted votes than others."

The *practical argument* is that EG is easy to calculate and to understand. Stephanopoulos and McGhee (2015, 834) explain that "the efficiency gap essentially aggregates all of a district plan's cracking and packing choices into a single tidy number." It can be derived from simple arithmetic and does not require the use of computers or any knowledge of the underlying electorate or geography of the state. Additionally, it can be calculated based merely on the results of a single election cycle, and as it does not rely on simulation or hypothetical elections, it assuages the concern of former Supreme Court swing justice Anthony Kennedy · about using partisan symmetry or any other method "based on unfair results that would occur in a hypothetical state of affairs" (845, quoting *LULAC*, 548 U.S. at 420). Additionally, it is easy to back out a calculation of seat share given EG and vote share if another proposed method is desired. EG also perhaps comes closest to a unified standard under which to analyze competitive and noncompetitive states. By prescribing a 2:1 seats/votes curve that would apply at any vote share, it joins the partisan bias notion that a party winning 50% of the vote should win 50% of the seats and a symmetrical number of seats at any other vote share with a specific and constant expectation of responsiveness as vote share deviates from 50%. Just as we would expect a fair map in a 50/50 state to yield a 50/50 vote share, EG demands that a fair map in a 65/35 state yield an 80/20 vote share—no more, no less.

The *historical argument* might be summarized as "the electoral ideal implied by a metric should not be too different from the historical norm in the United States" (Stephanopoulos and McGhee 2018, 1509). And indeed, the 2:1 seats/votes curve prescribed by a fair map under the EG metric has the (somewhat coincidental) advantage of tracking with historically average results for congressional elections, which have closely followed a seats/votes curve with a slope of 2 for at least the past century, as discussed in Chapter 2 (Tufte 1973; Goedert 2014, 2015). Thus, shortcut EG gives us a good, but not perfect, approximation for how much the partisan balance of a delegation deviates from the long-term historical average that a party would expect to win given a certain vote share.

This method does have a few well-documented flaws. It obviously is inapplicable to elections where one party wins *more* than 75% of the vote, and even seems somewhat unrealistic as that threshold is approached. But it is also extremely sensitive to variations in single observed election results in a way that

Table 5.1 Highest Efficiency Gap Bias Observed in 2012 and 2018

		2012				2018		
	State	Control	GOP % Gap	GOP Seat Gap	State	Control	GOP % Gap	GOP Seat Gap
Republican Bias								
1	AR	D	22.9	0.9	NC	R	21.8	2.8
2	OH	R	21.7	3.5	AR	D	20.8	0.8
3	NC	R	20.3	2.6	OH	R	20.3	3.3
4	PA	R	20.3	3.7	IN	R	17.3	1.6
5	VA	R	20.1	2.2	AL	R	15.6	1.1
Democratic Bias								
1	CT	B	−21.4	−1.1	CT	B	−26.0	−1.3
2	MA	D	−12.4	−1.1	IA	N	−20.9	−0.8
3	OR	D/B	−11.9	−0.6	NJ	B	−19.7	−2.4
4	AZ	N	−11.3	−1.0	NV	B	−15.5	−0.6
5	MD	D	−8.6	−0.7	OR	D/B	−11.1	−0.6

approaches like McDonald et al. (2018), who employ a robust collection of statewide elections and hypothetical maps, will not be.

For example, I calculate the actual EG for every state with at least four districts in each cycle, 2012–2018, using the *average vote by district* with an imputed vote of 75% for the winner of unopposed races as a substitute for total statewide vote.[2] Table 5.1 shows the states with the highest EG by percentage in two actually observed elections: 2012, the first cycle after redistricting and a closely balanced national environment, and 2018, a significant Democratic wave.[3] Because Stephanopoulos and McGhee suggest a threshold of two congressional seats for presumptive unconstitutionality, Table 5.2 also shows all instances during this decade in which a map was biased by more than two seats in either direction (seats with Democratic bias in italics). In this table as well as all tables throughout the book, I express Republican bias as a positive number and Democratic bias as a negative number.

These tables reveal that observed EG seems to function well in tagging severe partisan gerrymanders in the close national environment of 2012 but draws some perplexing conclusions following the 2018 wave election. The six maps exceeding

Table 5.2 Congressional Delegations Exceeding
Two-Seat EG Threshold, 2012–2018

Year	State	Control	GOP % Gap	GOP Seat Gap
2012	PA	R	20.3	3.7
2012	OH	R	21.7	3.5
2012	NC	R	20.3	2.6
2012	MI	R	17.5	2.4
2012	VA	R	20.1	2.2
2012	FL	R	8.1	2.2
2014	NC	R	18.3	2.4
2014	MI	R	15.9	2.2
2014	*CA*	*N*	*–10.1*	*–5.3*
2016	TX	R/C	9.6	3.5
2016	NC	R	19.7	2.6
2016	PA	R	13.8	2.5
2018	TX	R/C	12.8	4.6
2018	OH	R	20.3	3.3
2018	NC	R	21.8	2.8
2018	*CA*	*N*	*–9.4*	*–5.0*
2018	*NJ*	*B*	*–19.7*	*–2.4*

the two-seat bias threshold in 2012 were all Republican gerrymanders that were subject to litigation, and each was eventually at least partially overturned by at least one court. But only *one* of these states (NC) remains over the threshold in each subsequent election, with the other states dropping off either because Republicans improved on their vote total without improving their seat total in 2014 (e.g., in PA and OH) or because the map at least somewhat backfired in the 2018 wave (e.g., in VA and MI). In 2018, the maps with the greatest bias include Texas, which saw an exceptionally high level of competition resulting from the Democratic wave but where Republicans won nine of eleven close elections in the state, and California and New Jersey, commission maps where Democrats turned over seven and four close Republican seats, respectively.[4] Applied to 2018, EG would mostly not flag enduring and egregious partisan gerrymanders but rather highly competitive maps where one party got particularly lucky, showing that the success of EG as a metric is highly sensitive to the electoral environment in which it is applied.

The great instability of the EG measure across election environments greatly diminishes the *practical argument* for its single-election simplicity. Moreover, EG was largely designed specifically mindful of Justice Kennedy's concerns expressed in *Vieth v. Jubelirer* (2004). But Kennedy's 2018 retirement, coupled with the apparent dismissal of statewide partisan gerrymandering claims in the Court's majority opinion in *Whitford*, has largely mooted this specific target. Therefore, in designing a new measure derived from EG, I see no reason to confine my data to a single election cycle or to avoid using data to simulate elections under a range of possible conditions.[5] I propose that future standards will be more useful if they take a wider view in terms of using historical data, anticipating future trends, and adjusting for the political realities of each state. Additionally, given the different competing but potentially valid democratic claims that citizens might make (outlined in Chapter 2), I don't find EG's *normative argument* that a court should define good representation under a particular narrow definition of wasted votes particularly convincing (see Plener Cover (2018) for how even the concept of wasted votes could plausibly be defined differently; see also Chamber, Miller, and Sobel (2017)).

However, the *historical argument*, that EG can be employed to describe how a map differs from what is *typical* rather than what is good or bad, is still compelling. Therefore, this chapter leverages this attribute of EG merely descriptively, without recommending any particular threshold as indicating a presumptively inappropriate or unlawful gerrymander.

Benefits and Limitations of HWEG

While the HWEG measure described in the next section has many strengths, including flexibility, ease of understanding, and connection to both short-term real election results and longer-term electoral trends, it is also important to acknowledge its limitations.

The biggest benefit of HWEG is its flexibility in depicting how a map will react to as yet unobserved election environments and swings. It both allows for easy visual depiction of bias and responsiveness under the entire range of possible national environments and also creates summary scalar measures of bias and responsiveness that synthesize all these environments, weighted by how likely they are to occur. In this sense, I believe HWEG represents a modest but substantively important innovation in both the actual measurement and the visual depiction of a map's attributes. This assessment is derived from as many relevant elections as possible, leveraging recent congressional, presidential, and statewide elections data to estimate partisan averages and variances in each individual district, and historical congressional election data to estimate the distribution of national tides. As will be seen in examples later in this chapter, HWEG permits us to easily visualize not just overall bias but traits such as the aggressiveness and backfire potential of the partisan map and the competitiveness of a bipartisan compromise.

One fundamental aspect of HWEG that might be considered both a benefit and a drawback is its very simple and straightforward judgment of what constitutes a fair map. This is not an innovation of HWEG but instead the basic idea behind EG itself: that under any fair map, a party will not just win 50% of seats when it wins 50% of the vote, but will also win a specific number of seats given any vote share based on a responsiveness slope of 2. As mentioned, I see this as a benefit of EG due both to its ease of understanding and calculation and to its very strong congruence with historical evidence in U.S. congressional elections.

However, there are also reasons why some might find this unsatisfying. First, while both the basic balance in partisan strength and the responsiveness rate embodied by EG reflect long-term historical averages (over the past fifty years, as shown in Figure 2.2, as well as a longer period found in other research), they may not reflect the reality of the political climate in the short term. For example, analyzing a subset of the elections shown in Figure 2.2, such as only the 2000s decade, might suggest an overall balance tilted toward Republicans and lower responsiveness.

More importantly, HWEG demands that all states conform to the same concept of what constitutes an unbiased map and what constitutes average competitiveness. Thus, it does not attempt to account for differences in geography, ethnicity, political culture, or partisan dispersion that may lead to certain types of maps being more "natural" in some states. While HWEG can draw general assessments about the interacted effect of gerrymandering method and tides across a sample of multiple states, any conclusion about individual states must be made with knowledge of the geography, demographics, and culture particular to that state (as we will see in our exploration of commission states in Chapter 7).

Although I am generally skeptical of the use of simulated districts as a legal standard (for reasons discussed in Chapters 3 and 8), this is one area where simulations may give important additional insight into the factors contributing to the HWEG estimates in individual states. For example, while Chen and Rodden (2015) famously found that maps of Florida drawn through unbiased algorithms would still produce Republican majorities due to patterns of partisan dispersion, HWEG (and any measure leveraging EG) would still assess these simulated maps as biased toward Republicans. Along the same lines, a map in a southern state that is constrained to draw an overwhelmingly Democratic Black-majority district might also be assessed as being biased toward Republicans even if motivated more by Voting Rights Act compliance than partisanship.

I would argue that this aspect of HWEG is not really a drawback, though this is largely a normative argument that I can see reasonable disagreement with. As I discuss more in my conclusion, I do not see why a map should be considered fair or unbiased simply because it is drawn through an algorithm that is non-partisan on its face. Just because an algorithm has generated a map of Florida that produces Republican majorities does not necessarily mean that this is what a map drawn by humans with no partisan motivations would produce or should produce. Just as a real map of Florida could be easily drawn to produce much larger Republican majorities than algorithmic maps (seen in the Republican gerrymanders of the past two decades), a real map could also be drawn to be unbiased, though this map may be slightly less compact than a purely algorithmic map. And I would hold that EG represents a better guideline for fundamental fairness than geographic compactness.

Similarly, a map that produces bias due to Voting Rights Act constraints should still be considered a biased map. But it is a map that has chosen to privilege the representation of a previously underrepresented minority group over balance in partisan composition. As discussed in Chapter 2, there are many situations in which trade-offs in representation claims must be made. We might assess this to sometimes be a very reasonable trade-off, but one that should be acknowledged. Additionally, in its assessment of what constitutes an unbiased map, HWEG considers only the estimated partisan composition of a delegation. It gives no attention to the ideology or descriptive characteristic of members, certainly factors that may influence various measures of representation quality discussed in Chapter 2.

A final potential drawback of HWEG is that, unlike basic EG, it relies on hypothetical election results. One of the initial perceived benefits of EG as a potential constitutional test was its pure rooting in real congressional election data, potentially satisfying some judges' (specifically, Justice Kennedy's) wariness toward any use of simulated or counterfactual elections. But as I am not advancing HWEG as a constitutional test for courts, I do not see this as a significant point against it. Many other proposed tests rely on counterfactual elections, and I believe such reliance is necessary to realistically assess how a map might react to future trends. And in using all available data from congressional, presidential, and statewide elections (which will often depict an election environment not yet observed in an immediately recent federal election), I believe HWEG's assessment is more nuanced in how it assesses counterfactual environments than measures that rely on some smaller subset of these data.

Nevertheless, in several states, the HWEG measure is calculated based on a relatively small selection of publicly available statewide election results (supplementing the presidential and congressional results easily available for all states). Particularly with respect to estimating independent variance for each district, this measure could be improved with the addition of data from more statewide elections.

Methodology for Historically Weighted Model for Bias and Responsiveness

The method developed in this chapter, HWEG, is designed to capitalize on the advantages of EG, including its correspondence to historical seats/votes patterns, its ease of calculation, and its robustness to application in noncompetitive states, while addressing its greatest failings, its unpredictability and sensitivity to idiosyncratic election results. Instead of measuring bias under a single observed election or under a predetermined range of hypothetical statewide vote, HWEG seeks to assess bias under a plausible range of electoral conditions, drawing this range from the distribution of historical results. Fundamentally, the HWEG measure asks: How much will the partisan delegation resulting from a map deviate from the results observed over a nationally average range of historical conditions? Along with a single HWEG bias measure, this method also generates an EG curve and range of responsiveness slopes for each map.

HWEG breaks down this process into four questions:

1. What is a historically average relationship of two-party seats to votes?
2. What is a historically average distribution of national partisan swings?
3. For each state, how does the partisan balance in this state in recent national elections deviate from the national average? (What is the state's "normal vote"?)
4. For each district in each state, how does the partisan balance in the district and the variation in that balance in recent elections deviate from the statewide average?

Breaking the process down in this way allows us to employ different appropriate data in each stage. For example, to measure how much a district deviates from other districts within the same state, it may be informative to use gubernatorial election results. But the results of such state elections would not be appropriate to compare districts across different states, since the candidates in these elections, and indeed the partisan political culture in many cases, would be different in each state. Note that the estimates presented here involve only a first cut at a plausible historically weighted measure. Each step of this process involves choices of data and methods that may be refined as additional data are incorporated.

As presented here, HWEG uses a simple method to calculate steps 1 through 3, but a much more involved one for step 4. For reference, several definitions of measurements used throughout the chapter are summarized in Appendix Table 5.5.

Historically Average Seats/Votes Curve

As may be obvious from its name, HWEG adopts EG's 2:1 seats/votes curve as the historical average rate of responsiveness, in line with past evidence discussed in Chapter 2.[6] In other words, HWEG expects that a party that wins 50% of the two-party vote in a state should win 50% of the seats, and for every additional 1% of the vote, that party should win an additional 2% of the seats. Any difference between this expectation and the actual estimated partisan composition resulting from a map would be considered partisan bias. If HWEG estimates that when Republicans win 60% of the vote in a state they would win an average of 65% of the seats (instead of the expected 70%), it would consider this map *biased toward Democrats* by 5% at that particular point. The bias measured at this point would then be weighted along with bias measured at all plausible percentages of Republican statewide vote, based on how historically likely that percentage of statewide vote was.

Using EG also gives us an easy standard for measuring the competitiveness of a map by assessing the responsiveness slope (i.e., the percentage of seats each party would be expected to gain given a 1% increase in vote) of any map under any electoral condition. EG suggests a scenario of average responsiveness would have a seats/votes slope of 2; a scenario where the slope was substantially under 2 would be considered unresponsive, while a slope substantially greater than 2 would be hyperresponsive.

Historically Average National Two-Party Vote

The weight given to any point on the continuum over Republican statewide vote is broken down into two calculations: first, the likelihood of any particular *national* vote balance; second, the average *statewide vote* for a party in each state *given a particular national vote*. The first of these, the distribution of national vote, is a single estimate based on the variation in national congressional vote over the past fifty years, with a mean national vote of 50% (so there is no bias inherent in the calculation). The standard deviation of the national congressional vote during this period is 3.48%, so national vote weights are derived from a normal curve where the mean of the curve is 50% and the standard deviation is 3.48%. Weights are calculated for the range of national Republican vote from 35% to 65%, though 99% of the resulting weights lie within a range of Republican vote between 41% and 59%, with a full description of weights shown in Appendix Table 5.3.

Average Statewide Swing from National Vote

I refer to the estimated average amount by which a state deviates from the nation as a whole as the "statewide normal vote." A "normal vote" is a general term for expected vote for a party reflecting long-term party loyalties under "normal" conditions (i.e., absent tides or shifts favoring one party) (see, e.g., Converse 1966). In a two-party system, it might also be considered the share of the vote expected in a specific constituency when the party received 50% of the two-party vote among the wider electorate. For each state, I calculate the normal vote as equal to the mean two-party Republican vote share in the state over six elections: the presidential elections in 2012 and 2016 and the total congressional vote in the state in 2012, 2014, 2016, and 2018. Nationwide, the Republican vote share across these six elections was 49.25%, so this average is rescaled by adding 0.75% to the Republican total in each state to reflect an exactly tied national environment. Statewide normal vote ranges from 29.7% (in Massachusetts) to 72.7% (in Wyoming), with Wisconsin, Colorado, and Virginia coming closest to the national average. All statewide normal votes are shown in Appendix Table 5.1.

Average District Swing Compared to Statewide Vote, and Variance in That Swing

The most detailed step in creating the historically weighted measure is the estimation of the distribution of the vote share in each district given a statewide vote share. This is done by estimating both a mean vote share for each district in relation to the statewide vote and a variance composed of both a constant component and a district-specific component. This yields a probability of the district voting Republican under any given statewide vote share; within this constant statewide vote share, variance within a district is presumed to be independent of other districts, and thus these probabilities are summed to estimate statewide seat share.

My estimates for the mean and variance of the two-party vote in each U.S. congressional district following the 2010 round of redistricting are based on presidential, statewide, and congressional data from 2012 to 2018 collected at the district level.[7] I did not compile data for the fifteen states with three or fewer congressional districts and do not attempt to analyze the maps in these small states. For the remaining thirty-five states, I was able to assemble some statewide election data by district (beyond presidential elections) in thirty-one states, including all states with at least eight districts.

For the nineteen states that are either too small for a district-by-district deviation analysis to be useful or for which sufficient statewide election data were not available to conduct such analysis, each congressional district is assigned a district normal vote equal to the mean deviation from the two-party statewide average vote of the previous four congressional elections and the previous two presidential elections (the same elections used to calculate the statewide normal vote). Additionally, each district is assumed to have a normal variance equal to the nationally average variance in congressional vote relative to the statewide mean over the past decade (SD = 3.84%). Because of the paucity of data, these states are not subject to detailed individual analysis.

For the remaining thirty-one states, each district is assigned a *district-specific normal vote*. The normal vote is the district's mean deviation from the statewide average of the two-party vote over all available elections (numbering a minimum of seven and an average of eleven, with details in Appendix Table 5.1). As with all states, these elections always include the previous four congressional elections and previous two presidential elections. Additionally, major statewide elections where data are available at the district level are also included in this average.[8] Thus, district information is drawn not only from recent national elections where the national vote was close but also, in many cases, elections where the state's vote deviated wildly from its average in national elections (e.g., the 2017 Senate race in Alabama won by Democrat Doug Jones and the 2014 governor's race in Massachusetts won by Republican Charlie Baker). Note that these elections are *not* used in calculating the *state's* normal vote but are merely used as additional information in determining how a district deviates from the statewide average.

Each district in these thirty-one states is also assigned a *district-specific variance*. This estimate is based on the Pythagorean theorem of statistics, that the square of a variable's overall deviation is equal to the sum of the squares of individual components generating that deviation. We might imagine that there are three general sources of variance in a congressional election's result:

A. Variance in the national election environment that will affect all districts.
B. Factors related to the electorate in specific districts (i.e., some districts might include more persuadable voters and thus be generally more elastic, or some districts might be more amenable to appeals beyond party label).
C. Factors specific to an individual race, campaign, or candidate.

Among these three, source (A) will be deliberately manipulated in this analysis and is aggregated in a previous step of the HWEG calculation, and thus it will not be included in the district-specific variance calculation. (As discussed in step 2, over the past several decades the average deviation in two-party vote share has been about 3.5%.) To calculate source (B), we use the average sample deviation in the difference between a district's vote and the statewide vote in *presidential and statewide elections only*. Note that for this component, we cannot include any information drawn from congressional races, since those would incorporate variance from both sources (B) and (C), without any information on how to disentangle these sources. However, in the case of presidential and statewide races, the national and race-specific factors will be held constant across the state, so any variance should be due to district-specific factors.

In developing our congressional seat estimates, we must be agnostic as to the size or direction of any campaign-specific variance. For example, we do not know which seats will be open or which districts will get quality challengers. However, we do want to acknowledge that this variance exists, and it will differ from district to district within a state; as a result, there will be more variance in congressional election results (compared to the district normal vote) than there is in statewide elections where the same candidate is running in every district. As we have an estimate for district-specific variance, and we can also estimate the *total* variance across all congressional elections (as always, compared to the statewide average), we can use the Pythagorean theorem to estimate an additional variance component that we must include in every district in order to simulate the greater variance in congressional elections. Thus:

$$(\text{Total Variance}) = (\text{District-Specific Variance}) + (\text{Campaign-Specific Variance})$$

The average deviation from a district's normal vote across all congressional elections during this decade has been 3.84%, while the average deviation from normal vote in statewide elections with available district-level data has been 2.24%. Solving for the third term in the equation yields an average campaign-specific deviation of 3.12%. This additional term is added to the district-specific normal variance (in statewide elections) in each district to produce a variance estimate in each district for congressional elections.

Thus, given a total statewide vote share, we can estimate the probability that each district will vote for the Republican candidate, derived from the distribution produced by the district's estimated mean and variance relative to the statewide normal vote, and these probabilities can be summed to estimate the mean EG produced under any given election environment.[9] The next section applies this method to three prominent state examples.

Three State Examples

In this section, I demonstrate in detail how the HWEG model evaluates three maps from the 2010s decade: the Republican gerrymander in the swing state of Pennsylvania, the Democratic gerrymander in heavily Democratic Maryland, and the map drawn by a nonpartisan commission in Republican-leaning Arizona. I have chosen these three states because they represent three very different redistricting contexts and also because each has been at the center of recent redistricting litigation: the Pennsylvania and Maryland maps will be recalled from the discussion of the *LWV* and *Benisek* cases in Chapter 3, while the legality of the commission drawing the Arizona map was narrowly upheld by the Supreme Court in 2015 in *Arizona State Legislature v. Arizona Independent Redistricting Commission*, discussed further in Chapter 7.

The HWEG model first estimates the underlying "normal vote" of each state by averaging the two-party statewide vote in the 2012 and 2016 presidential elections with the 2012–2018 congressional elections, and rescaling this based on 50% national Republican vote. This calculation estimates the normal vote to be 51.0% in Pennsylvania (or 1 point more Republican than the national average); 37.4% in Maryland (about 13 points more Democratic than the nation); and 54.7% in Arizona (about 5 points more Republican than the nation).

We then proceed to calculate the district partisanship of each state *relative to the statewide average* drawing from all available congressional, presidential, and statewide election data conducted while the map was in effect. In addition, we estimate variance of this relative vote in each district, based on the presidential and statewide data, scaled up to simulate the higher variance in congressional elections as described earlier. In Maryland, these district estimates are based on a total of fifteen elections between 2012 and 2018 (four U.S. House, two presidential, three U.S. Senate, and six other statewide elections). In Arizona, the estimates are based on twelve elections between 2012 and 2018 (four U.S. House, two presidential, two U.S. Senate, and four other statewide elections). In Pennsylvania, the estimates are based on fourteen elections between 2012 and 2016 (three U.S. House, two presidential, two U.S. Senate, and seven other statewide elections); 2018 is excluded because it was conducted over a different map.

Given the underlying statewide partisanship and the mean and variance estimates for each district relative to that partisanship, we can then estimate the probability that each district will elect a Republican under a wide range of national conditions. Tables 5.3 through 5.5 show these estimates for each district in these three states, and the statewide summaries, under three conditions:

1. The likely composition of the delegation when each party wins exactly 50% of the two-party vote in the *state*. This is useful to estimate partisan bias measures anchored to the statewide 50/50 point.
2. The delegation when each party wins a share of the vote equal to the state's estimated normal vote, thus simulating a *tied national* election. We would expect the delegation to be similar to this in a close national environment like 2012 or 2016.
3. The delegation under a Democratic wave where the Democrats win 7% more of the statewide vote than their normal vote. Such a wave represents about the 97th percentile of historical vote performance and would be slightly stronger than the 2008 or 2018 waves but weaker than the 1974 wave.

Figures 5.1 and 5.2 show the average efficiency gap and slope of each map under the range of 35%–65% Republican statewide vote to visualize how the bias and competitiveness of the map changes with the electoral environment. In the panel for each individual state (Figures 5.3 through 5.5), I also overlay the distribution of likely statewide vote based on the state's normal vote and

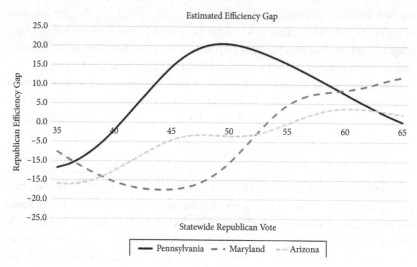

Figure 5.1 Estimated Efficiency Gap in Three States

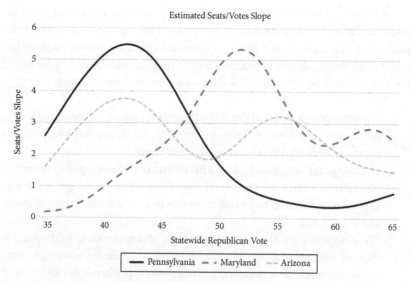

Figure 5.2 Estimated Seats/Votes Slope in Three States

historical trends in wave strength. By referencing this distribution, we can see which points along the statewide vote range we should expect to actually observe with any frequency. Putting the steps of HWEG together, we can show how this measure evaluates these maps under a weighted average of all these conditions.

Looking only at the EG and slope curves anchored to the statewide vote and the bias measures at the statewide 50/50 point, we would draw some conclusions that are mostly accurate. For example, the Pennsylvania map is heavily biased toward Republicans both at the 50/50 point and at a large range of statewide votes on either side of this point. But this would also lead us to other conclusions that are largely misleading. For example, the slope curves indicate that the map in Maryland, a state that has seen very few close congressional races, is much more competitive around the 50/50 point than the map in Arizona, which was specifically drawn to foster competition. One arrives at a fuller picture by overlaying the expected vote distribution on the graphs of each state and examining them under different realistic conditions.

Pennsylvania

Because Pennsylvania is a swing state, its estimates under the first two conditions, a tied statewide vote and a tied national vote, are very close to each other. The Republican-drawn map is both nonresponsive and heavily biased in favor of the Republicans in both cases, with a pro-Republican EG of around 20% and a slope of around 1.5. But under the Democratic wave condition, the map becomes both more responsive and less biased, as Democrats become favored in the three seats intended for Republicans in the Philadelphia suburbs (Districts 6, 7, and 8) and turn three additional districts (12, 15, and 16) into swing seats. In this way, Pennsylvania follows the expected pattern of a partisan gerrymander almost perfectly: it maximizes bias in favor of Republicans at around a statewide or nationwide vote of 50%, with bias declining steadily in both directions from that point; this bias does not backfire into a pro-Democratic efficiency gap until Democrats win at least 59% of the vote. We will see this pattern and shape of EG curves repeatedly as we examine partisan gerrymandering in *swing states* specifically in Chapter 6. When the vote is pro-Republican or close to 50/50, the map is fairly unresponsive, but it becomes steadily more competitive as Democratic tides increase, maximizing at around a 57% Democratic vote share. Thus it is unsurprising that many Republican-held seats in Pennsylvania were considered prime Democratic targets in 2018 even before the map was redrawn.

Table 5.3 HWEG Model in Pennsylvania

Normal Vote: R +1.0

CD	Seat Properties		Probability of GOP Seat under Different Scenarios		
	Avg. GOP Vote Relative to State	St. Dev. of Relative Avg	Tied Statewide (GOP wins 50%)	Normal Vote (GOP wins 51%)	Democratic Wave (GOP wins 44%)
1	−29.1%	3.4%	0%	0%	0%
2	−35.7%	3.8%	0%	0%	0%
3	10.0%	3.5%	100%	100%	88%
4	11.6%	3.4%	100%	100%	95%
5	11.2%	3.9%	100%	100%	91%
6	4.3%	3.8%	87%	92%	32%
7	5.1%	4.1%	89%	93%	41%
8	3.6%	3.5%	85%	90%	25%
9	13.7%	4.4%	100%	100%	96%
10	15.1%	3.6%	100%	100%	99%
11	8.3%	3.5%	99%	100%	75%
12	6.9%	3.8%	96%	98%	59%
13	−16.3%	3.7%	0%	0%	0%
14	−20.5%	3.9%	0%	0%	0%
15	6.0%	3.2%	97%	99%	50%
16	6.3%	3.6%	96%	98%	53%
17	−4.0%	4.5%	19%	25%	1%
18	10.2%	3.8%	100%	100%	86%
GOP Seats			12.7	12.9	8.9
GOP Seat %			70	72	50
Efficiency Gap			20.4	19.9	11.5
Seats/Votes Slope			1.7	1.3	5.1

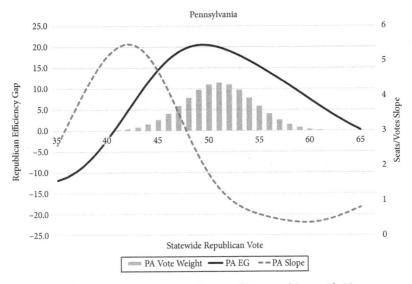

Figure 5.3 Efficiency Gap, Seats/Votes Slope, and Expected Statewide Vote Distribution under Republican Gerrymander of Pennsylvania

Maryland

Since Maryland is a noncompetitive state that will almost always vote far to the left of the nation as a whole, the first two conditions differ drastically in their results. As we might expect of a Democratic gerrymander, the map is extremely nonresponsive and heavily biased in favor of the Democrats under the (second) normal vote condition. By contrast, the map is very responsive under the 50/50 condition, where Republicans entirely flip District 6 (the district specifically at issue in the *Benisek* case) and have a strong chance to win three additional districts virtually guaranteed to go Democratic in the normal condition. The outcome of the Democratic-wave condition is almost identical to the normal condition (an almost certain 7–1 Democratic majority), but the map is no longer biased, as Democrats would be expected to win at least seven seats under an average map with a 70/30 vote majority. The map shows a Democratic bias around 10% at both the normal and tied statewide condition, but this bias is both lower than we see in either condition in Pennsylvania and lower than the bias expected around a range of Democratic vote share from 52% to 60%. The map backfires into pro-Republican bias at a Democratic vote share around 48%. Yet because Maryland is such a heavily Democratic state, the vote is much more likely to be in the range of high Democratic bias than the backfire range. This is a pattern we will see repeatedly in our analysis of partisan gerrymanders of *noncompetitive* states in Chapter 6.

Table 5.4 HWEG Model in Maryland

Normal Vote: D+12.6

CD	Seat Properties		Probability of GOP Seat under Different Scenarios		
	Avg. GOP Vote Relative to State	St. Dev. of Relative Avg	Tied Statewide (GOP wins 50%)	Normal Vote (GOP wins 37.4%)	Democratic Wave (GOP wins 30.4%)
1	25.6%	4.9%	100%	100%	89%
2	−1.2%	3.8%	37%	0%	0%
3	−1.5%	3.5%	33%	0%	0%
4	−14.2%	3.7%	0%	0%	0%
5	−4.0%	3.5%	13%	0%	0%
6	6.6%	3.4%	97%	4%	0%
7	−12.6%	3.3%	0%	0%	0%
8	−1.3%	3.5%	35%	0%	0%
GOP Seats			3.2	1.0	0.9
GOP Seat %			40	13	11
Efficiency Gap			−10.5	−11.9	0.3
Seats/Votes Slope			4.8	0.4	0.5

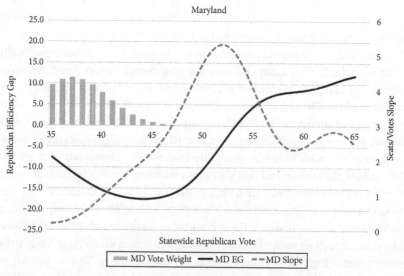

Figure 5.4 Efficiency Gap, Seats/Votes Slope, and Expected Statewide Vote Distribution under Democratic Map of Maryland

Arizona

The map in Arizona seems more clearly drawn with the normal condition in mind (see Table 5.5). Winning 55% of the vote yields Republicans an average of just over five of Arizona's nine seats, and the map is hyperresponsive, two seats being evenly matched seats and a slope of 3.5. Under both the 50/50 and Democratic-wave conditions, these two seats usually go Democratic, and the map is much less responsive. But note that under the 50/50 condition, the typical outcome of five Democratic seats and four Republican seats biases the map slightly toward the Democrats, likely the source of Republican complaints about the map's fairness. Nevertheless, the map never shows an EG nearly as large as either Pennsylvania or Maryland.

Table 5.5 HWEG Model in Arizona

Normal Vote: R+4.7

	Seat Properties		Probability of GOP Seat under Different Scenarios		
CD	Avg. GOP Vote Relative to State	St. Dev. of Relative Avg	Tied Statewide (GOP wins 50%)	Normal Vote (GOP wins 54.7%)	Democratic Wave (GOP wins 61.7%)
1	−4.2%	3.4%	11%	56%	3%
2	−4.0%	3.7%	14%	58%	4%
3	−15.7%	3.7%	0%	0%	0%
4	12.7%	3.8% .	100%	100%	100%
5	10.5%	3.4%	100%	100%	99%
6	5.5%	3.4%	95%	100%	83%
7	−24.6%	3.7%	0%	0%	0%
8	6.7%	3.3%	98%	100%	91%
9	−8.4%	3.7%	1%	15%	0%
GOP Seats			4.2	5.3	3.8
GOP Seat %			47	59	42
Efficiency Gap			−3.5	−0.6	−3.2
Seats/Votes Slope			1.9	3.2	2.0

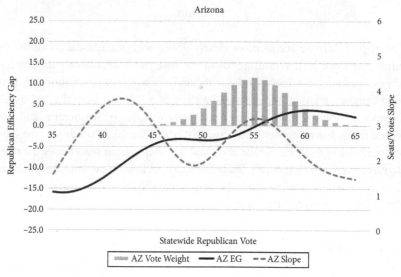

Figure 5.5 Efficiency Gap, Seats/Votes Slope, and Expected Statewide Vote Distribution under Nonpartisan Commission Map of Arizona

The Arizona commission is charged with drawing a nonbiased and competitive map. On the first count, it seems they have succeeded, as EG never significantly exceeds 5% in either direction unless Democrats unrealistically win more than 60% of the vote. The map is indeed highly competitive around the normal vote (55% Republican), but it becomes less competitive as the vote deviates significantly in either direction. Thus, while under most balanced conditions Arizona will see multiple seats closely contested by both parties, it may actually be less of a target than a Republican map like Pennsylvania's during a heavily partisan wave. These elements of partisan balance and hypercompetitiveness will appear across several *nonpartisan commission* maps discussed in Chapter 7.

Extreme Bias and Slope Estimates

We now move to an analysis of all thirty-one states where we have independent mean and variance estimates for each district's electoral performance. I categorize each state according to which party or process was in control of drawing the map: (D)emocratic, (R)epublican, (B)ipartisan, (C)ourt, or (N)onpartisan (typically a commission). In a few states, control is ambiguous or debatable, and these states are given multiple codes, with details shown in Appendix Table 5.2. This analysis is mostly exploratory and looks for patterns common to states with similar districting control and statewide vote share.

I analyze estimated efficiency gaps and slopes under three different measures:

1. *Statewide 50/50 Point:* To account for possible discontinuities as a single point, this is a weighted average of the range from 48% to 52% Republican statewide vote, with the most weight placed on the 50% Republican vote point.
2. *55/45 Range:* The unweighted average across the range from 45% to 55% statewide Republican vote.
3. *Historically Weighted Efficiency Gap:* The weighted average centered around the state's normal vote, as described in the definitions.

Table 5.6 shows the ten states most biased toward Republicans and the five states most biased toward Democrats under the three measures.[10] The differences across these measures highlight how the choice of measurement can alter our perceptions of what constitutes a fair map. The last set of columns showing the historically weighted normal distribution yields the most intuitive list. Republican maps struck down by courts in North Carolina and Pennsylvania top the "most-Republican list," while the remainder of the top ten consists of other Republican gerrymanders interrupted only by the Democratic "dummymander" in Arkansas. By contrast, the states appearing as most biased at the 50/50 point are Louisiana, Tennessee, and Missouri. These states have strongly Republican delegations, but, as explored further in Chapter 6, those delegations do not strike us as particularly biased given the strong Republican leaning of these states. However, the electorate is also highly racially polarized in these states, and their delegations would be similarly Republican as, and even more biased than, states like Pennsylvania if the statewide vote were tied. The 55/45 range measure is something of a midpoint between the other two measures, though more similar to the 50/50 list, still led by noncompetitive, strongly Republican states rather than the more controversial Republican maps or swing states.

On the Democratic side, Maryland stands out as the most biased state under all measures, though Maryland is still less biased under any measure than the top ten Republican states on each list. There are a few differences across the measures: Democratic maps in Massachusetts and Oregon show up as having Democratic bias when centered around their normal (pro-Democratic) vote, but not when centered around the 50/50 point. A few nonpartisan maps in Arizona, Iowa, and Washington appear slightly biased toward the Democrats under some measures, but the observed EG in each of these cases is quite small compared to the reverse gap under most of the Republican maps. Most strangely, the Arkansas map appears on the first two lists as biased toward Democrats despite having an

Table 5.6 Highest and Lowest Efficiency Gaps under Different Measures

	Highest Republican Bias								
	Around 50/50 Point			Across 55/45 Range			HWEG		
	State	Control	EG	State	Control	EG	State	Control	EG
1	LA	R	26.3	TN	R	22.8	NC	R	19.3
2	TN	R	25.2	LA	R	21.8	PA	R	17.8
3	NC	R	24.2	NC	R	21.5	UT	R	14.9
4	PA	R	20.1	PA	R	18.2	AR	D	14.2
5	MO	R	19.6	MO	R	17.8	OH	R	13.5
6	OH	R	18.0	OH	R	14.8	VA.	R	12.2
7	IN	R	17.2	IN	R	14.5	MI	R	11.6
8	VA	R	15.2	VA	R	12.3	WI	R	11.3
9	MN	B	14.8	GA	R	12.2	IN	R	10.9
10	MI	R	13.1	MI	R	11.9	OK	R	10.6

	Highest Democratic Bias								
	Around 50/50 Point			Across 55/45 Range			HWEG		
	State	Control	EG	State	Control	EG	State	Control	EG
1	MD	D	−10.2	MD	D	−8.6	MD	D	−11.0
2	IA	N	−5.4	AR	D	−3.9	OR	D/B	−9.8
3	AR	D	−5.0	NV	N	−2.9	MA	D	−9.2
4	NV	B	−3.4	IA	N	−2.5	WA	N/B	−2.4
5	CA	N	−2.1	CA	R	−1.9	NV	B	−1.1

entirely Republican delegation throughout the decade and appearing among the most Republican states in the HWEG column.

Table 5.7 analyzes responsiveness, showing the states with the ten highest and five lowest slopes under the "50/50 point" and "historically weighted" conditions. This table again reveals the drawbacks of using the tied statewide vote hypothetical to judge a map. Among the *most* competitive states under this measure is Alabama, where under typical conditions we normally expect to see almost no competitive elections. However, under the highly unusual condition of a close statewide vote, as was observed in the 2017 Senate race, many of Alabama's usually safely Republican districts are also very competitive. Massachusetts's

Table 5.7 Highest and Lowest Responsiveness Slopes under Different Measures

Most Responsive States

	Around 50/50 Point			HW Slope		
	State	Control	Slope	State	Control	Slope
1	IA	N	6.5	IA	N	6.2
2	AR	D	6.4	MN	B	4.4
3	OK	R	6.3	NV	B	3.9
4	AL	R	6.1	WA	N/B	3.4
5	MA	D	5.3	VA	R	2.8
6	OR	D/B	4.9	NJ	B	2.6
7	NV	B	4.7	CO	B	2.5
8	MD	D	4.7	AZ	N	2.5
9	WA	N/B	3.9	NY	B	2.3
10	IN	R	3.5	MI	R	2.2

Least Responsive States

	Around 50/50 Point			HW Slope		
	State	Control	Slope	State	Control	Slope
1	WI	R	1.1	LA	R	0.0
2	NJ	B	1.1	AL	R	0.1
3	MI	R	1.2	MA	D	0.1
4	TN	R	1.4	TN	R	0.2
5	NC	R	1.4	AR	D	0.4

inclusion on this list is the mirror image, a state in which almost all districts are usually safely Democratic, but which would become competitive in the abnormal hypothetical of a tied statewide congressional vote.

The right-hand side of this table, responsiveness slope weighted around the state's normal vote, depicts results much closer to what we might expect to be a reasonable measure of competition. The most competitive states are all maps drawn by courts or nonpartisan commissions. It is led by Iowa, where partisanship is not considered in drawing the map, and also the nonpartisan commission states of Arizona and Washington, as well as several other states drawn by courts or bipartisan commissions. The "least responsive" list contains mostly southern states, many of which are obliged by Voting Rights Act considerations to draw a majority-minority district, and which have a generally inelastic electorate. Note that three states judged among the top five *most* responsive by the 50/50 point metric appear on the *least* responsive list using the normal vote metric.

National Bias and Responsiveness

Since HWEG generates an expected delegation composition for every state under all plausible election conditions, we can take a composite of all these states to estimate the bias and responsiveness of the nation as a whole, and also test how closely the projections of HWEG resemble recently observed election outcomes.[11] Table 5.8 shows the actual vote and seat results in U.S. House elections from 2012 to 2018, along with the national seat outcomes projected by HWEG given the popular vote in each cycle and the overall bias and responsiveness expected from the national composite. With the exception of 2014, where HWEG actually overestimates the size of the Republican majority by close to 2.5%, the HWEG seat projection is within 1% (four seats) of the actual election outcome in each cycle.[12]

Figure 5.6 shows expected EG of the nation as a whole under various national electoral conditions. Across the expected range of electoral conditions (drawn from weights shown in the bar graph in Figure 5.6), the nation is biased toward Republicans by an average of 5 points, with a seats/votes slope of 1.6, reflecting responsiveness slightly lower than the historical average. The national EG and slope curves strongly resemble a somewhat muted version of the Republican gerrymander in Pennsylvania shown in Figure 5.3, with some Republican bias

Table 5.8 Projected vs. Actual U.S. House Results Using HWEG, 2012–2018

Year	House GOP 2-Party Vote	Actual GOP Seats	HWEG Projected GOP Seats
2012	49.4%	234	238
2014	52.9%	247	258
2016	50.5%	241	243
2018	45.6%	199	203
National Projected HWEG (2012 Maps)			5.0
National Projected HW Slope			1.6

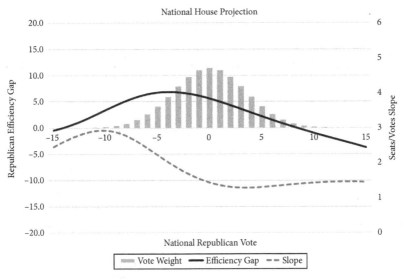

Figure 5.6 Efficiency Gap, Seats/Votes Slope, and Expected Vote Distribution of National U.S. House Delegation

across almost all plausible election scenarios, peaking under modest Democratic waves and slowly declining in both directions. The responsiveness of the map is particularly low under Republican waves (reflected in relatively few Republican gains during their wave election in 2014), but it grows rapidly under Democratic waves (reflected in the large Democratic gains in 2018). HWEG estimates that under the 2012 maps, Democrats would need to have won the popular vote by about 7 points to have an even chance to win the seat majority (though this threshold dropped to around 6 points by 2018 due to changes in the maps in Pennsylvania, Virginia, and Florida).

Given this, it does appear that the congressional landscape throughout the 2010s decade is significantly biased in favor of the Republicans, a bias manifested in every election cycle during the decade. Additionally, this national composite map is less competitive than most historical congressional maps, except under strong Democratic tides. But it is worth noting that in the fifteen small states with three or fewer districts, and thus less incentive or ability to gerrymander, we actually observe even greater Republican bias, with an HWEG average of 7.3 points. So is the Republican bias of the current congressional landscape a result of deliberate partisan gerrymandering or an inevitable result of other factors such as the geographic dispersion of partisans? The next chapter breaks down the results in each state with a partisan map, with a focus on the interaction of gerrymandering and the underlying partisanship of each state.

6

Bias and Responsiveness in Partisan Maps

The previous chapter described a new tool, HWEG, to measure the bias and responsiveness of legislative maps across an expected range of electoral environments. When applied to the enacted U.S. congressional maps in the 2010s cycle, HWEG estimates that the U.S. House was biased in favor of Republicans by 5 points on average. The natural next step would be to ask: How much is partisan gerrymandering specifically responsible for this bias? And are certain types of partisan gerrymanders more responsible than others?

Analysis by Redistricting Institution

As a first cut, we can estimate the average EG and slope curves of states with different redistricting institutions to make some generalizations about what goals each regime is trying to attain through the map. Figure 6.1 shows average EG and seats/votes slope under various conditions among five groups of states:

- Thirteen states with maps drawn by Republicans (including four maps drawn at the start of the decade that have since been overturned or modified by courts).
- Five states with maps drawn by Democrats.
- Four states with maps drawn by a nonpartisan commission or process (AZ, CA, IA, and WA).
- Eight states with maps drawn by a court or bipartisan compromise or legislative commission.
- Five states in the Deep South (AL, GA, LA, MS, and SC).[1]

The average of Republican maps mirrors what was previously seen in the single graph of Pennsylvania, perhaps reflecting a consistency of purpose and effect. The Republican maps show large Republican bias under all but the most extreme national conditions, with bias peaking between 45% and 50% Republican national vote, reflecting maps that will strongly favor the gerrymandering party both under tied election conditions and under moderate Democratic waves. Responsiveness under the Republican maps is extremely low (less than 1.0) when the Republican national vote share is 50% or greater, but increases steadily as

Ground War. Nicholas Goedert, Oxford University Press. © Oxford University Press 2022.
DOI: 10.1093/oso/9780197626627.003.0006

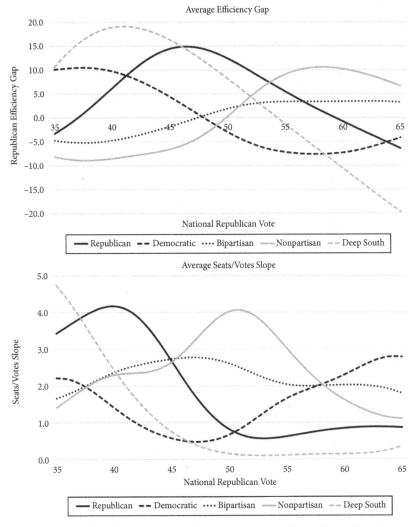

Figure 6.1 Average Efficiency Gap and Responsiveness by Party Control under Range of National Vote Conditions

Republican vote share declines. This mirrors both the theory and findings from Chapter 4 with respect to the effects of tides on competition under Republican maps since the 1970s and suggests that the current decade's maps would also create more close elections and turnover as Democratic tides rise.

The average of nonpartisan commission maps reflects a hyperresponsiveness, consistently over 2.0 under most plausible conditions and peaking around 4.0, approximately double the average threshold, when the national vote is close to even. This responsiveness generates a Democratic EG under Democratic waves and a Republican EG under Republican waves, though the average commission map is almost exactly unbiased when the national vote is tied. The techniques and goals of individual nonpartisan commissions and other procedures are explored in greater detail in Chapter 7, but these figures suggest that commissions on the whole are succeeding in producing maps that are both unbiased and highly competitive. The shape of the slope curve also matches the theory and empirical findings in Chapter 4 about the propensity of commission maps toward close elections.

We might expect the average of Democratic maps to show the *reverse* of Republican maps. But instead, they come closer to the *reverse of the nonpartisan maps*, with Democratic bias under Democratic tides, and Republican bias under Republican tides, and low responsiveness overall. This is likely due to the small number and diversity of Democratic maps offsetting each other, particularly the unusual trends in Illinois, Massachusetts, and Arkansas, explored later in the chapter. Unlike the Republican gerrymanders, none of the Democratic gerrymanders occur in swing states, where we see the most consistent pattern of partisan bias and responsiveness.

We can contrast the patterns seen in both partisan and nonpartisan maps to the average of bipartisan and court maps, which represents something of a control condition. The bipartisan maps are never severely biased in either direction, although the average is very slightly biased toward Republicans under close conditions, perhaps reflecting a modest geographic asymmetry explored in other research (e.g., Chen and Rodden 2015). Additionally, these maps display average responsiveness under all conditions, with the slope curve hovering consistently around 2.0.

Finally, the states of the Deep South are generally mildly biased in favor of Republicans but share the overwhelming characteristic of being grossly noncompetitive under all conditions but the very strongest of Democratic waves. And this has played out in the actual congressional elections, with *only 4* of the more than 150 congressional seat elections across those five states decided by 9 points or less during this decade. This suggests a trade-off between competition and minority representation that has been debated over the past thirty years with respect to racial gerrymandering and application of the Voting Rights Act. But for our purpose it is largely noted only to explain the exclusion of these states from the analysis of partisan gerrymanders in the next chapter.

It would appear from Figure 6.1 that Republican gerrymanders in particular uniformly accomplish their goal of creating safe majorities for their party in each state under most election conditions, while being subject to the possibility of backfire under strong Democratic waves. But it would be a mistake to generalize uniformly about all Republican maps. Instead, a closer examination of the EG and responsiveness curves for individual partisan gerrymanders reveals that they don't all achieve the same goals or follow the same patterns. Instead, the underlying partisanship of the state seems to largely predict the shape of the gerrymander, and measurements that can account for both variation in state partisanship and national tides are essential to understand these patterns.

Bias in Republican Maps

With respect to Republican maps, the average EG curve shown in Figure 6.1 follows an unambiguous shape, with Republican bias under almost all plausible conditions, peaking when the national vote was close to even. But when we break this curve down into its constituent states, the pattern becomes more complicated.

Figures 6.2 and 6.3 show the EG curves generated by HWEG for eleven states that drew Republican gerrymanders in the 2010s cycle. Figure 6.2 displays *statewide* Republican vote on the x-axis, while Figure 6.3 rescales the same data to show *national* Republican vote on the x-axis. The eleven states are ordered and shaded by their statewide normal vote, ranging from leaning-Democratic Michigan (48.9% normal Republican vote) to overwhelmingly Republican Oklahoma (69.3% normal Republican vote).[2]

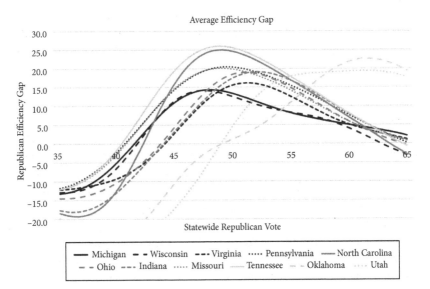

Figure 6.2 Bias under Range of *Statewide* Conditions—Individual Republican Maps

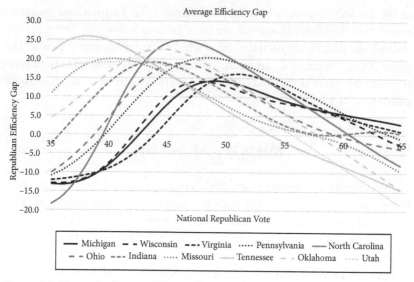

Figure 6.3 Bias under Range of *National* Conditions—Individual Republican Maps

When measured around the point where the statewide vote is tied (in Figure 6.2), nine of the eleven Republican maps unsurprisingly show heavy Republican bias. But curiously, the two maps that appear largely unbiased under tied statewide conditions are also the two that are most heavily dominated by Republicans: Oklahoma and Utah.

By contrast, when we shift the curves to measure bias in relation to the national vote (in Figure 6.3), the swing state maps will show large Republican bias when the national vote is tied or reasonably even. This should also be unsurprising since the swing state curves will move very little when changing our reference from state to national vote. However, the two heavily Republican states that showed no bias at the statewide 50/50 point now also show strong Republican bias under tied national conditions. But bias is *not* uniformly high. Rather, a handful of states show much smaller bias under the tied condition but maximize bias under strong Democratic tides, conditions under which many swing state gerrymanders would backfire. These states, including Tennessee and Missouri, also share a common characteristic: they are too heavily Republican to be considered swing states, but not as heavily Republican as Oklahoma or Utah.

These anecdotal patterns suggest that the shape of a partisan gerrymander is largely determined by the underlying partisanship of the state. To test this further, I typologize each state into one of three categories based on the state's normal vote (calculated as described in Chapter 5):

- *Competitive States:* States with a Republican normal vote between 42.5% and 57.5%. These states we would expect to be won by less than 15 points when the national vote is tied. They include true swing states such as Virginia, Wisconsin, and Pennsylvania, as well as states with a clear but modest partisan lean like Ohio and Oregon.
- *Noncompetitive States:* States with a Republican normal vote between 35% and 42.5%, or between 57.5% and 65%. These states we would expect to be won by between 15 and 30 points when the national vote is tied. They include Indiana, Missouri, and Tennessee on the Republican side, and Maryland on the Democratic side.
- *Extreme States:* States with a Republican normal vote less than 35% or greater than 65%. These states we would expect to be won by more than 30 points when the national vote is tied. They include Oklahoma and Utah on the Republican side, and Massachusetts on the Democratic side.

Factoring the partisan competitiveness of a state into a typology of gerrymandering has taken on much greater importance over the past ten to twenty years simply because growing geographic polarization has led to dramatic increases in the number of noncompetitive and extreme states in the current decade. Using these normal vote thresholds, Table 6.1 shows the number of states in each category over the past four decades. In the 1980s and 1990s, more than three-quarters of states would have fallen into the competitive category, and only Utah would have fallen into the extreme category. However, beginning in the 2000s, the number of competitive states dropped dramatically, first falling to the noncompetitive bin, and then into the extreme bin, such that in the 2010s the number of competitive states has nearly been cut in half, the number of noncompetitive states has doubled, and the extreme states have increased from one to ten. Thus, whereas in the 1980s and 1990s almost all states large enough for gerrymandering to be important would also be nationally competitive, in the 2010s there is wide variation on this measure among states with gerrymanders of all types.

Table 6.1 Number of States by Decade and Competitiveness Category

	Normal Vote Range	2010s	2000s	1990s	1980s
Competitive States	42.5–57.5	20	28	38	39
Noncompetitive States	35–42.5 or 57.5–65	20	19	11	10
Extreme States	<35 or >65	10	3	1	1

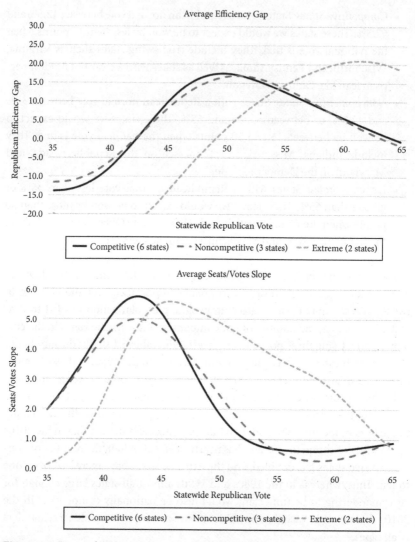

Figure 6.4 Bias and Responsiveness under Range of *Statewide* Conditions—Average of GOP Maps

Categorizing the eleven Republican gerrymanders shown in Figures 6.2 and 6.3 yields six competitive, three noncompetitive, and two extreme states. Figures 6.4 and 6.5 display the category averages for bias and responsiveness evaluated by statewide Republican vote (Figure 6.4) and national Republican vote (Figure 6.5). Table 6.2 summarizes bias and responsiveness evaluated at both the statewide 50/50 point and under historically weighted national conditions.

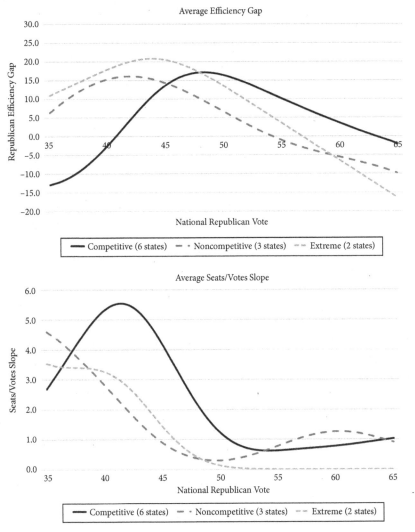

Figure 6.5 Bias and Responsiveness under Range of *National* Conditions—Average of GOP Maps

Table 6.2 shows both the important differences across these categories and also the importance of choice of measurement. Measured at the 50/50 point, the competitive and noncompetitive states look extremely similar, showing very high Republican bias and average responsiveness, while the extreme states don't look like gerrymanders at all, showing very high responsiveness but almost no bias. Yet when we weight our measurement around historic patterns of election results, we draw the same conclusions with respect to the competitive states, but

Table 6.2 Average Bias and Responsiveness of Republican Gerrymanders by Competitiveness Category

Category	Bias		Responsiveness	
	Statewide 50/50	HWEG	Statewide 50/50	HW Slope
Competitive	17.1	14.2	1.9	1.7
Noncompetitive	16.4	6.6	2.5	0.6
Extreme	2.9	12.7	4.9	0.4

much different ones with respect to the other two categories. Both the noncompetitive and the extreme states now reveal themselves to be very *non*responsive. And while the extreme states now show bias comparable to the competitive states, the noncompetitive states show only about half this bias on average.

Bias in Democratic Maps

In contrast to the obvious patterns shown in the average bias under Republican maps in Figure 6.1, the average of Democratic maps is more puzzling. The reasons for this ambiguity are revealed when we map out the projected bias in the five states with Democratic gerrymanders in the 2000s cycle. Figure 6.6 shows bias in Democratic gerrymanders anchored to *statewide* Republican vote share, while Figure 6.7 shifts the same data to be anchored to *national* Republican vote (analogous to Figures 6.2 and 6.3).

Unlike the Republican maps, the Democratic maps show no consistent patterns when the statewide vote is tied: Oregon and Illinois show very little bias, while Maryland is biased toward Democrats and Massachusetts is biased toward *Republicans*. Several of the maps, especially Arkansas, are highly competitive around this point, while Illinois is unusually noncompetitive. When the curves are rescaled to the national vote, much of this confusion is clarified. Unlike the Republican maps, none of the Democratic gerrymanders occur in the swing states, and thus Figure 6.7 shifts all of the curve dramatically, in some cases reversing the conclusions we might draw about the map. This graph shows that three of the Democratic maps, Massachusetts, Maryland, and Oregon, are all clearly biased toward the Democrats under tied national conditions and most likely conditions around this point. And among these three maps, the differences we do see are closely analogous to the differences observed across Republican maps based on the relative partisanship of the state, and each map is essentially a mirror image of the set of maps shown in Figure 6.4.

This leaves two exceptional cases that do not have Republican analogues, possibly reflecting the difficulty in drawing strongly Democratic maps in some states

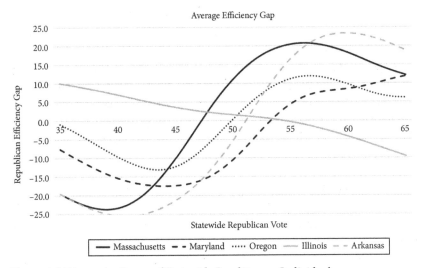

Figure 6.6 Bias under Range of *Statewide* Conditions—Individual Democratic Maps

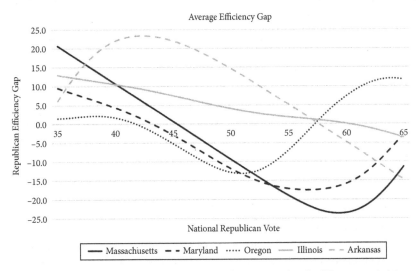

Figure 6.7 Bias under Range of *National* Conditions—Individual Democratic Maps

due to the asymmetric distribution of partisans. Arkansas is a stark Democratic dummymander whose curves curiously resemble those of Utah. Democrats in Arkansas declined to draw a single clearly Democratic district and ended up winning none of them, failing to anticipate the rapid shift of Arkansas from heavily Democratic to heavily Republican at the local level. As there were no Republican maps drawn in heavily Democratic states, we cannot tell whether Republicans would have been more successful gerrymandering a similarly hostile state. In Illinois, Democrats did not draw a map clearly biased toward one party or another; they did crack several districts around Chicago to make the map less biased than the one drawn by Republicans in the previous decade, but mostly this map incorporates a lot of safe seats for both parties, resulting in a map whose responsiveness slope lies consistently below the 2.0 threshold and which is actually slightly biased toward Republicans under normal or Democratic-leaning tides.[3]

Partisan Gerrymanders and the 2018 Election

Both the anecdotes and historical empirical analysis of past cycles have suggested that many partisan gerrymanders are vulnerable to backfires, signified by increased competition and turnover, during adverse waves. Given the numerous Republican maps drawn in the 2010s decade and the magnitude of the tide, the 2018 election seems exactly the sort of cycle where we should observe this pattern. Yet even this anecdotal evidence reveals that not all partisan gerrymanders react the same way, with the underlying partisanship or competitiveness of the state a key moderating variable.

Democrats gained forty seats nationwide in the 2018 election in which they won the popular vote by almost 9 points. Yet their gains among Republican-gerrymandered states were not spread consistently. At one end of the spectrum, the wave was strong enough to force some surprising competition in the extremely Republican states of Oklahoma and Utah, with the Democrats narrowly winning a seat in each to break up a previously unanimous Republican delegation, though in both cases the seats were recaptured by Republicans in 2020. At the other end, Republican gerrymanders in two states narrowly tilting to the Democrats backfired dramatically, with Democrats flipping two seats in Michigan and three in Virginia; three additional seats flipped in the newly redrawn Pennsylvania.

But for states whose partisanship lay in between these extremes, the effects of the wave were much more muted. Democrats failed to make seat gains in Republican-leaning North Carolina and Ohio, but at least they forced significant competition, with six Ohio races and seven North Carolina races decided by 9 points or fewer.

More significant, the wave seemed entirely absent in the strongly, but not overwhelmingly, Republican states of Indiana, Missouri, and Tennessee. These three states, each with a statewide Republican normal vote between 58% and 61%, not only saw no seat turnover, but saw only one competitive race among them (MO District 2). In this way, the complete nonresponsiveness of these three maps to waves actually makes them similar to the Democratic map of Maryland, which was drawn robustly enough to remain 7–1 in favor of the Democrats, even following the Republican wave in 2014. While Maryland has often been grouped with Pennsylvania, Virginia, and North Carolina as examples of egregious partisan gerrymanders, it actually has much more in common with the Republican maps in less competitive states coming under far less scrutiny.

Gerrymanders in Competitive States

Based on the patterns seen in Figures 6.4 and 6.5, bolstered by these anecdotal results of the 2018 cycle, we can detail the tactics and outcomes consistently observed in three categories of partisan gerrymanders, determined by the typology of the state normal vote outlined earlier. All partisan gerrymanders from the 2010s cycle, Democratic and Republican, fall into one of these three categories, with the exception of the ineffective Democratic maps in Arkansas and Illinois. Each of these categories embodies significant normative concerns about bias and noncompetitiveness, but each also manifests their most concerning traits under different conditions and in different ways. And thus there is no single metric or scenario that allows us to evaluate all partisan maps in the same framework.

The remainder of this chapter looks at a few gerrymanders in each category through several lenses. First, I examine the exact tactics used by the mapmakers in terms of packing and cracking particular cities or regions. Second, I look at the district results of a few statewide elections to assess how the gerrymander reacted to different statewide environments. And finally, I compare the map to hypothetical maps drawn by the Atlas of Redistricting project at the website FiveThirtyEight.com to maximize either partisan gain or district compactness.

The most straightforward category is the partisan gerrymandering of competitive states. These are the states where the bias is usually most obvious, and in particular where the "antimajoritarian" outcome is most likely. They are naturally also the states that tend to attract controversy and litigation, including recent cases in Pennsylvania, North Carolina, Michigan, and Ohio.

We've already seen an example of one such map in Pennsylvania in the previous chapter (Figure 5.3), the map that provided Republicans with a 13–5 majority in the delegation prior to being overturned in *LWV* in 2018. The partisanship of each district in this map displays the archetypical patterns of packing and cracking, yet also reveals the possibility of backfire broached in our first chapter. Democratic vote strength was packed into five districts: three around Philadelphia (Districts 1, 2, and 13), one around Pittsburgh (District 14), and one around Allentown (District 17), while smaller pockets of Democratic voting strength were cracked to spread Republican majorities around the remaining thirteen districts. The map also resembles other competitive partisan gerrymanders with an HWEG bias of 17.8% and an HW slope of 1.8. Table 6.3 shows the performance of each Pennsylvania district in three recent elections: the 2016 presidential race won by Trump by 1% (close to the state's normal vote), the

Table 6.3 Statewide Election Results in a Competitive State

	Pennsylvania Normal Republican Vote = 51.0% (R+1.0) HWEG = 17.8 HW Slope = 1.8			
Total	2012 Senate Smith % 45.4	2016 Senate Toomey % 50.7	2016 Pres. Trump % 50.4	14-election GOP Average vs. Statewide
District				
1	16.0	20.2	18.6	−29.1
2	8.7	10.7	7.7	−35.7
3	55.2	62.1	63.5	10.0
4	56.2	61.4	61.2	11.6
5	57.4	63.3	65.1	11.2
6	49.4	53.8	49.8	4.3
7	48.8	54.2	48.8	5.1
8	48.3	53.4	50.1	3.6
9	60.2	67.9	72.0	13.7
10	59.3	66.0	68.6	15.1
11	52.4	59.8	62.4	8.3
12	53.8	59.4	60.7	6.9
13	31.1	36.1	32.7	−16.3
14	28.4	31.1	31.6	−20.5
15	49.5	55.4	53.9	6.0
16	52.5	55.3	53.5	6.3
17	42.3	50.8	55.2	−3.4
18	54.4	59.1	60.1	10.2

2016 Senate race won by Republican Pat Toomey by a similar margin, and the 2012 Senate race in which Democrat Bob Casey defeated Republican Bob Smith by a more substantial 9%.[4]

Through the lens of these elections, we can see both the intended function of the map under normal conditions and the potential for backfire under an adverse wave. In the 2016 Senate election, Senator Toomey actually won fourteen of the eighteen districts, several narrowly, including the Democratic-held but Republican-trending 17th District by a narrow margin, while losing the remaining four districts in landslides. On the other hand, four of the Republican districts (6,

7, and 8 in suburban Philadelphia and 15 in the Lehigh Valley) voted for Senator Casey over his Republican rival in 2012, demonstrating that a strong enough wave could have overcome the gerrymander. Because the map was overturned prior to the 2018 election, we cannot know for certain whether the wave that year would have been sufficient. But given Democrat Conor Lamb's surprising special election win early that year in the heavily Republican 18th District and retirements by at least two incumbents in left-trending areas, it is likely that Democrats would have seen substantial gains in the state even in the absence of a new map.

Another way to look at the effectiveness of a gerrymander might be to compare its results to other possible maps drawn with different goals in mind. Early in 2018, the website FiveThirtyEight.com published an Atlas of Redistricting, depicting hypothetical congressional maps for all states under several different conditions. Three of these conditions included drawing maps to maximize Republican representation, Democratic representation, and district compactness. Figure 6.8 replicates the maps drawn in six states to maximize partisan advantage, including four Republican gerrymanders and two Democratic gerrymanders, including the map to maximize Republican representation in Pennsylvania in Figure 6.8a. While the exact contours of the lines are different (FiveThirtyEight drew four Democratic districts around Philadelphia and none in the Lehigh Valley), the net results are largely the same: thirteen Republican districts and five Democratic districts under average voting conditions.

So it looks like Republicans really did maximize their advantage in this case. By contrast, two "compact" maps of Pennsylvania drawn by FiveThirtyEight (one of which respects county lines, a second of which does not) both produce results with a Republican advantage, but a much smaller one, with nine Republican, five Democratic, and four "highly competitive" districts. So while some Republican bias may be explained by the asymmetric geography of the state, the extent of bias actually observed was intentional and close to maximal.

There were no comparable large swing states gerrymandered by Democrats, but Oregon provides something of a parallel. With five congressional districts, Oregon packs the eastern two-thirds of its land area into a single district that is 20% more Republican than the state as a whole. The state then strategically cracks Portland into two districts and centers the remaining two districts around Salem and Eugene to create one heavily Democratic district and three districts that lean Democratic, like the state as a whole. This produced a map with a Democratic HWEG bias of –9.7 (second highest in the nation) and, similar to many of the competitive state partisan gerrymanders, an HWEG slope of 1.9 (representing average responsiveness).[5]

And like the converse case in Pennsylvania, it appears Democrats maximized their partisan advantage in Oregon. The FiveThirtyEight Democratic gerrymander of the state (shown in Figure 6.8b) is highly similar to the actual map used, creating four Democratic districts by splitting Portland into two districts and

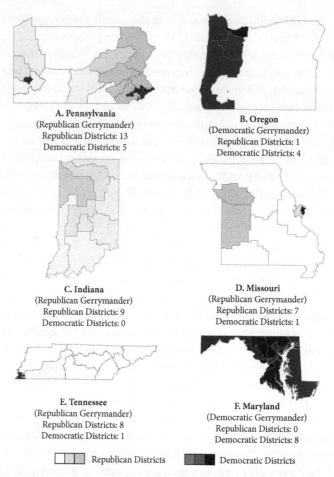

A. Pennsylvania
(Republican Gerrymander)
Republican Districts: 13
Democratic Districts: 5

B. Oregon
(Democratic Gerrymander)
Republican Districts: 1
Democratic Districts: 4

C. Indiana
(Republican Gerrymander)
Republican Districts: 9
Democratic Districts: 0

D. Missouri
(Republican Gerrymander)
Republican Districts: 7
Democratic Districts: 1

E. Tennessee
(Republican Gerrymander)
Republican Districts: 8
Democratic Districts: 1

F. Maryland
(Democratic Gerrymander)
Republican Districts: 0
Democratic Districts: 8

☐☐☐ Republican Districts   ██ Democratic Districts

Figure 6.8 Partisan Maps from the FiveThirtyEight Atlas of Redistricting
Source: Adapted from FiveThirtyEight Atlas of Redistricting by Robert Hildebrand from files made available by Aaron Bycoff at https://github.com/fivethirtyeight/redistricting-atlas-data.

centering another two around Salem and Eugene. The compactness-maximizing maps both create two Democratic, one Republican, and two "highly competitive" districts (again in mirror image to Pennsylvania), suggesting a slight Democratic advantage in the state geography, enhanced by intentional gerrymandering.

These two states exemplify the patterns of the competitive-state partisan gerrymander. On one hand, opposing partisans are packed to yield maximal bias under normal voting conditions. But on the other hand, affiliated partisans are spread more thinly over more districts, resulting in reasonable measures of competitiveness and the possibility that the map will be highly responsive to adverse wave elections. The 2010 REDMAP strategy ensured that these maps were much more prevalent and influential among Republicans, and the Illinois example suggests geography might make it harder for Democrats to draw such an effective map. But the Oregon example shows us that a similar gerrymander from both sides is still possible. Figure 6.9 displays the EG and responsiveness slope curves for the six competitive Republican gerrymanders alongside the Democratic gerrymander of Oregon. And here the common patterns are crystal clear, with Oregon the mirror image of the

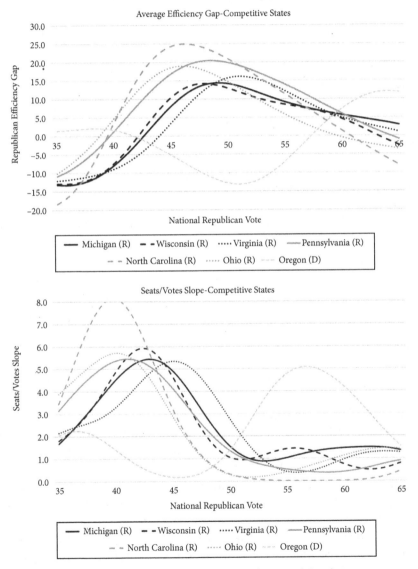

Figure 6.9 Bias and Responsiveness under Range of National Conditions— Competitive States

Republican maps. Each map displays high partisan bias under tied national conditions or slight adverse tides, with bias decreasing from either end of the peak. And each map displays average responsiveness, although it is asymmetrically distributed, with the maps being much more competitive under adverse tides than friendly ones.

Gerrymanders in Noncompetitive States

The next set of states I analyze are the "noncompetitive states"; these are states in which we would expect one party to consistently win relatively easily statewide when the national vote is close, but in which significant pockets or regions of adverse party strength still exist. If partisan mapmakers in all states were following the traditional packing-and-cracking strategy, we would expect these maps to show a large number of districts marginally favoring their party under a typical range of electoral conditions. But unlike partisan gerrymanders in swing states, maps in noncompetitive states do not display this pattern. The result in each case is a map that will measure as only moderately biased under nationally normal conditions but will also be especially fortified against adverse waves.

The patterns are most easily evident in the three noncompetitive Republican states shown in Figure 6.2: Indiana, Missouri, and Tennessee. These three maps share a number of traits in common: each drew one safely Democratic district, either majority African American or held by an African American, around one city in the state (Indianapolis, St. Louis, and Memphis). But each state also drew a second, white-majority but Democratic-leaning district around another city (Gary, Kansas City, and Nashville), while making the remaining districts in the state strongly Republican. In each of these three states, Republicans in control of the districting process did not choose to maximize their expected seat total, and in fact did not draw more Republican districts than the natural lean and geographic patterns of the state would suggest. It is likely that Republicans in each state could have cracked the Democrats in this second district while retaining the Republican lean of every other district had they chosen to be more aggressive, while remaining in compliance with the Voting Rights Act and other constitutional requirements. Instead, these maps more closely resemble maps that simply follow the natural partisan dispersion of the state.

Table 6.4 below shows results from three statewide elections in two Republican gerrymanders in noncompetitive states. In each case the results by congressional district are shown in (a) a close Democratic win, (b) a close Republican win, (c) the *nationally* close 2016 presidential election, and (d) the average of many congressional, statewide, and presidential elections from 2012 to 2018 *compared to the statewide result.*[6]

Table 6.4 Statewide Election Results in Two Noncompetitive States

	Missouri Normal GOP Vote = 58.8%			
Total	2012 SoS Schoeller % 49.2	2012 LG Kinder % 52.0	2016 Pres Trump % 59.8	13-election GOP Average vs. Statewide
CD				
1	16.8	19.7	19.6	−32.6
2	53.0	56.2	55.4	2.0
3	56.5	59.8	70.5	8.4
4	56.2	58.8	69.0	6.4
5	34.6	37.7	42.9	−15.2
6	53.2	56.6	66.6	6.8
7	66.6	65.5	74.0	13.0
8	59.1	63.7	78.2	12.4
	Indiana Normal GOP Vote = 58.3%			
Total	2012 Sen Mourdock % 47.0	2012 Gov Pence % 51.5	2016 Pres Trump % 60.1	9-election GOP Average vs. Statewide
CD				
1	31.9	34.4	43.4	−20.0
2	47.6	52.3	62.2	1.2
3	57.1	60.0	68.4	10.6
4	53.0	56.8	68.1	8.0
5	49.4	57.8	56.3	4.4
6	52.8	59.5	71.2	9.1
7	29.8	34.9	38.0	−18.2
8	49.5	49.8	67.7	4.3
9	50.2	55.4	64.1	3.0

The partisan nature of each of these gerrymanders appears in the 2016 presidential column as well. In this evenly divided national contest, no district in any of these three states is closely competitive: Trump won all but two districts by more than 10% in each state of Missouri and Indiana. But the other three columns depict a divergent story. Indiana and Missouri appear to be gerrymandered so the Republicans will win a supermajority of seats when their vote share is close to or even slightly below 50%. The Republican candidate in Missouri wins six of eight districts in cases of both a close loss (2012 Secretary of State) and a close win (2012 Lieutenant Governor). In Indiana, Richard Mourdock won just four of nine districts while losing statewide by 6%, but lost two districts by only 1 point, and a seventh district by 5%. Both cases appear to maximize Republican seats in an evenly contested *statewide* race, even though an evenly split statewide congressional vote in these states is unlikely. In this aspect, these gerrymanders follow a strategy adapted to Republican gerrymanders in swing states, but perhaps less effectively applied in a different context. Republicans will almost always win all but two seats in these states, even during a Democratic wave, but they fail to maximize their seats in a more typical environment. As seen in the overwhelming Trump support in most districts in 2016, these maps waste an enormous number of Republican votes during close national elections.

The map in Maryland, which we discussed in Chapter 3 (the *Benisek* case) and Chapter 5 (Table 5.4 and Figure 5.4), follows the inverse pattern. Maryland is heavily Democratic statewide but has two pockets of Republican strength: the Chesapeake Eastern Shore (traditionally the 1st District) and the Western panhandle (traditionally the 6th District). Maryland Democrats chose to crack the 6th District (which precipitated the *Benisek* litigation) but to keep the 1st District intact. The result is one very heavily Republican district (won by Trump in 2016 by almost 30 points) and seven heavily Democratic districts (Clinton won the 6th District by 18 points in 2016, and all remaining districts by at least 25 points). While many of the eastern Democratic districts are very strangely shaped, they are not efficiently drawn to maximize the Democratic delegation.

When we compared the actual gerrymander maps of Pennsylvania and Oregon to the maps drawn by FiveThirtyEight attempting to maximize partisan advantage (Figure 6.8a and b), we found the results of these efforts very similar, suggesting the real gerrymanders had approached the most effective gerrymander possible. But this is *not* true of the maps of the noncompetitive states. Instead, the FiveThirtyEight Atlas showed how Tennessee and Missouri could draw a compact map with only one Democratic district, while Indiana, lacking a legal mandate to draw a minority-influence district, could be drawn with *all nine* districts favoring Republicans. Conversely, in Maryland, several legally compliant and reasonably compact hypothetical maps have been drawn with all eight districts strongly favoring Democrats. While Maryland is one of the few states to show Democratic bias under the HWEG measure, even this map does not come close to maximizing the Democrats' advantage. The alternate, more aggressive gerrymanders of each state are shown in Figure 6.8c through 6.8f. Additionally, FiveThirtyEight found that Missouri, Indiana, and Tennessee would all tend to create at most two Democratic districts under algorithmic methods and methods designed to retain county borders. So the intentional gerrymander of these states did not gain the map-drawing party any additional seats beyond what we might expect from the geography of the state.

Figure 6.10 displays the EG and responsiveness slope curves for the three noncompetitive Republican gerrymanders alongside the Democratic

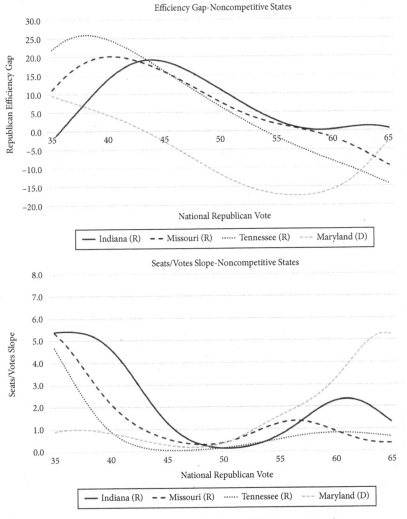

Figure 6.10 Bias and Responsiveness under Range of National Conditions—Noncompetitive States

gerrymander of Maryland. And just like the competitive gerrymanders shown in Figure 6.9, the patterns are clear, this time with Maryland the mirror image of the Republican maps. Each map displays moderate partisan bias when the national vote is tied, but this is not where bias peaks. Instead, bias gets steadily stronger under adverse partisan waves, suggesting a much more defensive gerrymander than those seen in the competitive states. Unlike the competitive states, these gerrymanders will not backfire unless a wave was so strong as to be almost historically unprecedented. And this is reinforced in Figure 6.10, showing responsiveness close to 0 in every case under close national conditions, and remaining very low under almost all plausible tides. These maps will be utterly noncompetitive in a normal election cycle and, as we observed in 2014 and 2018, almost entirely noncompetitive even in a wave cycle.

Bias in Extreme States

The final category of states we will analyze are what I term "extreme states," where we expect one party to win by at least 30 points on average when the national vote is close. This includes Oklahoma and Utah on the Republican side, and Massachusetts on the Democratic side. These states are so thoroughly dominated by one party that even the natural geography of the states suggests that this party might be favored in every district drawn even under a fair map. In the hypothetical maps drawn by the FiveThirtyEight Atlas of Redistricting to maximize compactness, Oklahoma includes five safely Republican districts; Utah includes three Republican districts and one competitive district around Salt Lake City; and Massachusetts includes eight Democratic and one competitive (but Democratic-leaning) district around Worcester in the middle of the state. They are separated here from the noncompetitive states because they look strikingly different when analyzed under a partisan bias metric that assesses outcomes when both parties win 50% of the statewide vote. Under this measure, maps in extreme states will often appear absurdly unbiased or even biased in favor of the party that, in practice, usually wins no seats (as seen in Figure 6.4 and Table 6.2).

Table 6.5 shows the results by congressional district in several statewide elections in Massachusetts and Oklahoma, including the 2016 presidential contest. In Oklahoma, the most competitive major statewide election was the 2018 governor's race, won by the Republican Kevin Stitt by 12 points. But Massachusetts shows a wider range of statewide results, including Republican Scott Brown's narrow loss to Elizabeth Warren in a 2012

Table 6.5 Statewide Election Results in Two Extreme States

	Massachusetts Normal GOP Vote = 29.7%			
Total	2012 Senate Brown % 46.2	2014 Governor Baker % 51.0	2016 Pres. Trump % 35.3	13-election GOP Average vs. Statewide
CD				
1	42.8	49.5	*39.0*	−1.2
2	48.6	**54.0**	*39.6*	2.1
3	*50.8*	**55.0**	*37.8*	5.0
4	*50.3*	54.3	*37.2*	2.7
5	41.2	44.8	27.0	−5.1
6	*53.6*	57.4	40.5	7.0
7	21.4	26.0	12.4	−16.8
8	*49.9*	**54.1**	*36.3*	0.8
9	*51.1*	55.5	*44.3*	8.4

	Oklahoma Normal GOP Vote = 69.3%		
Total	2018 Governor Stitt % 56.3	2016 Pres. Trump % 66.8	7-election GOP Average vs. Statewide
CD			
1	54.5	65.8	−1.8
2	*61.6*	67.8	5.3
3	*65.1*	73.9	8.8
4	55.7	67.1	−0.5
5	45.2	59.2	−11.0

Senate election and Republican Charlie Baker's narrow victory in the 2014 governor's race.

Comparing the Massachusetts gerrymander under two close statewide elections reveals a dramatic difference between the strategy used in this map and the noncompetitive state maps in Table 6.5. In the Massachusetts case, it appears that gerrymandering Democrats did not particularly care how this map would perform when the statewide vote is even or marginally favoring the Democrats. Even while losing the state by almost 8 points, Republican Senator Scott Brown won four districts and came within a point of winning two more. And in Republican Charlie Baker's 2-point 2014 gubernatorial win, he won six of the state's nine districts easily, and lost a seventh district by only 1 point. Similarly, the last column here reveals that over an average of many elections, six of nine districts are more Republican than the state as a whole, while a seventh district is within 1 point of average. In a case where the Republicans were competitive in the statewide congressional votes, this Democratic gerrymander would massively backfire. But Democrats appear willing to risk this unlikely event in exchange for safely winning every seat in a nationally average environment. In this average environment, such as the 2016 presidential election, Democrats win every seat by more than 10 points. Thus, unlike the Republican maps, this *is* a clear example of cracking the opposing party where the state is so noncompetitive that no packing is even necessary.

The Oklahoma map shows a similar strategy. Three of the five districts are actually slightly more Democratic than the statewide average, and one was actually lost, both at the congressional level and in the 12-point gubernatorial win in 2018. But in the average environment of 2016, Trump won every district by more than 15 points.

Just as we previously displayed the patterns for bias and responsiveness for competitive and noncompetitive states, Figure 6.11 shows the EG and slope of our three extreme states. And once again obvious patterns appear, with Massachusetts mirroring Oklahoma and Utah. In these maps, the gerrymandering party wins every seat in a tied national election, so bias is high when the election is close, but bias necessarily decreases under friendly tides, since there are no more possible seats for the party to win. As with the noncompetitive states, average responsiveness is extremely low. But unlike the noncompetitive states (and more like the competitive states), what little responsiveness we do see is asymmetrically distributed. These maps are actually slightly more responsive to adverse waves than Indiana or Missouri, as exemplified by the narrow Democratic gains in Oklahoma and Utah in 2018.

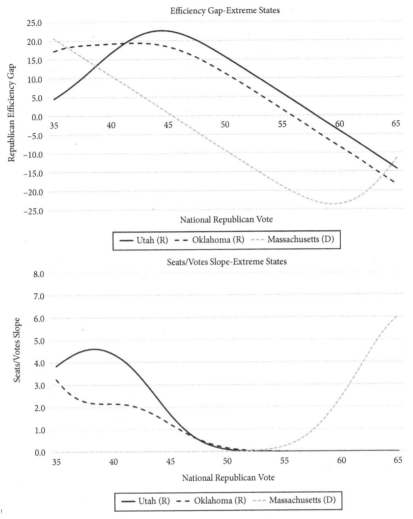

Figure 6.11 Bias and Responsiveness under Range of National Conditions—Extreme States

Regression Analysis

The final step we will take is to explore whether any of the anecdotal patterns drawn from observation of individual states translates to significant effect when the entire (admittedly small) data set of thirty-five states is analyzed. The results in Table 6.6 show the correlation between redistricting party and Republican EG (a) around the 50/50 statewide vote point (columns 1 and

Table 6.6 Effect of Redistricting Control and Normal Vote on Estimated Bias

	Republican Efficiency Gap			
	Around 50/50 Point		Historically Weighted EG	
Variables	(1)	(2)	(3)	(4)
Republican Vote Advantage	–	0.20 (0.25)	–	0.72** (0.19)
Republican Map	7.51 (3.73)	9.82* (4.54)	8.43* (3.70)	11.90** (3.34)
Rep. Vote* Rep. Map	–	−0.47 (0.41)	–	−1.05** (0.30)
Democratic Map	−7.60 (4.82)	−8.80 (5.20)	−3.87 (4.79)	1.04 (3.82)
Dem. Vote* Rep. Map	–	−0.45 (0.39)	–	−0.023 (0.29)
Nonpartisan Map	−6.56 (4.40)	−6.16 (4.50)	2.41 (4.37)	3.85 (3.31)
Constant	7.10* (3.11)	6.84* (3.18)	1.59 (3.09)	0.65 (2.34)
Observations	35	35	35	35
R-squared	0.409	0.449	0.266	0.625

Notes: Standard errors in parentheses; ** $p < 0.01$, * $p < 0.05$

2) and (b) the historically weighted average (columns 3 and 4). The control group here is maps drawn by a court or bipartisan compromise.[7] Table 6.7 shows analysis using the same independent variables with responsiveness slope as the dependent variable.

We see that Republican maps show significant Republican bias in almost all specifications, but the Democratic bias of the Democratic maps is less consistently significant. But note the significant positive constant; taken together with the negative coefficient on nonpartisan maps, this suggests the court and bipartisan maps are somewhat biased toward Republicans at the 50/50 point, possibly due to geographic dispersion, while nonpartisan commissions are more actively trying to draw a balanced map. The lack of significant Democratic bias in the Democratic maps may be a combination of geographic constraints, the impact of the Arkansas dummymander, and mapmakers in Maryland and Massachusetts drawing a map primarily with the normal vote split rather than

Table 6.7 Effect of Redistricting Control and Normal Vote on Estimated Responsiveness

Variables	Responsiveness Slope			
	Around 50/50 Point		Historically Weighted Slope	
	(1)	(2)	(3)	(4)
Republican Vote Advantage	–	0.023 (0.050)	–	−0.049 (0.031)
Republican Map	−0.59 (0.80)	−1.83** (0.89)	−0.77 (0.52)	−0.018 (0.56)
Rep. Vote* Rep. Map	–	0.14 (0.081)	–	−0.058 (0.051)
Democratic Map	1.19 (1.03)	1.43 (1.02)	−0.91 (0.67)	−0.97 (0.64)
Dem. Vote* Rep. Map	–	0.012 (0.077)	–	0.050 (0.048)
Nonpartisan Map	−0.100 (0.94)	−0.053 (0.89)	1.36* (0.61)	1.26* (0.56)
Constant	3.39** (0.66)	3.35** (0.63)	1.79** (0.43)	1.85** (0.39)
Observations	35	35	35	35
R-squared	0.114	0.299	0.382	0.539

Notes: Standard errors in parentheses; ** $p < 0.01$, * $p < 0.05$

50/50 split in mind. When the state's normal vote (expressed in Table 6.6 as positive in Republican-leaning states and negative in Democratic-leaning states) is included along with an interaction with Republican gerrymanders (columns 2 and 4), an intriguing result appears. There is a significant negative coefficient for interacted vote with Republican maps, indicating that, unlike for other maps, Republican-drawn maps are less biased under normal conditions in heavily Republican states. This is consistent with our anecdotal evidence contrasting average bias in competitive and noncompetitive states.[8]

Table 6.7, measuring partisan effects on responsiveness slope, shows few significant effects of partisan gerrymanders. We might expect lower responsiveness under Republican maps as Republican normal vote increases, and in column 4 the coefficient for this variable is in the expected direction, but not statistically significant. Instead, the one strong effect seen in the last two columns of Table

6.7 is the positive effect of nonpartisan maps on responsiveness. It does appear that nonpartisan procedures and commissions do on average produce a more competitive map than either partisan gerrymanders, courts, or bipartisan compromise. (The control coefficient for court and bipartisan maps is around 1.8, suggesting just below average responsiveness.) And nonpartisan gerrymanders achieve this heightened competitiveness without consistently increasing bias in either direction.

Given these patterns, it is unsurprising that the competitive states' gerrymanders attract the most controversy and litigation: their problems are most immediately visible in a single given election cycle, particularly one that is closely contested. Their bias is the highest in this scenario, and they are the only ones likely to produce the intuitively upsetting antimajoritarian outcome. But given the many different normative claims we might make on our system of representation, we should not let partisan gerrymandering in other states off the hook. Maps in noncompetitive states don't share the same bias under close conditions, but they almost completely foreclose on the possibility of the delegation responding to changes in the will of their own voters or holding representatives responsible for their positions and policies (at least in the general election). And while extreme states may quite reasonably elect a legislative majority in line with the majority of their voters, these states also contain substantial partisan minorities who are not just stuck in minority status but are given no voice at all in their state's delegation. Thus where competitive state gerrymanders might fail in creating fair compositional representation under some conditions, noncompetitive state gerrymanders equally fail at providing forms of responsive representation, while extreme state gerrymanders usually entirely fail to provide any discursive representation beyond the viewpoint of the majority party. As shown in Chapter 3, these competing claims contribute to the difficulty a court might have in resolving these issues using some universal standard. Another choice is to leave it to states to change the process itself. The next chapter explores how these same patterns play out in several nonpartisan state cases, detailing the similarities and differences across each with respect to goals, procedures, and outcomes.

7

Bias and Responsiveness in Nonpartisan Maps

In Chapter 6, we explored the choices made by the majority of states that draw district lines through the partisan legislative process, most of which in the past decade were controlled by a single party (usually the Republicans). While there was great variation in the tactics used by partisan mapmakers, largely governed by the political composition of the state, each map still violates some normative sense of what constitutes fairness or good representation, whether that be some form of proportionality, a responsiveness to changes in public will, or the desire to hear varied perspectives in debate. This chapter focuses on the handful of states that have made a different choice as to how to draw their district lines, turning the reins over to an independent commission or other nonpartisan actors, and explores whether this choice has improved the resulting districts on these varied normative dimensions.

As of the 2010s redistricting cycle, eight states included legal provisions for the use of a nonpartisan or bipartisan commission or bureaucracy in the drawing of congressional districts. This does not include several states in which ad hoc or partisan commissions are used only in advisory roles to the legislature. Among these eight states, one (Montana) had only a single congressional district, and two (Idaho and Hawaii) are noncompetitive states with only two congressional districts, both of which will heavily lean toward the same party regardless of the lines drawn. This chapter details the history, procedures, and results of the redistricting process in the remaining five states.

The five states I highlight in this chapter are Iowa, Arizona, California, New Jersey, and Washington. For each state, I look back at the HWEG bias and responsiveness scores going back to the 1990s. Two of the states (Arizona and California) adopted commissions in the middle of this period, giving us insight into how the change in process produced a change in district outcomes. The other three states have used a similar nonpartisan process during all three decades, allowing us to assess whether the maps produced by this process are consistent across time.[1]

Figures 7.1 and 7.2 show the bias and responsiveness across different national election conditions for these five nonpartisan or commission states in the current decade. Some differences and similarities are immediately apparent. First,

Ground War. Nicholas Goedert, Oxford University Press. © Oxford University Press 2022.
DOI: 10.1093/oso/9780197626627.003.0007

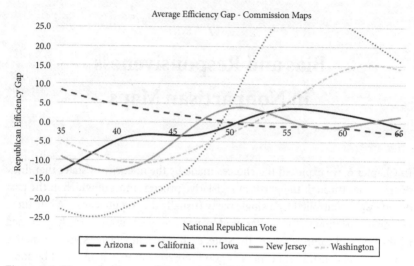

Figure 7.1 Bias under Range of National Conditions—Nonpartisan/ Commission Maps

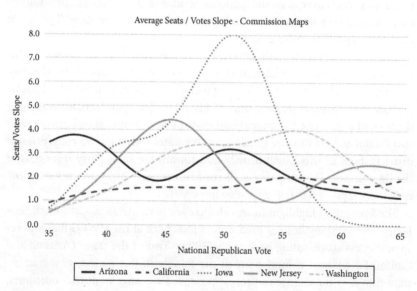

Figure 7.2 Responsiveness under Range of National Conditions—Nonpartisan/ Commission Maps

all of the maps appear relatively unbiased when the national vote is tied. Three states (Arizona, Washington, and especially Iowa) follow a hyperresponsiveness pattern of very high slope when the national vote is close, generating bias during wave elections in whichever direction the wave favors. New Jersey and California do not follow this pattern. California shows low bias and consistent, average responsiveness under all conditions, while New Jersey's curves in both graphs are idiosyncratic and not single-peaked.

The differences observed among the districts drawn in these commission-based or nonpartisan states may be partially explained by the widely varying demographics or political culture of each state. For example, Iowa is a moderate and homogeneous state (both ethnically and geographically) and has only four congressional districts, making it potentially much easier and more natural to draw more competitive seats. But some of the variation is also likely explained by the specific composition of the commission and the process used to select it, as well as the factors and values they are expected to privilege or exclude during their deliberations. The next several sections detail the process used by each of these five states, revealing two generalizations. First, each commission state has made different deliberate choices about one or two factors it will value above others, and the ramifications of these choices translate into different visions of a fair map. But also, despite these differences in values and vision, each nonpartisan process produced a map that performs well on our measures of bias and responsiveness. Moreover, these states have produced unbiased and responsive maps while also largely fulfilling nonrepresentational "traditional districting principles" (such as compactness and maintaining existing political boundaries) that concern the public but that this book has consistently downplayed. Despite the controversy and claims of hidden motives that tend to surround the adoption of nonpartisan districting systems, the results stand for themselves.

Iowa: Privileging Municipal Boundaries

Iowa's system for congressional and state legislative districting is unique among U.S. states, in that maps are not drawn by the state legislature, courts, or a designated commission. Instead, since 1981 district lines have been drawn by nonpartisan employees of the state's Legislative Services Bureau. LSB members are not permitted to look at the partisanship of voters or the residences of incumbent members when considering where the lines should be drawn, only population numbers and municipal boundaries. Once the LSB has proposed a set of maps, they must be approved by the state legislature and signed by the governor. If the legislature rejects a map, the process returns to the LSB to draw a new map unless the legislature rejects the LSB map for a third time.[2]

Despite the backstop of the political branch of state government, Iowa maps have been remarkably resilient to partisan or even personal influence on the part of members. Nonpartisan redistricting is seen as a point of pride within the Iowa government. The LSB's first congressional map in 2011 was approved by both houses of the state legislature in a bipartisan and nearly unanimous vote. The LSB's first map in 2001 was rejected, but the legislature's stated concerns were with the population deviations and competitiveness of the map, not its partisan implications. Although one might typically question the legitimacy of such stated "good government" motivations coming from partisan politicians, the Republican-controlled Iowa legislatures backed up their positions by promptly approving a second effort by the LSB which unnecessarily placed two Republican incumbents in the same district.

Additionally unusual to the Iowa process is that it privileges existing polit-ical boundaries, especially county lines, over virtually all other criteria *including population equality*. As discussed in Chapter 3, the Supreme Court has typically demanded almost *exact* population equality in the construction of congressional districts (e.g., *Karcher v. Daggett, Vieth v. Jubilirer*). As a result, all other states except West Virginia draw congressional districts so that the maximum popu-lation deviation drawn from U.S. Census figures is one or two *people*. But Iowa, leveraging the guidance from lower courts in other contexts that small popu-lation differences may be permissible if they serve legitimate state objectives (e.g., *Abrams v. Johnson*, 521 U.S. 74, 99–100 [1997]), specifies, "No congres-sional district shall have a population which varies *by more than one percent* from the applicable ideal district population" (Iowa Code 42.4.1.b, emphasis mine). Additionally, the Iowa Code demands, "The number of counties and cities di-vided among more than one district shall be as small as possible" (42.4.2). As a result, Iowa's congressional districts deviate in population by as much as 1% but never split county lines. Figure 7.3 shows the approved maps drawn by the LSB since it was given redistricting authority in 1981, showing the deep value placed on compactness and county boundaries. The most recent map, approved in 2011, is particularly intuitive, with the state's four districts essentially determined by bisecting the state twice, first north/south and then east/west, with deviations from this principle made merely to keep counties intact. Finally, Iowa uniquely nests their state legislative map within their congressional districts, requiring "so far as possible, each representative and each senatorial district shall be in-cluded within a single congressional district" (Iowa Code 42.4.6). In the 1990s and 2000s, when Iowa had five congressional districts, each district contained exactly twenty state house districts and ten state senate districts. Down to four districts after the 2010 census, this is not quite possible under the current map, but the LSB still got as close as they could, and each congressional district now contains twenty-five house districts and twelve and a half senate districts.

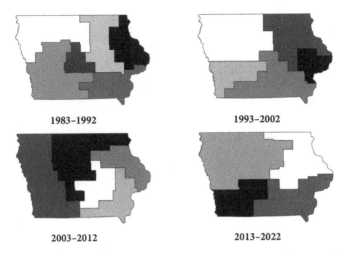

1983–1992   1993–2002

2003–2012   2013–2022

Figure 7.3 Maps Drawn by Iowa Legislative Services Bureau and Approved by State
Legislature since 1980

When combined with the closely competitive nature of Iowa's partisan politics and the demographic homogeneity of the state, the result of Iowa's process is
probably the closest in the country to the "nonpartisan gerrymander" defined in
Chapter 2 in which every district is a microcosm of the state. The toy nonpartisan
gerrymander in Chapter 2 shows no consistent bias when in a close election environment. However, this map is also exceptionally competitive and responsive
to changes in national tides. As a result, changes in the political environment
may result in significant turnover and a delegation that appears biased toward
whatever party the tides in a particular cycle favor.

The actual maps of Iowa over the past several cycles have consisted of one
clearly Republican district in the western portion of the state, with every other
district being politically balanced and similar. And historically Iowa districts
do display an exceptional amount of turnover that can at least temporarily
lead to an unbalanced delegation representing a politically balanced state.
The 1994 Republican wave resulted in a unanimously Republican delegation,
and Republicans held a 4–1 majority during the period of national narrow
Republican victories in Congress from 1996 to 2004. But conversely, the 2006
Democratic wave reversed this into a 3–2 Democratic majority. And the trend
has persisted in the current decade, with results including a tied delegation in
the close national environment of 2012, a 3–1 Republican majority following the
Republican wave in 2014, reversed into a 3–1 Democratic majority in an opposite wave in 2018, and then returned to 3–1 Republican in 2020.

This high anecdotal frequency of turnover bears out in the HWEG analysis of
Iowa's maps. Figures 7.4 and 7.5 show the projected bias and responsiveness of

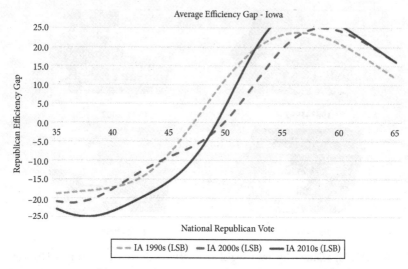

Figure 7.4 Bias under Range of National Conditions—Iowa 1991–2020

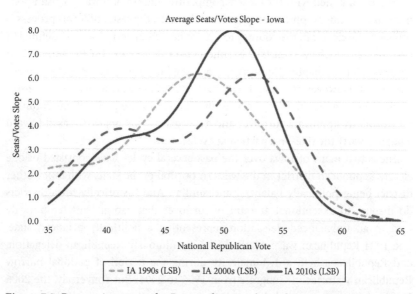

Figure 7.5 Responsiveness under Range of National Conditions—Iowa 1991–2020

Iowa's maps over the past three decades, each map drawn by the nonpartisan LSB using only raw population and municipal line data. Table 7.1 summarizes these measures both at the statewide 50/50 point and under historical weighting. Back in Chapter 5, we ranked states using the HWEG method by highest and lowest

Table 7.1 Bias and Responsiveness of Iowa Districts, 1991–2020

Decade	Gerrymander	Republican Norm Vote	Bias		Responsiveness	
			Statewide 50/50	HWEG	Statewide 50/50	HW Slope
1990s	LSB	54.2	−4.8	9.8	5.6	5.0
2000s	LSB	52.0	−4.3	2.6	4.1	4.8
2010s	LSB	52.0	−5.3	5.4	6.5	6.1

weight average responsiveness slopes; Iowa was found to have the highest responsiveness in the nation among the thirty-five states in the data set. As shown in Figure 7.5, Iowa is highly responsive under all plausible conditions, but is even more exceptionally competitive when the national vote is tied, with HW slope peaking around 8, which is four times the historic average. But this is not unique to the most recent map. The bias and responsiveness patterns for each of the past three Iowa maps are similar, with responsiveness slope being more than twice the historical average in every map under both measures. This results in the sort of hypercompetitive maps described by the nonpartisan gerrymander, with relatively little bias under tied conditions but very strong bias in favor of Republicans during Republican waves, and in favor of Democrats during Democratic waves. Under our normal vote formula, Iowa rates as a slightly Republican-tilting state in each decade, so each map rates as slightly biased toward Democrats at the statewide 50/50 point, but slightly biased toward Republicans using HWEG. But in all cases bias will be completely eliminated or reversed by a very modest wave due to the extraordinarily high responsiveness.

Thus the Iowa LSB probably serves as the best current example of a truly nonpartisan gerrymander, with mapmakers purely privileging compactness and county lines to the complete exclusion of any political factors. Of course, Iowa is also unusual among American states in other aspects, most relevant among them its homogeneity; an identical system adopted in other states would likely yield different results. So it is fortuitous that the next two states we analyze, each of which has recently adopted a nonpartisan districting process, lie at the opposite end of the diversity spectrum, beginning with Arizona.

Arizona: Privileging Competition

While the work of the Iowa LSB is a point of nonpartisan pride in the Iowa state government, the Arizona Independent Redistricting Commission (AIRC), more recently adopted by voters over the resistance of the legislature, has been the source of enormous partisan controversy. Nevertheless, its results share many of the same features, benefits, and drawbacks of Iowa's maps, an arguably much more impressive feat given the much greater size, diversity, and polarization of Arizona's population.

In the 1990s, split control of the Arizona state legislature resulted in a court-drawn map that largely preserved a Republican gerrymander from the previous decade, consisting of one solidly Democratic (and majority-Latino) district and five Republican-leaning districts. Following the 2000 census, Arizona gained two congressional seats, but more important, their redistricting procedure was changed by a state constitutional amendment passed by a ballot referendum known as Proposition 106.

Proposition 106, receiving 56% of the vote in the 2000 election, created the AIRC to redraw congressional and state legislative districts. Under Proposition 106, the commission consists of five members with state legislative leaders of the two largest parties each appointing two members, and those four members appointing a final member to serve as chair, "who shall not be registered with any party already represented" on the AIRC (Arizona Constitution, Art. IV, Part 2, § 1(8)). Current or recently elected public officials are not permitted to serve on the commission. The AIRC is charged with meeting six goals in the drawing of districts:

A. Districts shall comply with the United States Constitution and the United States Voting Rights Act;
B. Congressional districts shall have equal population to the extent practicable, and state legislative districts shall have equal population to the extent practicable;
C. Districts shall be geographically compact and contiguous to the extent practicable;
D. District boundaries shall respect communities of interest to the extent practicable;
E. To the extent practicable, district lines shall use visible geographic features, city, town, and county boundaries, and undivided census tracts;
F. To the extent practicable, *competitive districts should be favored where to do so would create no significant detriment to the other goals.* (Art. IV, Part 2, § 1(14), emphasis mine)

The first five of these goals are commonly set out in the constitutions of many states. But the final goal, the creation of competitive districts, is distinctive to Arizona and was seen as a key feature of the new Arizona commission.

But Proposition 106 did not define exactly what is meant by a "competitive district," and two interpretations have been common. The first is that, within the bounds of the other requirements, as many districts as possible should be structured to have *the same balance* between Democrats and Republicans, though not necessarily an equal balance. The second is that as many districts as possible should be structured to have *an equal balance* between Democrats and Republicans, though this goal might also lead to the creation of several safe districts on both sides.

Republicans in Arizona have generally favored the first interpretation, and in combination with Voting Rights Act compliance, it becomes apparent why. With a Latino population of around 30%, Arizona in both 2000 and 2010 was required to draw two Latino-majority districts, both of which would inevitably be heavily Democratic. Once these two districts are removed, the remainder of Arizona's population certainly leans Republican. So if six or seven districts were drawn to equally resemble this residual population, it is possible they would all be won by Republicans.

And this first approach is largely the approach taken by the AIRC in their first decade of drawing maps following the 2000 census. The commission drew two Latino-majority districts that were always won by Democrats, and then six Republican-leaning districts in the rest of the state (ranging from R + 2 to R + 12 in Cook's PVI). In 2002, the first election under this map and a Republican-leaning cycle, Republicans won all six districts, making this map look barely better than the de facto partisan gerrymander of the previous decade. Democrats filed suit in state court against the map, alleging it failed to create enough competitive districts, but their claim was rejected at both the lower and the appellate court levels (*Arizona Minority Coalition for Fair Redistricting v. Arizona Independent Redistricting Commission* 2004).

Nevertheless, as tides shifted, the commission's goal of creating competition also revealed itself. Democrats gained two seats in Arizona in 2006 and a third in 2008 to temporarily seize a 5–3 majority of the delegation. This shift might recall the reversal of the Pennsylvania Republican majority in 2006 and 2008 discussed in Chapter 1. But of course, in Pennsylvania the reversal was the result of an unintentional backfire of a partisan gerrymander. In Arizona the reversal was the deliberate result of the AIRC sacrificing occasional bias for potentially increased competition.

The second time the AIRC was asked to redraw maps, following the 2010 census, they largely took the second approach to competitiveness. Arizona gained another seat to give it nine districts, and again two districts were drawn with Latino majorities for Voting Rights Act compliance. But now, instead of drawing the remaining districts to lean Republican, the commission chose to draw four safe Republican districts in order to maximize competition in the remaining three (the 1st, 2nd, and 9th districts have PVIs of R + 1, R + 2, and D + 4, respectively, while four districts range from R + 9 to R + 21). Again, the map has achieved high competitiveness, especially in the 2nd District, which flipped to Democrats in 2012, Republicans in 2014, then back to Democrats in 2018. But such closely balanced districts can also lead to counter-majoritarian outcomes when one party gets lucky and wins several close races.

And this is exactly what happened in 2012, as Democrats won all three swing districts by less than 5 percentage points each to take a 5–4 majority of the delegation despite Republicans winning 54% of the congressional popular vote statewide. This left Arizona Republicans outraged (notwithstanding the fact that Republicans had achieved a nationwide counter-majoritarian House majority the same year), and they took several steps to overturn AIRC's work. First, Jan Brewer, the Republican governor of Arizona, impeached and removed AIRC chair Colleen Mathis in 2011, citing her husband's ties to Democratic politics and her decision to side with the Democratic members in choosing outside consulting and mapping firms. But this decision was overturned and Mathis was reinstated by the Arizona Supreme Court in *Arizona Independent Redistricting Commission v. Brewer* (2012), with the court finding that Mathis had not demonstrated the sort of misconduct required for such an impeachment. The Arizona legislature then moved to federal court to challenge the constitutionality of the commission itself.

In this case, *Arizona State Legislature v. Arizona Independent Redistricting Commission* (135 S. Ct. 2652 [2015]), the U.S. Supreme Court narrowly upheld the constitutionality of the AIRC as applied to U.S. congressional districts, with Justice Anthony Kennedy siding with the four liberals in a majority opinion written by Justice Ruth Bader Ginsburg. The Arizona legislature had challenged the constitutionality of AIRC under the Elections Clause, which provides that the "Time, Place, and Manner of holding Elections or Senators and Representatives shall be prescribed in each State by *the Legislature* thereof" (U.S. Constitution Art 1, § 4, emphasis mine). By taking the power of redistricting from the state legislature through ballot initiative, the plaintiffs claimed that Proposition 106 unconstitutionally removed part of the legislature's specifically delegated power to regulate congressional elections.

In her majority opinion in *Arizona State Legislature*, Justice Ginsburg interpreted "the Legislature" in the Elections Clause as "capaciously defined" to mean not just the state's *legislative process* but anywhere the state delegated the power to make laws, which could include other actors involved in passing state laws such as the executive or the voters (*Ariz. State Legislature*, 135 S. Ct. at 2671). By reserving some lawmaking power to the voters through the initiative process, the Arizona Constitution incorporates the voters into the framer's conception of the state's "legislature." In doing so, Ginsburg relies on precedent from three early twentieth-century cases, each recognizing that "the referendum was part of the legislative power" (*id.* at 2668, citing *Davis*

Table 7.2 Bias and Responsiveness of Arizona Districts, 1991–2020

Decade	Gerrymander	Republican Norm Vote	Bias		Responsiveness	
			Statewide 50/50	HWEG	Statewide 50/50	HW Slope
1990s	Republican	55.4	12.5	15.7	4.0	1.9
2000s	Nonpartisan	53.8	7.2	9.5	3.9	2.3
2010s	Nonpartisan	54.7	-3.4	-0.3	2.0	2.7

v. Hildebrandt 1916). Ginsburg also takes a functionalist approach in pointing to the underlying "dominant purpose" of the Elections Clause, which "was to empower Congress to override state election rules, not to restrict the way States enact legislation" (*Id.* at 2674). Chief Justice John Roberts issued a dissent in the case, joined by the three other conservatives, objecting to what he perceived as an expansive definition of "legislature" not supported by the text or historical interpretation.[3]

Had the plaintiffs prevailed in *Arizona State Legislature*, not only would the AIRC's congressional maps have been overturned but also potentially the work of other commissions created through voter initiative, such as in California. But note that such a ruling would not have affected a commission's power to draw state legislative maps, or any nonpartisan procedure created by the state legislature itself, such as in Iowa or New Jersey. But at least for the time being, the constitutionality of the AIRC and other present and future commissions enacted by voter initiative was upheld by a single vote.

Despite the protests of Republicans and legislators in Arizona, the HWEG analysis shows that the AIRC's maps for the 2010s decade do not resemble a Democratic gerrymander (shown in Figures 7.6 and 7.7 and summarized in Table 7.2). Rather, they recall the nonpartisan maps in Iowa, with high levels of competitiveness and responsiveness, especially when the national vote is close. This hypercompetitiveness can lead to unpredictability and bias, especially during wave elections, but this bias is symmetrically distributed for both parties. In contrast, the 1990s map, before the adoption of the AIRC, looks like a standard competitive-state partisan gerrymander despite being drawn by a court, with Republican bias approaching 20% in a tied national election, and seeing significant responsiveness only under the strongest of Democratic tides. The AIRC's first map for the 2000s decade represents something of a middle ground between these two, with mild Republican bias projected under close election conditions but with potential for high responsiveness and bias reversal under very plausible tides (which is exactly what happened in 2006 and 2008).

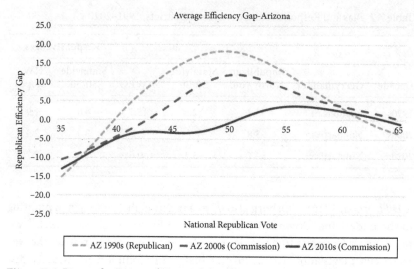

Figure 7.6 Bias under Range of National Conditions—Arizona 1991–2020

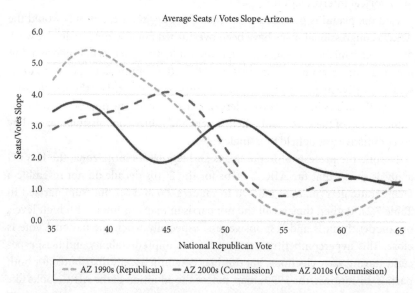

Figure 7.7 Responsiveness under Range of National Conditions—Arizona 1991–2020

California: Privileging Communities of Interest

As discussed in the introduction, the congressional map in California in the 2000s was a perfect exemplar of neither a partisan nor a nonpartisan gerrymander, but rather a bipartisan compromise that protected incumbents regardless of party. Unhappy with the lack of competition or responsiveness produced by this map, voters enacted a commission in 2010 that in many ways resembles the precedents set in other states discussed here, like Arizona and Washington, but in other ways follows a very different path in terms of its format and priorities. In doing so, California may have established a model for how to balance the multitude of competing interests inherent in drawing lines in a large and diverse state.

In the 1990s, split control of the state government led to a court adopting a map proposed by an ad hoc commission formed by Republican Governor Pete Wilson. This map generally led to narrow Democratic majorities in the delegation of around 28–24. But as the state continued its long and steady move toward the Democrats, the delegation took a sharp turn during the last election cycle of the decade, with Democrats flipping four seats. Following the 2000 census, Democrats had full control of the state's government but chose to consolidate their gains in this election rather than aggressively target Republicans. As recounted in Chapter 1, Democrats and Republicans in the state legislature joined to construct a map that would give the Democrats the one additional seat gained during that decade, but otherwise protect every incumbent of both parties, ossifying a 33–20 split of the delegation for the next decade.

Lacking any significant competition in federal elections during the 2000s decade, most of the interest in California politics came at the state level (famously including the recall of Governor Gray Davis and the election of Arnold Schwarzenegger). And much of the action came through ballot referenda, including three major reforms to California's electoral process, largely motivated by the perceived entrenchment of California representatives. First, the Voters First Act, creating a nonpartisan Citizens Redistricting Commission (CRC) for the drawing of state legislative districts, was put on the ballot in 2008 as Proposition 11, and narrowly adopted by the California electorate with 51% of the vote. Second, the Voters First Act for Congress, additionally including congressional districts under the authority of the CRC, was then placed on the 2010 ballot as Proposition 20 and adopted by a much wider margin, with 61% of the vote. Finally, Proposition 14 was also adopted in 2010; it transformed California's nonpresidential primary elections into nonpartisan blanket primaries in which all candidates run on the same open primary ballot and the top two candidates advance to the general election regardless of party.

The amendments enacted through the Voters First Act establish a fourteen-member CRC, which "shall consist of five who are registered with the largest political party in California based on registration, five who are registered with the second largest political party in California based on registration, and four who are not registered with either of the two largest political parties in California based on registration" (California Constitution Art. XXI, § 2(b)(2)). The composition of the CRC is thus considerably larger than that in Arizona and includes a greater proportion of independent members.

Members are also chosen through a much less partisan and more complicated process, established by the state auditor, employing a combination of voluntary application, expert review of qualifications, political veto, and literal lottery. The process begins with a public solicitation for applications, for which the state received over twenty-five thousand completed and eligible applications in 2010.[4] From these thousands of applications, a panel of auditors chose a pool of sixty possible candidates: twenty Democrats, twenty Republicans, and twenty not affiliated with either party. State legislative leaders are then permitted to reduce this pool of sixty down to thirty-six, so that partisan office holders may veto individual possible candidates but never actually install a preferred candidate on the commission. From this pool of thirty-six, eight members are chosen to actually serve on the commission, and these eight members choose the final six members themselves.[5]

Enacting a map requires the votes of at least nine of the fourteen commissioners and must include the votes of a majority of commissioners from each major party. The amendments to the California Constitution made by Propositions 11 and 20 also establish five criteria for the drawing of congressional districts, listed *in order of priority*:[6]

1. Districts shall comply with the United States Constitution. Congressional districts shall achieve population equality as nearly as is practicable. . . .
2. Districts shall comply with the federal Voting Rights Act.
3. Districts shall be geographically contiguous.
4. *The geographic integrity of any* city, county, city and county, local neighborhood, or local *community of interest shall be respected* in a manner that minimizes their division to the extent possible without violating the requirements of any of the preceding subdivisions. *A community of interest is a contiguous population which shares common social and economic interests that should be included within a single district for purposes of its effective and fair representation.* Examples of such shared interests are those common to an urban area, a rural area, an industrial area, or an agricultural area, and those common to areas in which the people share similar living standards, use the same transportation facilities, have

similar work opportunities, or have access to the same media of communication relevant to the election process. Communities of interest shall not include relationships with political parties, incumbents, or political candidates.

5. To the extent practicable, and where this does not conflict with the criteria above, districts shall be drawn to encourage geographical compactness such that nearby areas of population are not bypassed for more distant population (Art. XXI, § 2(d), emphasis mine).

Particularly notable is the fourth criterion, which demands that maps respect the integrity not just of existing formal subdivisions but also of "communities of interest," which could be any "population which shares common social and economic interests . . . for the purposes of effective and fair representation" and includes various geographic, economic, and cultural interests, but specifically excludes political partisanship. This criterion is placed ahead of compactness in the rank order, while factors such as partisan balance and competitiveness are not included at all.

In order to establish what constitutes a valid "community of interest," the CRC was required to hold a series of public hearings, and held thirty-four hearings across the state including testimony from almost three thousand citizens. About half of the comments from this public testimony and more than half of the submitted comments were specifically related to communities of interest (Donald and Cain 2013, 628). And there is evidence that the CRC took much of this testimony into account in distinguishing between culturally distinct regions that were nevertheless geographically proximate and economically comparable (for example, joining Marin with Sonoma County rather than San Francisco, or separating Beverly Hills from the San Fernando Valley) (628, 631).

The prominence given to communities of interest among the criteria may have allowed the CRC to preserve one of the major advantages of the previous incumbent-protecting gerrymander: the diversity of the delegation. The 2000s map may have suppressed interparty competition, but it did create many majority-minority districts and districts where candidates from previously underrepresented groups may have felt comfortable running. Following the 2010 election (the same year Proposition 20 passed), among the fifty-three incumbents protected by the bipartisan maps were nine Latinos, four African Americans, three Asian Americans, and nineteen women.[7] It included not only congressional leaders of both parties but also several members who are not afraid to represent lone voices for unpopular causes.[8] A safe congressional seat, while doing nothing to contribute to "responsive representation," may embolden unconventional candidates to run or legislators to express unconventional views, in turn enhancing personal and discursive representation.[9]

Table 7.3 Bias and Responsiveness of California Districts, 1991–2020

| Decade | Gerrymander | Republican Norm Vote | Bias | | Responsiveness | |
			Statewide 50/50	HWEG	Statewide 50/50	HW Slope
1990s	Court	45.6	0.9	1.5	1.7	1.8
2000s	Bipartisan	43.0	−10.6	0.7	0.7	0.5
2010s	Nonpartisan	37.5	−2.1	0.3	1.7	1.7

The CRC immediately improved competitiveness and responsiveness, tripling the rate of close elections compared to the previous decade. But its use of communities of interest also preserved or created many safe seats, enhancing the representation of the small but politically distinct communities they represented. The CRC did not *maximize* competition to the degree we see in Iowa or Arizona, but instead chose to *balance* competing democratic norms in a way that better fits the unique political composition of their state.

Table 7.3 and Figures 7.8 and 7.9 depict the bias and responsiveness of the past three California maps: the court-approved plan from the 1990s, the bipartisan compromise of the 2000s, and the commission map of the 2010s. The 2000s map shows the clear patterns of an incumbent-protecting "bipartisan" map in which almost every seat is safe for one party. Bias is close to 0 when the national election is close (HWEG of 0.7). But responsiveness is also extremely low under all likely conditions (HW slope of 0.5), which generates Republican bias under Democratic tides and Democratic bias under Republican tides, the mirror image to the nonpartisan maps in Arizona and Iowa.

The 2010s curve curiously differs both from other commission maps during the same decade and from the state's previous map. Given that California is a heavily Democratic state with enormous ethnic diversity and several large urban areas, it is unsurprising that many districts in the state will be overwhelmingly Democratic, especially when combined with an emphasis on uniting communities of common interest; Trump received less than 30% of the two-party vote in twenty-three of the state's fifty-three districts in 2016. But the state also contains many closely contested districts, as demonstrated by the seven Democratic pickups in 2018, and even a handful of heavily Republican districts. The resulting mix of competitive and noncompetitive districts creates a bias pattern that is extremely uncommon in the modern era. As shown in Figure 7.10, bias is not just close to 0 when the election is close, but remains similarly low across all plausible election environments. HWEG is 0.3 and bias does not exceed 5 points in

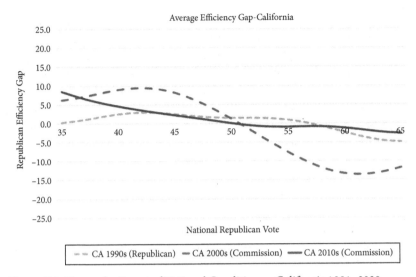

Figure 7.8 Bias under Range of National Conditions—California 1991–2020

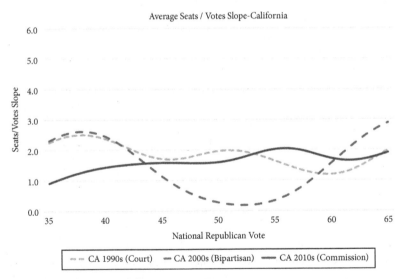

Figure 7.9 Responsiveness under Range of National Conditions—California 1991–2020

either direction within the 40% to 60% range of the national Republican vote. Responsiveness is close to the national average across the range of possible tides (HW slope of 1.7), though notably higher than the 2000s map. It appears that in California, the combination of a large and diverse electorate, a nonpartisan commission process, and the deliberate choice of that commission to account for the diversity of interests and communities in the state has resulted in a rare example of successfully balancing many representation interests and values under the full range of foreseeable conditions.

New Jersey: Privileging Partisan Balance

New Jersey was among the first states to establish a commission for redrawing state legislative seats through a voter-approved ballot referendum in 1966. The use of a commission was temporarily expanded to include congressional districts by the legislature in 1991, and then permanently established through a constitutional amendment referendum in 1996 (Public Question #1, amending New Jersey Constitution Art. II, § 2, ¶ 1). While New Jersey predated Arizona and California in the use of a commission for congressional maps, the procedures and qualifications for selecting commission members have tended to yield results that appear somewhat less nonpartisan than those states' commissions.

The New Jersey Redistricting Commission (NJRC) consists of thirteen members. Six members are chosen by legislative and party leaders of each of the Republican and Democratic parties, and these twelve then choose an "independent" member. In this sense, the procedures for selection resemble the AIRC. However, unlike AIRC members, who cannot be current or recently elected officials, only current members or employees of the U.S. Congress are disqualified from the NJRC. As a result, most of the appointees to the NJRC are current or former members of the state legislature. When combined with the larger size of the commission, this leads each party to organize its own caucus within the commission, with its own plans and leadership. This has led to one of two results: either a bipartisan compromise, in which both sides agree to protect incumbents of both parties (similar to the 2000s California example), or each side presenting a competing partisan plan that the tiebreaking member must choose between.

Table 7.4 and Figures 7.10 and 7.11 show the contrast between these two approaches. The resulting map from the 2000s decade followed the first path. After the 2000 election, Democrats held a narrow 7–6 majority in the New Jersey delegation. By 2000, New Jersey had swung from a toss-up to a Democratic-leaning state in national elections. But many of the six Republican incumbents were moderate senior members with strong personal brands (including Frank LoBiondo, Chris Smith, and Marge Roukema), who would routinely win

Table 7.4 Bias and Responsiveness of New Jersey Districts, 1991–2020

Decade	Gerrymander	Republican Norm Vote	Bias		Responsiveness	
			Statewide 50/50	HWEG	Statewide 50/50	HW Slope
1990s	Leg. Comm.	47.9	3.8	4.5	1.0	1.7
2000s	Leg. Comm.	45.2	−2.9	3.0	0.6	1.1
2010s	Leg. Comm.	45.0	0.9	1.1	1.1	2.6

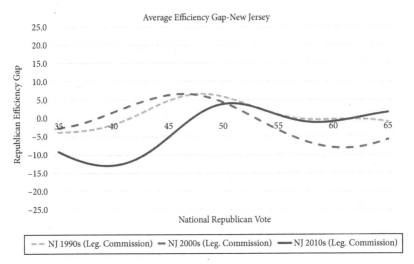

Figure 7.10 Bias under Range of National Conditions—New Jersey 1991–2020

easily in swing districts. The commission agreed to a map intended to maintain this balance, making relatively few changes to the previous map except for strengthening the most endangered incumbents of both parties. The result is a map with very slight Republican bias under close national conditions (HWEG of 3.0). But more notably, the map also shows very low responsiveness except under strong Democratic tides (HW slope of 1.1, about half the historical average). Indeed, this initial 7–6 balance was only once briefly interrupted during the decade, when the 3rd District flipped to Democrats in the 2008 wave before immediately flipping back to Republicans in 2010.

While the 2000s map was very similar to the 1990s map, and mostly just reinforced the existing partisan balance, the 2010s map would need to shake this up in one way or another. New Jersey lost a seat following the 2010 census, ensuring

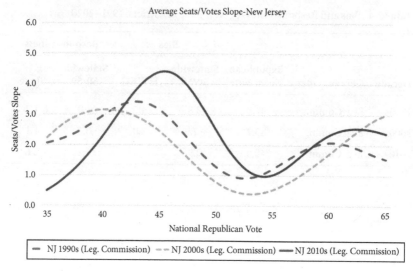

Figure 7.11 Responsiveness under Range of National Conditions—New Jersey 1991–2020

that at least one of the incumbents protected in the previous round would need to be sacrificed. And with this, the bipartisan agreement of the past decade fell apart. Democrats and Republicans instead presented competing maps, with the Democrats aiming for a 7–5 majority and Republicans hoping for a 6–6 split. The thirteenth commission member, former Republican attorney general John Farmer, cast his vote with the Republicans, and in the 2012 elections Republicans did achieve a tied delegation. Although the chain of events was slightly different, once again the outcome of the New Jersey commission seemed to place a "fair" partisan split of the delegation as its foremost criteria.

But unlike the previous iteration of the map, this partisan split would not hold for long, and the Republicans' apparent victory would backfire disastrously by the end of the decade. In a state that is both leaning and trending toward the Democrats, an even split of the delegation, rather than a nonpartisan incumbent-protection plan, might be viewed through the lens of an extremely risky Republican gerrymander. Among the six seats won by Republicans in 2012, only Chris Smith's 4th District had a PVI more secure than R + 3. After gaining one seat in 2016, Democrats won every seat in the state except for the 4th District in the 2018 wave on the back of 61% of the congressional popular vote, aided by two moderate Republican retirements. Had the commission gone with the 7–5 Democratic plan, almost certainly a fairer distribution given the Democratic tilt of the state, it is likely that most of the five remaining Republicans would have been more fortified and the competitiveness of the map would have remained lower. But in siding with Republicans, the commission adopted a hypercompetitive map much more like Iowa or Arizona than the bipartisan compromises of the past.

Thus, the bias and slope curves of the past two New Jersey maps (shown in Figures 7.10 and 7.11) neither resemble each other, nor do they resemble the unbiased but hypercompetitive curves of the recent maps in Iowa and Arizona. Instead, the 2000s New Jersey map recalls our California example from the same period, a bipartisan compromise protecting incumbents and partisan balance at the expense of competition. And the 2010s map, being the result of a victorious Republican proposal in a Democratic-leaning state, resembles an extremely risky partisan gerrymander, being slightly biased toward Republicans under tied conditions but easily backfiring into Democratic bias and hyperresponsiveness under even a modest Democratic tide.

Washington—Privileging Geographic Stability

Congressional redistricting in Washington has been conducted by the bipartisan Washington State Redistricting Commission (WSRC) since its establishment by state constitutional amendment in 1983. Like the AIRC, the WSRC consists of five members, two appointed by the leaders of each major party and a fifth appointed by the remaining four (or by the state supreme court if the partisan commissioners cannot agree). However, unlike in Arizona, this fifth member cannot vote, and in order to be enacted, a map must be approved by three of the four remaining members. Thus, a map can be passed only with truly bipartisan support, not merely the support of one party plus an independent tiebreaker. While officials serving in public office in the immediately previous two years cannot serve on the WSRC, former legislators are often chosen as commissioners. For example, Republican Slade Gorton, a former U.S. senator, served on WSRC in 2011–2012. Thus, we might expect maps coming out of the WSRC to more closely resemble a bipartisan legislative compromise than the more nonpartisan maps coming from Iowa or California. The commission's plans may be overridden by a two-thirds vote of both houses of the state legislature, though this had not been a concern during any redistricting cycle, with partisan control of the Washington legislature usually closely contested.

The Washington Constitution specifies several standard guidelines for drawing districts, including compactness, contiguity, and respect for existing boundaries. The constitution also requires that "[t]he commission's plan shall not be drawn purposely to favor or discriminate against any political party or group" (Washington Constitution Art. I§ 43), though nothing is specified with respect to competitiveness, communities of interest, incumbency, or even federal Voting Rights Act requirements.

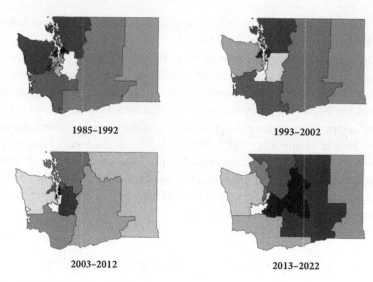

1985–1992   1993–2002

2003–2012   2013–2022

Figure 7.12 Maps Drawn by Washington State Redistricting Commission since Establishment in 1984

The results of the WSRC's process have generally been maps that, like other commission maps, generate minimal bias under most typical election conditions, and occasionally (but not always) foster competition. However, looking at the four rounds of maps created by the commission gives one the sense that their overriding concern was simply to change as little as possible. In particular, the commission has striven to retain the overall geographic and political essence of each district wherever possible. Figure 7.12 shows the maps ratified by the WSRC in each of the past four decades. Note how little has changed despite Washington's gaining a district in both the 1990s and the 2000s. In particular, Districts 3, 4, 5, 7, and 8 all cover largely the same territory in the 2010s that they did in the 1980s. Even when the geography of districts must be changed substantially, the commission tries to retain its political core; while the territory of the 2nd District has shrunk dramatically as two additional districts have been added, it remains fundamentally the district of the northeastern and San Juan Islands. Between the two decades when the state did not gain a district (after the 2000 census), only minor adjustments were made to any districts (note the extreme similarities between the 1990s and 2000s maps). Contrast this with the 1990s and 2000s maps in Iowa shown in Figure 7.5. Though Iowa had only five districts in both decades, all districts were drastically changed across those two maps.

But although the commission has seemed to value geographic stability, this is not the same as incumbent protection. While the New Jersey commission in the 2000s sought to protect a specific partisan split by strengthening the districts of endangered members of both parties, the WSRC has been happy to allow competitive districts to remain competitive. In particular, the 8th District, containing Seattle exurbs, had been evenly balanced for decades, generally being represented by a moderate Republican before being captured by Democrats in 2018. This has led to some periods of extreme turnover, particularly in 1994, when Republicans flipped six of the state's nine seats, but also some periods of low competition, including most of the 2000s. Where there is competition, it is due to naturally competitive districts and not to a shake-up immediately following a redistricting round. The WSRC has never placed two incumbents running for reelection into the same district, and all turnover since 1990 has occurred during mid-decade wave elections.

Table 7.5 and Figures 7.13 and 7.14 show the bias and responsiveness in the results of this geographic stability over the past thirty years. In the one case

Table 7.5 Bias and Responsiveness of Washington Districts, 1991–2020

Decade	Gerrymander	Republican Norm Vote	Bias Statewide 50/50	Bias HWEG	Responsiveness Statewide 50/50	Responsiveness HW Slope
1990s	Nonpartisan	46.9	6.1	−0.4	4.2	3.8
2000s	Nonpartisan	44.9	−6.5	−7.1	3.4	1.9
2010s	Nonpartisan	45.0	7.7	−2.4	3.9	3.4

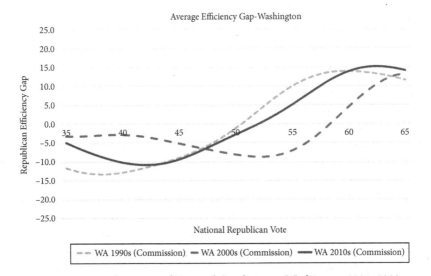

Figure 7.13 Bias under Range of National Conditions—Washington 1991–2020

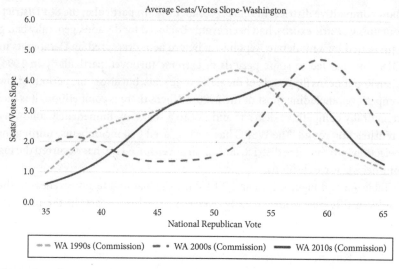

Figure 7.14 Responsiveness under Range of National Conditions—Washington 1991–2020

where no districts were added and the map remained almost entirely the same (the 2000s), responsiveness is average (1.9 HW slope) and the map is moderately biased toward Democrats, who retained a 6–3 majority for most of the decade. The two years when the commission made more substantial changes by adding a district more closely resemble the nonpartisan model seen in Iowa and Arizona, with high responsiveness (HW slope of 3.8 and 3.4 in the 1990s and 2010s) and low bias under typical conditions (HWEG of –0.4 and –2.4).

Summary

Across these five major states with commissions or nonpartisan redistricting procedures, we see several instances of commonality (e.g., the way commissioners are appointed in Arizona and New Jersey) but also many important differences, both in formal procedures and in the goals and norms that are most valued. And these norms often include aesthetic factors like compactness or voter convenience considerations like respecting county lines or district stability, all of which often fall under the umbrella of traditional districting criteria but have been mostly overlooked in this book in lieu of directly representational objectives. But despite the varied goals and norms, the results produced by commissions almost universally share a few desirable common features.

First, projected bias is almost always very low both in close national election environments and under the historical range of results.[10] Across the twelve nonpartisan or commission examples in this chapter (five states in three decades, excluding Arizona and California before adopting a commission), the average of the *absolute value* of HWEG was 3.9. This compares to an average absolute value HWEG of 8.6 for all states in the 2010s with at least three districts. Second, as suggested by the regression tables in Chapter 6, commissions draft maps that are consistently more responsive than maps drawn by legislators. The average HW slope across the twelve commission instances is 3.1, almost double the 1.6 average responsiveness of all states in the 2010s with more than three districts. Finally, all of these maps at least discursively represent both major parties in their delegations, with at least one Democrat and one Republican being elected in all but one of the fifty-six election cycles conducted under commissions, with several state commissions (especially in California and Arizona) being especially effective at electing a diverse delegation within the major parties. And to the extent that we observe variation in competitiveness among commission states, these case studies suggest that commissions with a more nonpartisan composition (e.g., in Iowa and Arizona) may produce more competitive seats than commissions with a bipartisan composition of former and current elected officials (e.g., in New Jersey and Washington).

Despite protests from legislators and partisans, commissions have mostly succeeded at simultaneously reducing bias, increasing competition, and serving political culture and interests unique to their own states. So are commissions the obvious answer across the nation? Or even the possible answer? Although complete reform of the districting process may not be feasible in every state, recent movement, both through citizen referenda and legislative action, suggests that we may be further along that road than we realize. The next and final chapter discusses this recent activity and prospects for reform in the near future.

8

Conclusion

The Road to Reform

Summary

The evidence throughout this book has confirmed the widely held belief that partisan gerrymandering is indeed a problem for American democracy but demonstrates it is a multifaceted problem that does not manifest in the same way in every context. The bias and competitiveness produced by partisan gerrymandering varies greatly with the competitiveness of the state in which it was enacted and the environment in which each election is being held. Moreover, individual voters might demand that representation be measured on completely different but equally valid dimensions, and a map that appears fair under one measure might seem outrageously unjust under another. We should be as vigilant about maps drawn to ossify incumbents or completely exclude certain viewpoints as we are about maps that produce countermajoritarian delegations. These complications have made partisan gerrymandering an impossible task for our federal court system to resolve. Instead, the only effective alternative may be to fundamentally change the institutions drawing maps through the political process.

Fortunately, the response to the perceived increased prominence of partisan gerrymandering in the 2010s has led not just to litigation but also to serious efforts to reform procedures at the state level, often in the model of one or more of the states discussed in Chapter 7. In 2018 alone, five states passed ballot initiatives altering their process for congressional or state legislative districting prior to the 2020 census. Just like the five states covered in Chapter 7, each of these five has chosen a slightly different process incorporating different goals and priorities, yet taken together they constitute significant and promising progress toward a solution covering most, if not all, of the nation.

Ground War. Nicholas Goedert, Oxford University Press. © Oxford University Press 2022.
DOI: 10.1093/oso/9780197626627.003.0008

Reform Referenda in 2018

Michigan

In November 2018, Michigan voters passed Proposal 2, establishing an independent redistricting commission to draw congressional and state legislative maps, composed of thirteen members: four Democrats, four Republicans, and five members not affiliated with either party.[1] In order to be approved, at least two members of each partisan group must vote in favor of a plan. Proposal 2 also lays out seven ranked-order criteria for the commission to consider, including compliance with the Voting Rights Act (VRA), respect for communities of interest, lack of partisan bias, subdivision boundaries, and (last) compactness. In all these aspects, the Michigan proposal resembles the Citizens Redistricting Commission in California.

But what truly sets Michigan's commission apart is the way commissioners are chosen. Rather than soliciting applications from all members of the public from which an expert panel chooses a small number of possible candidates (as in California), or asking state legislative leaders to make most selections (as in several other commission states), the Michigan commission is intended to reflect a truly representative group of citizens. The new procedure first sends out applications to ten thousand citizens *at random*, while making lobbyists, recent officeholders, and their relatives ineligible. From among the completed applications, two hundred are chosen *at random* and submitted to state legislative leaders, who may strike a small number from the pool. Finally, four Democrats, four Republicans, and five unaffiliated members are chosen from the remaining pool, once again *at random*, to form the commission. Thus, with the exception of a handful of partisan vetoes, the commission is composed of an almost entirely random selection of willing citizens. This thorough use of a lottery to choose officeholders is not entirely unknown in democratic history, being used extensively in the proto-republics of ancient Greece and medieval Venice. But the degree of independence from not just partisan elected politics but the unelected state bureaucracy in the case of Michigan's new commission is striking. In the previous chapter, I suggested that California may represent a model for a truly independent redistricting commission. Michigan's proposal takes a somewhat radical step even beyond California's process in promoting involvement from average citizens. Whether this is a step in the right direction or a step too far remains to be seen in the next redistricting cycle.

Missouri

Also in November 2018, voters in Missouri approved Constitutional Amendment 1 with 62% of the vote. In addition to making changes in state campaign finance and lobbying rules, Amendment 1 altered the way in which state legislative districts (but not congressional districts) are to be drawn in the future. Previously, legislative districts in the state were drawn by a bipartisan legislative commission. Amendment 1 created a new position of state demographer, appointed by a process jointly involving the state auditor and the majority and minority leaders of the state senate. The demographer is charged with drawing state legislative maps following each census, which can be amended only with a 70% supermajority vote by the existing bipartisan commission.[2]

The most original and provocative part of Amendment 1 is the criteria established to guide the demographer in drawing districts. After equal population and compliance, the next criterion listed is "Districts shall be designed in a manner that achieves both partisan fairness and, secondarily, competitiveness" (Amendment 1, Sec 3(1)(b)). The text then goes on to define how fairness and competitiveness should be calculated:

> To this end, the non-partisan state demographer shall calculate the average electoral performance of the two parties receiving the most votes in the three preceding elections for governor, for United States Senate, and for President of the United States. . . . Using this index, the non-partisan state demographer *shall calculate the total number of wasted votes for each party*, summing across all of the districts in the plan. Wasted votes are votes cast for a losing candidate or for a winning candidate in excess of the fifty percent threshold needed for victory. In any plan of apportionment and map of the proposed districts submitted to the respective apportionment commission, *the non-partisan state demographer shall ensure the difference between the two parties' total wasted votes*, divided by the total votes cast for the two parties, *is as close to zero as practicable.*
>
> To promote competitiveness: the non-partisan state demographer shall use the electoral performance index to simulate elections in which the hypothetical statewide vote shifts by one percent, two percent, three percent, four percent, and five percent in favor of each party. . . . The non-partisan state demographer shall ensure that in each of these simulated elections, the difference between the two parties' total wasted votes divided by the total votes cast for the two parties, is as close to zero as practicable. (*Id.*, emphasis mine)

In other words, the initiative implements an efficiency gap standard calculated under a range of hypothetical election environments using presidential and statewide election data. Certainly, this is by far the closest that a state has come to using a measure similar to HWEG to evaluate both the bias and the competitiveness as mapped.

As Missouri's Amendment 1 did not deal with congressional districting, it represented only a partial solution to the problem of partisan gerrymandering in the state; as noted in Chapter 6, the existing congressional map was only modestly biased toward Republicans but was extremely noncompetitive. Nevertheless, the very creative solution implemented by this amendment, combined with the unique embrace of efficiency gap to reduce bias and enhance competitiveness, represented both procedural and substantive progress toward fairness in a state that had become increasingly dominated by one party. However, at least in this particular instance, this progress proved fleeting, as the state demographer position was eliminated by Missouri's Amendment 3, passed in 2020 with just 51% of the vote.

Colorado

On the same day that Michigan and Missouri voted for changes to their redistricting process, Colorado voters enacted referenda creating nonpartisan commissions by even more overwhelming margins, approving of Amendment Y (for congressional districts) and Amendment Z (for state legislative districts) with 71% of the vote each.

These amendments create separate twelve-member commissions for congressional and state legislative redistricting that largely follow the California model.[3] In the case of the congressional redistricting committee, public applications are solicited and randomly reduced to a pool of about one thousand, which are then reviewed by a panel of former judges following public hearing. The panel chooses fifty possible members based on skills, experience, and impartiality, and from these, six commissioners are chosen randomly. The panel then chooses (nonrandomly) six more commissioners, including two each from a list recommended by the leaders of each major party. The judicial panel is also instructed to ensure that the panel reflects the racial, gender, and geographic diversity of the state. Though slightly different in details, the selection process largely mirrors California's in balancing public participation, partisan input, expert review, and a significant dose of luck (though still much less randomness than Michigan's process).

To enact a map, the commission must get agreement from a supermajority of eight commissioners. The criteria the commission uses include respect for communities of interest, existing subdivisions, compactness, and (finally) competitiveness. The amendment here again largely follows California's priority list, with the addition of borrowing from Arizona in encouraging competitive elections once all other criteria have been satisfied.

Utah

Among the states with redistricting reform on their November 2018 ballots, Utah was the only one where the outcome was seriously in doubt. Given the overwhelming Republican balance of the electorate and the state government, it is understandable why a majority of voters may have been hesitant to wrest control of redistricting from their favored party. Nevertheless, the Better Boundaries Proposition 4 passed after all votes were counted by a margin of 0.6%.

Proposition 4 creates a bipartisan commission of seven members, six of whom are selected by partisan state legislative leaders (but two of whom cannot be affiliated with a political party), and one of whom is selected by the governor. The result is that the party of the governor actually appoints a majority of the commission, with the caveat that the "unaffiliated" members will still hold the balance of power, and approval of a map requires the vote of five of the seven commissioners.[4]

The commission established by Proposition 4 definitely falls much closer to the bipartisan end (with New Jersey and Washington) than the nonpartisan end of the continuum (with California and now Colorado). Indeed the Utah commission is arguably the *least* truly independent of all the proposed or enacted commissions, with even the unaffiliated members appointed by partisan legislative leaders and the partisan members not being evenly balanced.

As Republicans have held Utah's governorship since 1985, this almost certainly gives an advantage to Republicans, but it may be that nudging the partisan split in this direction (while still retaining the supermajority approval requirement) allowed the heavily partisan electorate in Utah to feel comfortable enough with the reforms to push it just over the top at the ballot box.

Almost all of the seven criteria the commission is instructed to follow deal with compactness or respecting existing political or geographic boundaries, with no requirement for competitiveness or partisan balance. Nevertheless, the specific data the commission is *prohibited* from considering, including the political party affiliation of voters and residencies of incumbents and candidates (similar to Iowa), would seem to make a nonpartisan outcome more likely. So while in many ways Utah's proposal is among the most conservative we have seen in recent years, it too represents significant progress toward a nonpartisan process in a political context where this might seem most difficult.

Ohio

Among the five states reforming their redistricting process in 2018, Ohio was actually the first, passing State Issue 1 in the May *primary* elections with 75% of the vote. This was a state constitutional amendment that, unlike referenda in other states initiated by citizens or advocacy groups, had first received the support of both parties in the state legislature.[5] Ohio's reform is also the most complicated, and the one that seems (at least to me) least likely to produce effective change.

While Ohio's Issue 1 does create a nonpartisan redistricting commission, this commission does not have sole or even primary authority over drawing congressional maps. Instead, they are merely one alternative step in a four-step process under which a map might be approved, with the other three steps still involving the legislature. First, the legislature is given the opportunity to draw a map that will get support from the majority of both major parties. If this fails, responsibility falls to the commission, which includes the governor, other statewide elected officials, and members appointed by legislative leaders. The commission can approve a map only with the support of two members of each party. If the commission fails to receive that support, the state legislature gets another shot to pass a map with a 60% majority, including one-third support of each party.

If all of these steps fail, the state legislature is permitted to pass a map by simple majority. But in this case, additional rules apply, including that "[t]he general assembly shall not pass a plan that unduly favors or disfavors a political party or its incumbents" (Ohio Constitution, Article XIX, Section 1 (C)(3)(b)). Further, such a map would be in place for only two election cycles before a new map would need to be drawn.

Ohio's reform creates a commission that is dependent on and very much subsidiary to the existing state legislature. The new rules do make a bipartisan outcome more likely, although as we saw in the California example and the analysis in Chapter 4, these outcomes tend to hinder competitiveness and responsiveness at the same time as they reduce bias. Further, the possibility for a partisan outcome still exists. Although a map drawn to favor one party is now prohibited in the law, such prohibitions are hard to interpret and may lead to both biased maps and prolonged litigation, as we have recently seen in Florida (discussed later in the chapter). So while future maps in Ohio might not see the same extreme bias as their current Republican gerrymander, this reform seems further from an ideal solution than the moves made in other states.

Redistricting Reform without Referendum

The five states that voted for redistricting reform in 2018 ranged from the large and Democratic-leaning Michigan to the small and solidly Republican Utah, but they do all share one crucial attribute: they allow citizen-initiated referenda for legislation and/or constitutional amendments as part of their legislative process. Citizen initiatives are largely the product of the early twentieth-century Progressive Era and have been adopted in only about half of the states, including most states in the western half of the county.[6] Given that redistricting reform almost always involves taking away powers from the state legislature, powers that closely contribute to legislators' own abilities to retain office, it is entirely intuitive that legislators may be very hesitant to initiate redistricting reform on their own, and the best prospects will come through a public referendum. But that does not mean that all hope is lost in the half of states without ballot initiatives. Indeed, under some circumstances, legislatures may indeed be willing to hand over the redistricting process, as recent efforts in two states suggest.

Virginia

Virginia's initial congressional and state legislative maps in the 2010s were partisan gerrymanders made possible when Republicans took control of all branches of the government in the state's 2011 election. These maps were effective at preserving Republican majorities in the first half of the decade, but by 2019 both the congressional map (*Wittman v. Personhuballah*, 136 S. Ct. 1732) and the state assembly map (*Bethune-Hill v. Virginia Board of Elections*, 137 S. Ct. 788) had been partially overturned by federal courts as unconstitutional racial gerrymanders. Additionally, as the Virginia electorate became steadily more Democratic, Republican control began to disintegrate. The 2017 state elections saw Democrats win the governorship and gain ten seats in the state assembly, and in the 2018 midterms, Democrats gained three congressional seats to take a 7–4 majority. Democrats completed the trifecta by winning narrow majorities in both houses in the 2019 state legislative elections.

Faced with the prospect of possible Democratic control of the state going into the 2020 census, both houses of the state legislature passed constitutional amendments implementing a bipartisan commission for future redistricting. And in February 2019, one such amendment passed with overwhelming support in the House of Delegates and *unanimous* support in the state senate. The bill creates a sixteen-member commission charged with drawing congressional and state legislative maps. Members of the commission are chosen from among state legislators, retired court judges, and citizens. But almost all members are chosen *by* the legislative leaders of the major parties, creating a commission whose composition is much closer to the bipartisan New Jersey than the nonpartisan California. Additionally, few of the considerations valued by existing nonpartisan commissions (discussed in Chapter 7), such as communities of interest, partisan balance, competitiveness, and respect for subdivisions, are included among the criteria the proposed Virginia commission is required to consider. After the commission proposes a map, it must be approved without amendment by the state legislature, but repeated failures to pass a map will result in a map adopted by the state supreme court.[7]

But the 2019 passage of this amendment was not the end of the process. In Virginia, constitutional amendments must be passed by both houses of the state legislature in *two consecutive sessions*, and then also ratified by the voters. When Democrats took control of both houses of the state legislature in 2019, it seemed the party might get cold feet. Nevertheless, the amendment passed again in the 2020 session, with an overwhelming majority in the state senate and a narrow 54–46 vote in the House of Delegates, over the objections of most members of the Black caucus. The commission was finally enacted into law after being approved by voters by an almost 2–1 margin on the November 2020 ballot.

Even after passage, the legislature remains heavily involved in the commission selection process and ultimate approval of the maps. But despite its imperfections and still uncertain prospects, the recent actions of the Virginia legislature demonstrate that reform is indeed possible even in a polarized era and even without the prospect of a citizen initiative.

Maryland

Like Virginia, Maryland was subject to a partisan gerrymander following the 2010 census (this time with Democrats in control) but faced federal litigation and a divided government by the middle of the decade. And as in Virginia, the Maryland state government took steps toward establishing a nonpartisan redistricting committee in the last years of the decade. Due to conflict between the Republican governor and Democratic supermajorities in the legislature, these steps fell short of those taken in Virginia, but the model established by the legislature does point to one potential way forward in states that are still dominated by one party: a strategy of "multilateral disarmament."

Governor Larry Hogan, a Republican elected in 2014 and 2018, unsurprisingly favored taking away redistricting power immediately from the safely Democratic legislature. This took the form of a proposed constitutional amendment creating a redistricting commission consisting of three Democrats, three Republicans, and three independents, who would be prohibited from considering the partisanship of voters or the location of incumbents in drawing maps.[8] But Hogan's proposals never made it out of committee in either house of the legislature. Hogan also put together an executive redistricting commission to redraw the current map in light of the district court decision in *Benisek*, but the state legislature adjourned without considering their proposed map.

The failure of Hogan's efforts suggests the routine impediment of partisan politics in reform of a state dominated by one party. But even before Hogan's most recent efforts, the governor had vetoed legislation that passed both houses of the Maryland state legislature in 2017, suggesting a different path. This bill proposed an "interstate compact," creating a nonpartisan commission for congressional redistricting that "is contingent on the enactment of a nonpartisan districting process for representatives . . . in the mid-Atlantic region in each of the states of New York, New Jersey, Pennsylvania, Virginia, and North Carolina" (Maryland 2017 SB1023 Section 2).[9] Thus, the commission would not take effect unless similar commissions were in place in five other states in the region, allowing Maryland to disarm from partisan redistricting simultaneous to a few previously Republican or bipartisan states.

As it was proposed, this may seem a very unlikely scenario, and thus really just an effort by Democrats to sidestep true reform. But in some form or other, it has perhaps more likelihood for success than it initially appears. Of the five other states, only New Jersey's current maps were drawn by a nonpartisan or bipartisan commission. But along with Virginia, New York voters already approved such a commission in 2014 for use after the 2020 census, at least in an advisory capacity. Pennsylvania was subject to a controversial Republican gerrymander in each of the past two decades, but their most recent congressional map was overturned in *LWV*, and the state will have a divided government going into the 2020 cycle. North Carolina perhaps presents the biggest obstacle. The state elected a Democratic governor in 2016, but the state legislature remains solidly Republican, and the governor's redistricting role in North Carolina is minimal.[10] A previous Democratic proposal in Maryland would have established a less ambitious "Potomac Compact" between Maryland and Virginia only, though this version died in committee in 2017.[11] Had this version passed, it seems very likely Maryland would now be on the same path as Virginia. But even an "interstate compact" bill with unlikely immediate prospects may place pressure on other states that could eventually lead to reform across multiple states.

Less Promising Prospects

While several states have moved down the promising path of a more nonpartisan process, I remain more doubtful of a few other proposed changes. We have already seen that using the judicial process may be foreclosed for the foreseeable future. But I am also skeptical about two other classes of reforms: legislative or state constitutional provisions prohibiting partisan advantage and the use of algorithmic or automated redistricting.

Legislative Criteria

On a few occasions, rather than changing their fundamental process of districting, states have changed the criteria the legislature is expected or required to use in drawing districts. Instead of producing less biased and more competitive districts, as most commission systems have done, this reform has been more likely to yield political controversy and prolonged litigation while failing to solve the underlying problems.

The most prominent example of this reform is Florida. At the same time that California was adopting a nonpartisan commission, Florida also voted for redistricting reform on the 2010 ballot. This Fair Districts Amendment (or Amendment 6) did not change the process for drawing districts, but in addition to VRA compliance, compactness, and respect for subdivisions, required that "congressional districts or districting plans may not be drawn to favor or disfavor an incumbent or political party" (Florida Constitution, Article 3, Section 20) without defining how this new standard should be evaluated.[12] Amendment 6 passed with 63% of the vote and was upheld in a court challenge from members of both parties in early 2012.

In response, the Republican-controlled state legislature approved maps that they claimed were drawn without partisan intent. Nevertheless, the enacted map had an HWEG bias of 9% in favor of Republicans, who won seventeen of the state's twenty-seven congressional districts with 52% of the average district vote in 2012 (as noted in Chapter 5, an EG bias of greater than two seats). Despite some evidence that Florida's political geography favors Republicans, Democrats filed suit in state court for violating the Fair Districts Amendment. The state supreme court agreed and, by a 5–2 margin, ordered the state to redraw several congressional districts (as well as the state senate map) (*League of Women Voters of Florida v. Dentzner*, 2015). The new map was again drawn by a Republican-controlled legislature, and while it likely led to one additional Democratic seat, Republicans still won a narrow majority of the congressional delegation in 2018 despite winning a minority of the average district vote along with a clear majority of state senate seats and more than 60% of seats in the lower state house.

While Florida is now *de jure* prohibited from drawing a map to favor one party, their lines are still drawn by partisan legislators, with very little preventing a *de facto* partisan gerrymander beyond litigation with no established standards. Although the new criteria may prevent the most glaring and notorious partisan maps, they most likely increase the secrecy and complication of the process without changing the underlying incentives of political actors. The result in Florida suggests that the best way to reduce partisanship from districting is to remove elected partisans from the process rather than simply asking elected partisans to act in a nonpartisan way.

Automated Districting

The notion of automated districting by computer algorithm has appealed to scholars at least going back to Weaver and Hess (1963) and has increased steadily over time with both improved technology and the increased visibility of gerrymandering as a political issue (see Ricca, Scozzari, and Simeone 2013 for an overview). As discussed in Chapter 3, various districting simulation procedures have been proposed as standards for courts to evaluate partisan gerrymanders (e.g., Tam Cho and Liu 2016; Magleby and Mosesson 2018; McDonald and Best 2015; Wang 2016), with political scientists developing open-source software for the purpose (Altman and McDonald 2011), and have actually been used as crucial counterfactual evidence by appellate courts to temporarily strike down partisan gerrymanders in cases in North Carolina, Michigan, and Ohio. Many of these procedures include a random component and thus produce a wide distribution of possible plans, but others, such as the "shortest splitline" method, produce a single map that advocates argue is the uniquely fairest plan that a state could adopt.[13]

Although such automated plans might superficially seem like an obvious way to produce fair districts, they present at least three problems. First, while an algorithm might be easily written to comply with many federal requirements (especially equal population), simultaneous compliance with the VRA and the Equal Protection Clause with respect to minority vote dilution is much more difficult. When giving no consideration to race, many such algorithms will fail to draw districts that give ethnic minorities sufficient influence to elect representatives of their choice, thus violating the VRA (e.g., Magleby and Mosesson 2018 find that automated districting draws fewer majority-minority districts than human districting in several states). Some proponents of specific algorithms attempt to remedy this by constraining acceptable maps to only include those that draw a certain number of districts with a certain percentage minority population. But as we have seen in recent cases like *Bethune-Hill v. Virginia Board of Education*, the federal courts have generally struck down maps that set definitive quotas on racial population percentages as violations of the Equal Protection Clause. The jurisprudence in this area is complicated and hazy, but this does seem to be an area where the nuance of human hands is more acceptable than pure reliance on data and algorithms.

Second, such algorithms tend to strongly privilege compactness over other normative considerations and criteria. This focus seems to me misplaced given the many competing values discussed throughout this book. Chief Justice Earl Warren memorably opened his landmark opinion in *Reynolds v. Sims* by remarking, "Legislators represent people, not trees or acres." This principle seems to be satisfied much better through the process of public hearings to define communities of interest enacted in California than a computer program that simply matches random census tracts with other adjoining census tracts. The computer process will naturally create aesthetically pleasing districts, but these are not the sort of districts that human decision-makers tend to adopt, as people do not often naturally populate in aesthetically pleasing patterns.

Finally, the choice of algorithms itself is a political one, which may imbue bias on the system as a whole. Famously, Rodden and Chen (2015) found that drawing randomly generated compact districts produces maps consistently biased toward Republicans because such maps tend to pack Democrats living in urban areas. But this does not mean that an algorithmic map must pack urban voters. Other methods, notably the splitline, will have a tendency to split densely populated areas (e.g., the splitline map of Colorado is mostly generated from a radial split of Denver, and Indiana's proposed map features a four-way split of Indianapolis). In choosing which algorithm to adopt, states would also be choosing how they wish to systematically pack or crack voters, based not specifically on partisanship but on population clustering. Yet given the current geographic polarization of the American electorate, even facially neutral decisions about how to treat population densities will be inherently partisan.

For similar reasons, it should be apparent that I am also skeptical of the use of simulated or automated districts as evidence in gerrymandering litigation. In Chapter 3, I describe the "stylized test" from *Rucho* as employing simulation evidence. But I do not try to cross-apply this test to other cases, as there is little consensus as to what set of algorithms should actually constitute a reasonable simulation. Moreover, while simulations employed in these cases may formally comply with the districting laws of their respective states, there is little evidence that they are a plausible counterfactual, in the sense that they would resemble the range of maps that would actually be drawn by human but nonpartisan actors. As noted earlier, the United States is unique among democratic countries in allowing single-member districts to be drawn by elected officials. But none of these other countries uses automated districting to draw maps. Among the several states discussed in the previous two chapters that have adopted nonpartisan reforms, none has chosen to employ automated districting. And in none of these cases involving simulation evidence was any evidence presented that automated districts actually did resemble human-drawn nonpartisan districts with respect to factors like compactness (which algorithmic maps will typically privilege) and communities of interest (which they will typically ignore). Throughout this book, I have emphasized the diversity of legitimate representation claims involved in districting. As seen in Chapter 7, real commissions have shown themselves adaptable to such diverse claims; algorithms by nature will conform only to whatever standards or objectives they are programmed to incorporate.

National Overview

Despite the recent Supreme Court decision in *Rucho*, looking at both the current state of redistricting and the progress of reform efforts across the nation should still make us optimistic. In the western region of the country, where the use of citizen initiative to enact policy is most common, almost every multidistrict state has now adopted a commission process for drawing congressional maps, and many of the commissions are among the most nonpartisan in the country in their selection procedures (including California and Colorado). Even in heavily partisan states in the region (e.g., Utah), we see voters willing to compromise toward a more nonpartisan system. In the Midwest, a handful of states have adopted a nonpartisan process (Iowa and Michigan), and others are moving significantly in that direction (Missouri and Ohio). Even among states that have not enacted process reforms, several that were controlled by Republicans in the previous decade are now under split control (Pennsylvania and Wisconsin) and thus will at least need a bipartisan compromise to enact new maps. Although such compromises in the past have led to maps with both low bias and low responsiveness, this could also create an incentive to enact a nonpartisan procedure in the near future. In the Mid-Atlantic, many states have also moved toward a commission process (New York and Virginia), although these commissions tend to be more bipartisan than nonpartisan (in the New Jersey model).

This largely leaves the South as the lone holdout for partisan legislative districting. Districting in this region is so profoundly influenced by factors beyond partisanship that I have mostly ignored the Deep South throughout this book. But a few brief observations are appropriate. Voting in these states is characterized by deep racial polarization, and election laws are strongly constrained by VRA compliance. As we observed back in Figures 6.1 and 6.2, this has resulted mostly in drawing districts that were moderately biased toward Republicans but severely noncompetitive, almost regardless of control of the process. These maps clearly sacrifice responsive representation (and perhaps policy median representation at the national level) for greater personal and discursive representation. This also gives us some reason to believe that a nonpartisan commission would provide less of a remedy in this region. First, because of the need for VRA compliance, both partisans in the legislature and a hypothetical commission would be much more constrained in the districts they can draw. Second, although the federal courts will no longer review partisan gerrymandering claims, they remain very active in policing racial gerrymandering, as seen in the *Bethune-Hill* case concluded by the Supreme Court just days before their *Rucho* decision, and racial gerrymanders are largely congruent with partisan gerrymanders among these electorates. Certainly, normative issues of representation remain at least as important in the South as in the rest of the nation, if not more important. But taken together, this suggests that (a) partisanship is not as much of a weapon in these states, (b) commissions would not be as effective a solution, and (c) courts might continue to provide a remedy for the most egregious maps. So while nonpartisan commissions are indeed least feasible in this region, they are also likely to be least helpful.

But even in states where a nonpartisan process seems impossible, there might still be hope at the national level. Upon winning control in early 2019, U.S. House Democrats quickly approved a sweeping electoral reform bill, the For the People Act of 2019 (H.R. 1).[14] Among these reforms is a requirement for states to draw congressional districts through a fifteen-member nonpartisan commission, largely in the mold of California.[15] These commissions would be required to consider communities of interest and would be prohibited from considering the partisanship of voters or residencies of candidates. This bill immediately died in the Republican-controlled Senate, but it does show a willingness to tackle this issue at the national level should partisan control of other branches change in the near future. The bill again passed the House in 2021, but as of this writing, it faces an uphill battle in the currently deadlocked Senate.

Final Thoughts

Throughout this book, I have emphasized my sentiment that federal courts are not well-adapted to tackle the issue of partisan gerrymandering. This emphasis is *not* meant to suggest that partisan gerrymanders are either an unimportant problem or an unsolvable one. And I hope my exploration of modern congressional maps through the HWEG measure has shown why. Rather than being unimportant, my analysis of recent partisan maps suggests the pathologies created by partisan maps are both wide and deep, touching on many different yet equally fundamental aspects of democratic representation. Partisan gerrymandering does hurt our democracy in several ways, but the harms produced are diverse and inconsistent, such that a simple and politically neutral constitutional test is impossible. Additionally, the harms produced by partisan gerrymanders are often temporary, with bipartisan compromise maps presenting the biggest threat to electoral competition; on a nationwide basis, our elections for Congress are still overall responsive to the will of the voters, as seen in the 2018 midterms wave. All these factors lead me to accept that Chief Justice Roberts was correct in concluding that partisan gerrymanders are an issue that must be addressed by the political branches of government rather than the courts.

But most important, voters do indeed have the power to change their political system within their states. Where it has happened, the change has been real, with commissions effectively producing representation that is fairer, more competitive, and better adapted to the political culture of each state. My analysis of nonpartisan maps suggests that recently adopted commissions can indeed successfully address the diversity of representational claims evoked by the process of districting. And where change has not yet happened, the signs of progress are there. Perhaps the definitive exit of the Court from this political stage will prove exactly what was necessary to get us over the top.

Appendix

Appendix Table 3.1 Wisconsin 2011 Legislative Redistricting: Percentage of Old Districts Population Retained by Incumbent Party

Incumbent Name	Incumbent Party	Old District Number	New District Number	Population % Retained
Garey Bies	R	1	1	94.7
Andre Jacque	R	2	88	34.2
Al Ott	R	3	3	94.8
Chad Weininger	R	4	4	55.7
Jim Steineke	R	5	5	79.3
Gary Tauchen	R	6	6	59.4
Peggy Krusick	D	7	7	30.9
Jocasta Zamarripa	D	8	8	55.3
Josh Zepnick	D	9	7	13.9
Elizabeth Coggs	D	10	10	66.3
Jason Fields	D	11	11	47.8
Fred Kessler	D	12	22	11.8
Dave Cullen	D	13	14	31.8
Dale Kooyenga	R	14	14	35.8
Tony Staskunas	D	15	15	47.3
Leon Young	D	16	16	68.5
Barbara Toles	D	17	17	61.4
Tamara Grigsby	D	18	18	58.6
John Richards	D	19	19	88.4
Cristine Sinicki	D	20	20	79.7
Mark Honadel	R	21	21	96.8
Sandy Pasch	D	22	23	36.1
Jim Ott	R	23	23	36.9

(continued)

Appendix Table 3.1 *Continued*

Incumbent Name	Incumbent Party	Old District Number	New District Number	Population % Retained
Dan Knodl	R	24	24	47.7
Bob Ziegelbauer	I	25	25	88.3
Mike Endsley	R	26	26	57.1
Steve Kestell	R	27	27	60.7
Erik Severson	R	28	28	97.5
John Murtha	R	29	29	96.6
Dean Knudson	R	30	30	87.9
Steve Nass	R	31	33	29.9
Tyler August	R	32	31	26.2
Chris Kapenga	R	33	99	61.3
Dan Meyer	R	34	34	86.6
Tom Tiffany	R	35	35	86.0
Jeff Mursau	R	36	36	60.4
Andy Jorgensen	D	37	33	45.3
Joel Kleefisch	R	38	38	34.9
Jeff Fitzgerald	R	39	39	79.4
Kevin Petersen	R	40	40	77.3
Joan Ballweg	R	41	41	49.8
Fred Clark	D	42	81	57.6
Evan Wynn	R	43	43	78.3
Joe Knilans	R	44	44	92.3
Amy Loudenbeck	R	45	31	45.4
Gary Hebl	D	46	46	99.9
Keith Ripp	R	47	42	54.9
Chris Taylor	D	48	76	10.5
Travis Trannel	R	49	49	95.8
Ed Brooks	R	50	50	97.7
Howard Marklein	R	51	51	68.3
Jeremy Thiesfeldt	R	52	52	82.5
Dick Spanbauer	R	53	53	83.9

Appendix Table 3.1 *Continued*

Incumbent Name	Incumbent Party	Old District Number	New District Number	Population % Retained
Gordon Hintz	D	54	54	95.7
Dean Kaufert	R	55	55	51.5
Michelle Litgens	R	56	56	65.2
Penny Schaeber	D	57	57	57.4
Pat Strachota	R	58	58	88.4
Dan Lemahieu	R	59	59	46.5
Dewey Stroeber	R	60	60	69.3
Robert Turner	D	61	66	59.7
Corey Mason	D	62	62	8.6
Robin Vos	R	63	63	40.4
Peter Barca	D	64	64	48.9
John Steinbrink	D	65	61	36.1
Samantha Kerkman	R	66	61	63.9
Tom Larson	R	67	67	93.8
Cathy Bernier	R	68	68	44.8
Scott Suder	R	69	69	69.0
Amy Sue Vruwink	D	70	70	43.7
Louis Molepske	D	71	71	89.1
Scott Krug	R	72	72	74.0
Nick Milroy	D	73	73	92.3
Janet Bewley	D	74	74	67.3
Roger Rivard	R	75	75	88.3
Terese Burceau	D	76	77	36.1
Brett Hulsey	D	77	78	32.1
Mark Pocan	D	78	76	68.0
Sondy Roberts	D	79	79	31.4
Janis Ringhand	D	80	45	32.1
Kelda Roys	D	81	48	50.6
Jeff Stone	R	82	82	81.3

(continued)

Appendix Table 3.1 *Continued*

Incumbent Name	Incumbent Party	Old District Number	New District Number	Population % Retained
David Craig	R	83	83	79.3
Mike Kuglitsch	R	84	84	33.1
Donna Seidel	D	85	85	84.4
Jerry Petrowski	R	86	86	81.0
Mary Williams	R	87	87	67.1
John Klenke	R	88	88	47.9
John Nygren	R	89	89	82.3
Karl Van Roy	R	90	89	17.7
Chris Danou	D	91	92	70.8
Mark Radcliffe	D	92	92	29.2
Warren Petryk	R	93	93	35.8
Steve Doyle	D	94	94	97.9
Jill Billings	D	95	95	92.1
Lee Nerison	R	96	96	90.5
Bill Kramer	R	97	97	76.4
Paul Farrow	R	98	98	37.9
Don Pridemore	R	99	22	35.7
Average of All Districts				61.7
Average of Democratic Districts				54.7
Average of Republican Districts				65.9

Appendix Table 4.1 Codings for State Gerrymandering Regimes

2000s Cycle

Democratic: AL, AR, CO, GA (2002–2004), MA, MD, NC, OR, TN, TX (2002), WV

Republican: FL, GA (2006–2010), KS, MI, NE, OH, PA, UT, TX (2004–2010), VA

Bipartisan (Split Control): CA, CT, ID, IL, IN, KY, LA, ME, MO, NH, NJ, NV, NY, OK, RI, SC, WA, WI

Nonpartisan: AK, AZ, DE, HI, IA, MT, ND, SD, VT, WA, WY

Court: AL, AR, CO, CT, MN, MS, NM, OK, TX (2002)

1990s Cycle

Democratic: AR, GA, IN, KY, LA, MD, MS, NC, OK, TN, TX, VA, WV

Republican: AL, IL, UT

Bipartisan (Split Control): AZ, CO, CT, ID, KS, MA, MO, NE, NH NJ, NM, NV, OH, OR, RI, SC, WA, WI

Nonpartisan: AK, DE, HI, IA, MT, ND, SD, VT, WA, WY

Court: AL, AR, CA, FL, IL, MI, MN, NC, NY, OR, PA, SC

1980s Cycle

Democratic: AL, AR, CA, FL, GA, KY, MA, MD, NC, NJ, OK, SC, TN, TX, VA, WV

Republican: IN, NE, PA, UT

Bipartisan (Split Control): AZ, ID, LA, ME, MT, NH, NM, NV, NY, OH, OR, RI, TN, WA, WI

Nonpartisan: AK, DE, IA, ND, SD, VT, WY

Court: AL, AR, CO, CT, HI, IL, KS, MI, MN, MO, MS, SC, TX

1970s Cycle

Democratic: AL, AR, CT, FL, GA, MD, MS, NC, OK, PA, SC, TN, TX

Republican: AZ, CO, IA, IL, IN, KY, LA, NJ, NY

Bipartisan (Split Control): HI, ID, KS, MA, ME, MN, MT, MH, OH, OR, RI, SD, UT, VA, WI, WV

Nonpartisan: AK, DE, ND, NE, NM, VT, WY

Court: AL, AR, CA, CT, IL, MI, MO, NJ, WA

Appendix Table 4.2 Effects of Gerrymandering Regime on District-Level Competition

District-Level Presidential Competition	(1)	(2)	No South (3)
Statewide Competition	0.31***	0.32***	0.31***
	(0.028)	(0.028)	(0.035)
Democratic Gerrymander	–	–0.40	0.55
		(0.45)	(0.74)
Republican Gerrymander	–	0.96	0.90
		(0.56)	(0.64)
Court Gerrymander	–	0.77	0.81
		(0.43)	(0.58)
Nonpartisan Gerrymander	–2.76***	–2.59***	–2.52**
	(0.94)	(0.97)	(1.05)
Constant	6.74	6.34	6.50
	(0.30)	(0.42)	(0.53)
Observations	1,740	1,740	1,237
R-squared	0.071	0.076	0.062

Notes: Dependent variable is the absolute value of a district's deviation from the national average in previous presidential elections, with lower values indicating swing districts. ** = $p<.05$, *** = $p<.01$

Appendix Table 4.3 Alternate Analysis: OLS on Means of State Delegations, Weighted by State Size

Pr(Close Race)	Bipartisan Maps Control			Small States Control	
	(1)	(2)	(3)	(4)	(5)
Statewide Competition	–0.00030	–0.00024	–0.00049	–0.00022	–0.00012
	(0.00085)	(0.00086)	(0.00078)	(0.00083)	(0.00084)
National Tides	0.0076***	0.0074***	0.0075***	0.0077***	0.013***
	(0.0013)	(0.0019).	(0.0019)	(0.0013)	(0.0032)
Democratic Gerrymander	–0.031**	–0.019	–0.026	–0.063***	–0.022
	(0.015)	(0.022)	(0.021)	(0.017)	(0.027)
Republican Gerrymander	–0.0086	–0.013	–0.017	–0.046**	–0.028
	(0.016)	(0.021)	(0.022)	(0.018)	(0.026)
Bipartisan Gerrymander	–	–	–	–0.052***	0.0025
Court Gerrymander	0.020	0.0047	0.013	–0.0071	0.00079
	(0.014)	(0.019)	(0.020)	(0.016)	(0.023)

Appendix Table 4.3 *Continued*

Pr(Close Race)	Bipartisan Maps Control			Small States Control	
	(1)	(2)	(3)	(4)	(5)
Nonpartisan Gerrymander	0.083*** (0.030)	0.12** (0.046)	0.098** (0.047)	0.094** (0.043)	0.16*** (0.034)
Democratic Gerrymander* Tides	–	–0.0019 (0.0028)	–0.0018 (0.0028)	–	–0.0069** (0.0035)
Republican Gerrymander* Tides	–	0.00062 (0.0030)	0.0011 (0.0030)	–	–0.0035 (0.0035)
Bipartisan Gerrymander* Tides	–	–	–	–	–0.0092** (0.0036)
Court Gerrymander* Tides	–	0.0026 (0.0027)	0.0018 (0.0029)	–	–0.0011 (0.0029)
Nonpartisan Gerrymander* Tides	–	–0.0061 (0.0067)	–0.0063 (0.0068)	–	–0.013* (0.0078)
CDs	–	–	–0.0014*** (0.00048)	–	–
Constant	0.13*** (0.016)	0.13*** (0.017)	0.16*** (0.019)	0.17 (0.021)	0.13 (0.027)
Observations	1,000	1,000	1,000	1,000	1,000
R-squared	0.062	0.065	0.080	0.071	0.080

Notes: Robust standard errors in parentheses. * = $p < .10$, ** = $p < .05$, *** = $p < .01$. This table structures the data set such that each data point is a statewide proportion of close races, ranging from 0 to 1, as opposed to a discrete dummy for each race. Data points are weighted by state size.

Appendix Table 4.4 Coefficient for Effect of National Tides on Close Races by Redistricting Institution (Congressional Races 1972–2010)

Institution	Coefficient	Std. Err.	n
Democratic	.017**	.008	2663
Republican	.041***	.010	1627
All Partisan	.028***	.006	4290
Bipartisan	.004	.009	2536
Nonpartisan	.003	.020	385
Overall	.019***	.005	8700

Appendix Table 4.5 Coefficient for Effect of National Tides on Close Races under Democratic Gerrymanders (Congressional Races 1972–2010)

Institution	Coefficient	Std. Err.	n
Democrats win popular vote	.012	.009	2041
Republicans win popular vote	.089***	.022	622
All elections	.017***	.008	2663

Appendix Table 4.6 Close Races by Wave, Gerrymandering, and Party Holding Seat

Pr(Close Race)	(1) All Elections	(2) Exclude GOP Waves	(3) Exclude Democratic Waves
Statewide Competition	−0.0040 (0.0033)	−0.0024 (0.0033)	−0.011** (0.0046)
National GOP Vote Margin	0.025*** (0.0041)	−0.0020 (0.0049)	0.064*** (0.010)
Republican Gerrymander	0.17** (0.080)	0.17** (0.087)	0.12 (0.11)
Democratic Gerrymander	−0.034 (0.064)	−0.015 (0.068)	−0.040 (0.089)
Republican Seat	−0.0036 (0.059)	0.25*** (0.071)	0.20** (0.079)
Republican Gerrymander* Republican Seat	−0.65*** (0.14)	−0.70*** (0.16)	−0.63*** (0.17)
Democratic Gerrymander* Republican Seat	−0.20* (0.11)	−0.21* (0.12)	−0.19 (0.13)
Republican Seat* GOP Vote Margin	−0.058*** (0.0069)	−0.025*** (0.0084)	−0.13*** (0.019)
Republican Gerrymander* Republican Seat* GOP Vote Margin	−0.038*** (0.012)	*−0.044*** (0.013)*	−0.0021 (0.036)
Democratic Gerrymander* Republican Seat* GOP Vote Margin	−0.0057 (0.011)	−0.0057 (0.013)	*0.028 (0.030)*
Constant	−1.03*** (0.052)	−1.26*** (0.058)	−1.09*** (0.070)
Observations	8,700	7,830	3,915

Notes: Entries are probit coefficients. Standard errors clustered by district interacted with decade.
* = p < .10, ** = p < .05, *** = p < .01

Appendix Table 4.7 Probability of Republican Seat Controlling for Redistricting Institution and State and National Electoral Trend (Non-South Congressional Races 1972–2008)

Pr(GOP seat)	Probit Model 1	Probit Model 2	OLS w/State Proportions[a]
Statewide Presidential Vote	.028**	.029**	.011**
	(.003)	(.003)	(.001)
National Congressional Tides	.026**	.019**	.007**
	(.004)	(.006)	(.002)
Democratic Gerrymander	–	−.246*	−.090*
		(.121)	(.035)
Republican Gerrymander	–	.140	.055**
		(.106)	(.020)
Court Gerrymander	–	−.052	−.020
		(.087)	(.021)
Nonpartisan Gerrymander	–	.242	.093
		(.177)	(.063)
Small States	–	−.100	−.044
		.132	(.045)
Democratic* National Tides	–	−.001	.000
		(.013)	(.004)
Republican* National Tides	–	.018†	.007*
		(.010)	(.003)
Court* National Tides	–	.008	.003
		(.009)	(.003)
Nonpartisan* National Tides	–	.022	.009
		(.018)	(.007)
Small State* National Tides	–	−.007	−.003
		.013	.005
Constant	.039	.068	.524
	(.038)	(.064)	(.015)
n	5886	5886	722

Notes: Entries are probit coefficients, except for Model 3. The dependent variable is 1 if a seat was won by a Republican, and 0 otherwise. Standard errors, clustered by congressional district interacted with decade, are in parentheses. † = p < .10; * = p < .05; ** = p < .01

[a] Each data point in this model is a proportion of races that were competitive within a state, weighted by the number of CDs in the state; see Chapter 4, n7.

Appendix Table 4.8 Probability of Republican Win by Redistricting Institution, 2005–2009

	2005		2009	
Statewide Presidential Vote	.026** (.357)	.029** (.006)	.028** (.005)	.029** (.006)
Bipartisan	.357* (.177)	.329† (.202)	.491* (.186)	.473* (.210)
Republican	.597** (.188)	.658** (.201)	.501* (.189)	.517** (.202)
Nonpartisan/Court	.357† (.207)	.385† (.234)	−.082 (.215)	−.035 (.241)
Small State	.222 (.278)	.243 (.335)	.037 (.287)	.103 (.341)
Constant (Democrat)	−.356 (.150)	−.477 (.271)	−.385 (.151)	−.536 (.277)
South	–	−.339 (.267)	–	−.096 (.281)
% Black	–	.016 (.014)	–	.009 (.014)
% Hispanic	–	.001 (.006)	–	.005 (.007)
n	435	435	435	435
R-squared	.078	.082	.087	.088

Notes: Entries are probit coefficients. Standard errors are in parentheses. The dependent variable is coded 1 if the election was won by the Republican candidate. p < .10†, .05*, .01*

Appendix Table 4.9 Probability of Partisan Flip by Redistricting Institution, 2005–2009

	Probability of Change	
Statewide Presidential Vote	−.005	−.001
	(.006)	(.007)
Presidential Margin Change	.004	.011
	(.017)	(.017)
Bipartisan	.005	.027
	.232	.249
Republican	.454†	.572*
	(.243)	(.260)
Nonpartisan/Court	.686**	.769**
	(.243)	(.277)
Small State	.502	.611
	(.340)	(.398)
	(.239)	(.381)
South	–	−.386
		(.321)
% Black	–	.022
		(.169)
% Hispanic	–	−.003
		(.008)
n	435	435
R-squared	.033	.045

Notes: Entries are probit coefficients. Standard errors are in parentheses. The dependent variable is coded 1 if the election was held by different parties in 2005 and 2009. $p < .10$†, $.05$*, $.01$**

Appendix Table 4.10 Probability of Republican Win by Redistricting Institution, 1973–1975

	1973		1975	
Statewide Presidential Vote	.021*	.033**	.020*	.034**
	(.009)	(.010)	(.010)	(.011)
Bipartisan	.680**	.458*	.515**	.260
	(.194)	(.209)	(.195)	(.212)
Republican	.381*	.071	.045	−.315
	(.169)	(.202)	(.177)	(.212)
Court	.341*	.037	.139	−.210
	(.168)	(.201)	(.176)	(.209)
Small State	.583*	.141	.653*	.147
	(.270)	(.316)	(.269)	(.316)
Constant (Democrat)	−.723	−.495	−.862	−.603
	(.164)	(.183)	(.168)	(.188)
South	–	−.599**	–	−.692
		(.217)		(.223)
n	392	392	392	392
R-squared	.035	.049	.031	.050

Notes: Entries are probit coefficients. Standard errors are in parentheses. The dependent variable is coded 1 if the election was won by the Republican candidate. California has been excluded. p < .10†, .05*, .01**

Appendix Table 4.11 Probability of Partisan Flip by Redistricting Institution, 1973–1975

	Probability of Change	
Statewide Presidential Vote	.002	.000
	(.012)	(.013)
Bipartisan	.254	.285
	(.252)	(.273)
Republican	.560**	.604*
	(.202)	(.253)
Court	.303	.344
	(.210)	(.252)
Small State	.189	.252
	(.355)	(.414)
Constant (Democrat)	−1.438	−1.472
	(.216)	(.245)
South	–	.085
		(.289)
n	392	392
R-squared	.030	.030

Notes: Entries are probit coefficients. Standard errors are in parentheses. The dependent variable is coded 1 if the election was held by different parties in 1973 and 1975. p < .10†, .05*, .01**

Appendix Table 4.12 Probability of Republican Win by Redistricting Institution, 1993–1995

	1993		1995	
Statewide Presidential Vote	−.009	−.009	−.028**	−.033**
	(.007)	(.008)	(.008)	(.009)
Bipartisan	.331	.319	.256	.108
	(.195)	(.232)	(.196)	(.233)
Republican	–	–	–	–
Nonpartisan/Court	.354*	.346*	.248	.153
	(.170)	(.188)	(.170)	(.188)
Small State	.233	.219	.049	−.121
	(.257)	(.297)	(.264)	(.303)
Constant (Democrat)	−.426	−.411	.127	.137
	(.119)	(.198)	(.115)	(.198)
South	–	−.019	–	−.239
		(.201)		(.202)
n	435	435	435	435
R-squared	.008	.008	.024	.026

Notes: Entries are probit coefficients. Standard errors are in parentheses. The dependent variable is coded 1 if the election was won by the Republican candidate. $p < .10$†, .05*, .01**

Appendix Table 4.13 Probability of Partisan Flip by Redistricting Institution, 1993–1995

	Probability of Change	
Statewide Presidential Vote	−.027**	−.033**
	(.010)	(.011)
Bipartisan	−.160	−.346
	(.236)	.283
Republican	–	–
Nonpartisan/Court	−.179	−.285
	(.206)	(.226)
Small State	−.086	−.312
	(.297)	(.355)
Constant (Democrat)	−.804	−.583
	(.130)	(.225)
South		−.282
		(.237)
n	435	435
R-squared	.048	.051

Notes: Entries are probit coefficients. Standard errors are in parentheses. The dependent variable is coded 1 if the election was held by different parties in 1993 and 1995. $p < .10$†, .05*, .01**

Appendix Table 4.14 Replication of Table 4.2 Including Endogenous District-Level Controls

Pr (Close Race)	Open Seat Control		District Competitiveness Control	
	(1)	(2)	(3)	(4)
Statewide Competition	−0.0032	−0.0029	0.016***	0.016***
	(0.0032)	(0.0033)	(0.0034)	(0.0034)
National Tides	0.020***	0.014*	0.019***	0.013
	(0.0046)	(0.0084)	(0.0046)	(0.0083)
Democratic Gerrymander	−0.12**	−0.14	−0.10**	−0.12
	(0.054)	(0.092)	(0.052)	(0.089)
Republican Gerrymander	−0.0090	−0.23**	0.047	−0.15
	(0.061)	(0.11)	(0.059)	(0.10)
Court Gerrymander	0.053	0.069	0.085*	0.079
	(0.052)	(0.084)	(0.050)	(0.081)
Nonpartisan Gerrymander	*0.32****	*0.39***	*0.26****	*0.32**
	(0.10)	*(0.16)*	*(0.098)*	*(0.17)*
Democratic Gerrymander* Tides	–	0.0046	–	0.0034
		(0.011)		(0.011)
Republican Gerrymander* Tides	–	*0.030***	–	*0.028***
		(0.012)		*(0.012)*
Court Gerrymander* Tides	–	−0.0025	–	0.0011
		(0.010)		(0.010)
Nonpartisan Gerrymander* Tides	–	−0.013	–	−0.011
		(0.020)		(0.021)
Open Seat	0.78***	0.79***		
	(0.045)	(0.045)		
District Competition	–	–	−0.063***	−0.063***
			(0.0040)	(0.0040)
Constant	−1.30***	−1.27***	−0.90***	−0.86***
	(0.060)	(0.075)	(0.062)	(0.075)
Observations	8,700	8,700	8,700	8,700

Notes: Robust standard errors in parentheses. *** p<0.01, ** p<0.05, * p<0.10

This table shows robustness checks including two district-level variables excluded from the original analysis because they are endogenous and causally posterior to the gerrymander. Columns (1) and (2) include a dummy variable for open seats, while (3) and (4) include District Presidential Competition (the DV in Appendix Table 4.2). Both drastically impact competition (e.g., 34% of open-seat races are close, compared to 11% of races including an incumbent), but neither significantly impacts the effects of tides or the differences between redistricting regimes.

Appendix Table 5.1 States Included in Gerrymandering Analysis Using Statewide Elections

	States with full analysis						
State	CDs	Normal GOP Vote	Statewide Elections	State	CDs	Normal GOP Vote	Statewide Elections
Alabama	7	64.6	3	Minnesota	8	47.3	6
Arizona	9	54.7	8	Missouri	8	58.8	9
Arkansas	4	67.4	10	Nevada	4	51.0	4
California	53	37.5	4	New Jersey	12	45.0	7
Colorado	7	49.7	7	New York	27	36.6	3
Georgia	14	56.1	4	Ohio	16	55.0	9
Illinois	18	44.2	10	Oregon	5	42.6	5
Indiana	9	58.3	5	Oklahoma	5	69.3	3
Iowa	4	52.0	8	Tennessee	9	60.8	7
Kentucky	6	64.4	8	Texas	36	59.0	10
Louisiana	6	66.5	3	Utah	4	67.1	7
Maryland	8	37.4	11	Washington	10	43.8	17
Massachusetts	9	29.7	9	Wisconsin	8	49.6	9
Michigan	14	48.9	7				

(continued)

Appendix Table 5.1 *Continued*

States with partial analysis due to overturned map mid-decade

State	CDs	Normal GOP Vote	Statewide Elections
Florida	27	53.4	5
North Carolina	13	52.8	6
Pennsylvania	18	51.0	11
Virginia	11	50.2	6

States with partial analysis due to lack of available statewide election data

State	CDs	Normal GOP Vote	Statewide Elections
Connecticut	5	40.2	N/A
Kansas	4	64.8	N/A
Mississippi	4	57.6	N/A
South Carolina	7	59.7	N/A

States with partial analysis due to having 3 or fewer CDs

State	CDs	Normal GOP Vote	Statewide Elections
Alaska	1	59.5	N/A
Delaware	1	39.9	N/A
Hawaii	2	30.3	N/A
Idaho	2	66.8	N/A
Maine	2	44.4	N/A
Montana	1	57.8	N/A
Nebraska	3	65.4	N/A
New Hampshire	2	48.4	N/A
New Mexico	3	45.0	N/A
North Dakota	1	64.6	N/A
Rhode Island	2	38.7	N/A
South Dakota	1	63.4	N/A
Vermont	1	31.8	N/A
West Virginia	3	63.8	N/A
Wyoming	1	72.7	N/A

Appendix Table 5.2 Average Efficiency Gaps and Slopes for All States under Difference Measures

State	CDs	Normal		Average GOP Efficiency Gap			Average Slope	
		GOP Vote	Districting Control	50/50 Point	55/45 Range	HWEG	50/50 Point	HW Slope
Alabama	7	64.6	R	11.3	9.4	6.5	6.0	0.1
Arizona	9	54.7	N	-3.4	-2.9	-0.3	2.0	2.7
Arkansas	4	67.4	D	-5.0	-3.9	14.1	6.3	0.4
California	53	37.5	N	-2.1	-1.9	0.3	1.7	1.7
Colorado	7	49.7	B	1.3	1.5	1.5	2.4	2.5
Florida	27	53.4	R/N	9.2	7.8	8.7	2.7	1.9
Georgia	14	56.1	R	13.1	12.2	7.4	1.8	0.8
Illinois	18	44.2	D	1.6	1.6	4.4	1.7	1.4
Indiana	9	58.3	R	17.1	14.4	10.9	3.5	0.6
Iowa	4	52.0	N	-5.3	-2.5	5.4	6.5	6.1
Kentucky	6	64.4	B	12.9	10.5	6.7	2.7	1.1
Louisiana	6	66.5	R	26.1	21.7	0.2	3.3	0.0
Maryland	8	37.4	D	-10.1	-8.6	-11.0	4.7	0.6
Massachusetts	9	29.7	D	10.7	8.6	-9.2	5.3	0.1
Michigan	14	48.9	R	13.1	11.8	11.6	1.2	2.2
Minnesota	8	47.3	B	14.7	11.8	6.3	3.5	4.4

(continued)

Appendix Table 5.2 *Continued*

State	CDs	Normal		Average GOP Efficiency Gap			Average Slope	
		GOP Vote	Districting Control	50/50 Point	55/45 Range	HWEG	50/50 Point	HW Slope
Missouri	8	58.8	R	19.6	17.7	8.2	1.6	0.6
Nevada	4	51.0	B	-3.4	-2.9	-1.1	4.7	3.9
New Jersey	12	45.0	B	0.9	1.1	1.1	1.1	2.6
New York	27	36.6	B	1.7	1.5	1.9	1.4	2.3
North Carolina	13	52.8	R	24.1	21.4	19.3	1.4	0.9
Ohio	16	55.0	R	17.9	14.7	13.4	3.0	0.9
Oklahoma	5	69.3	R	4.5	3.0	10.6	6.2	0.4
Oregon	5	42.6	D/B	0.3	0.0	-9.7	4.9	1.9
Pennsylvania	18	51.0	R	20.1	18.1	17.8	1.8	1.8
Tennessee	9	60.8	R	25.1	22.7	6.9	1.4	0.2
Texas	36	59.0	R/C	3.8	2.6	0.5	3.3	0.8
Utah	4	67.1	R	1.3	1.0	14.8	3.5	0.4
Virginia	11	50.2	R	15.1	12.2	12.2	2.9	2.8
Washington	10	43.8	N/B	7.7	7.5	-2.4	3.9	3.4
Wisconsin	8	49.6	R	12.4	11.5	11.2	1.1	1.9

Districting Control Key: R = Republican; D = Democratic; N = Nonpartisan; B = Bipartisan; C = Court

Appendix Table 5.3 Relationship of Vote to Expected Seats under Efficiency Gap and Historical Probit (Including Weights Used to Simulate Historically Average Swings in National Tides)

Vote %	Expected Seats % under		Difference	Weight under Weighted Normal
	Historical Probit	Efficiency Gap		
50	50.0	50.0	0.0	11.5
51	52.1	52.0	0.1	11.0
52	54.1	54.0	0.1	9.7
53	56.2	56.0	0.2	7.9
54	58.2	58.0	0.2	5.9
55	60.3	60.0	0.3	4.1
56	62.2	62.0	0.2	2.6
57	64.2	64.0	0.2	1.5
58	66.1	66.0	0.1	0.8
59	68.0	68.0	0.0	0.4
60	69.8	70.0	−0.2	0.2
61	71.6	72.0	−0.4	0.1
62	73.4	74.0	−0.6	0.0
63	75.0	76.0	−1.0	0.0
64	76.7	78.0	−1.3	0.0
65	78.2	80.0	−1.8	0.0
66	79.7	82.0	−2.3	NA
67	81.2	84.0	−2.8	NA
68	82.5	86.0	−3.5	NA
69	83.8	88.0	−4.2	NA
70	85.1	90.0	−4.9	NA
71	86.3	92.0	−5.7	NA
72	87.4	94.0	−6.6	NA
73	88.4	96.0	−7.6	NA
74	89.4	98.0	−8.6	NA
75	90.3	100.0	−9.7	NA

Appendix Table 5.4 Efficiency Gap Calculations Based on Total Statewide Congressional Vote vs. Average District Vote, 2012–2018

State	2012 EG Based on		2014 EG Based on		2016 EG Based on		2018 EG Based on	
	Total Vote	Average Vote	Total Vote	Average Vote	Total Vote	Average Vote	Total Vote	Average Vote
AL	7.7%	10.5%	−0.3%	6.6%	3.2%	10.6%	2.4%	15.6%
AR	14.7%	22.9%	16.7%	24.4%	−24.5%	6.8%	22.0%	20.8%
AZ	−14.4%	−11.3%	−11.6%	−3.9%	−4.4%	2.3%	−7.9%	−4.4%
CA	2.3%	−3.3%	−7.7%	−10.1%	6.0%	−0.4%	−4.1%	−9.4%
CO	4.3%	5.3%	3.8%	3.1%	6.2%	5.4%	3.7%	2.6%
CT	−21.4%	−21.4%	−31.4%	−31.6%	−25.7%	−25.7%	−26.0%	−26.0%
FL	6.9%	8.1%	0.9%	2.5%	0.7%	3.9%	−6.6%	5.2%
GA	−4.2%	0.9%	4.4%	6.5%	0.9%	7.0%	6.8%	7.5%
IA	3.1%	2.9%	17.2%	17.1%	15.6%	15.6%	−20.9%	−20.9%
IL	−5.8%	−5.5%	−2.7%	−0.8%	−3.2%	−1.6%	0.0%	−1.7%
IN	27.8%	19.7%	5.6%	7.0%	12.1%	10.6%	16.8%	17.3%
KS	−8.2%	12.1%	23.1%	22.9%	12.8%	18.4%	15.4%	13.5%
KY	13.3%	12.5%	6.2%	6.4%	−8.1%	2.8%	12.5%	11.7%
LA	−18.8%	0.0%	−10.2%	1.3%	−4.6%	0.0%	7.4%	5.1%
MA	−0.2%	−12.4%	15.4%	−11.1%	17.7%	−5.8%	−16.0%	−9.1%
MD	−6.6%	−8.6%	−21.2%	−19.6%	−11.6%	−12.0%	−3.7%	−4.9%
MI	19.7%	17.5%	16.0%	15.9%	13.2%	13.0%	8.0%	7.1%
MN	0.1%	0.9%	−8.7%	−7.9%	−8.9%	−8.2%	11.6%	10.1%
MO	11.7%	9.5%	1.0%	1.8%	8.2%	8.3%	12.2%	10.7%
MS	−1.2%	6.2%	7.3%	4.8%	4.6%	5.0%	11.9%	12.9%
NC	21.1%	20.3%	15.4%	18.3%	20.3%	19.7%	26.4%	21.8%
NJ	11.3%	12.7%	2.1%	6.2%	0.0%	2.3%	−20.5%	−19.7%
NV	−0.4%	2.9%	6.6%	12.8%	−24.0%	−20.1%	−19.5%	−15.5%
NY	5.2%	−0.8%	0.8%	0.5%	15.8%	6.0%	3.5%	−0.9%
OH	20.9%	21.7%	5.0%	8.6%	8.7%	9.3%	20.2%	20.3%
OK	14.8%	16.5%	5.1%	5.8%	6.2%	6.6%	3.9%	3.4%
OR	−8.2%	−11.9%	−15.7%	−16.9%	−13.2%	−18.6%	−9.7%	−11.1%
PA	23.7%	20.3%	11.1%	11.3%	14.0%	13.8%	5.9%	4.8%

Appendix Table 5.4 *Continued*

State	2012 EG Based on Total Vote	2012 EG Based on Average Vote	2014 EG Based on Total Vote	2014 EG Based on Average Vote	2016 EG Based on Total Vote	2016 EG Based on Average Vote	2018 EG Based on Total Vote	2018 EG Based on Average Vote
SC	17.8%	17.6%	3.6%	12.3%	14.6%	15.7%	11.4%	12.0%
TN	11.8%	6.0%	9.6%	3.4%	9.8%	1.0%	7.4%	8.5%
TX	–3.4%	5.5%	–9.7%	5.1%	–1.9%	9.6%	10.4%	12.8%
UT	–8.3%	–7.1%	18.7%	18.7%	16.8%	17.1%	0.5%	–0.7%
VA	20.8%	20.1%	7.8%	10.3%	14.1%	12.0%	–5.2%	–2.6%
WA	–1.1%	–3.8%	–6.8%	–6.3%	0.5%	–3.8%	6.7%	–1.6%
WI	14.0%	14.6%	6.9%	7.8%	16.6%	11.5%	7.4%	15.3%

Appendix Table 5.5
Measures and Definitions

Republican Two-Party Vote: The total votes of the Republican candidate for office divided by the sum of votes for the Republican and Democratic candidates for office. All our measures focus only on votes cast for the two major parties, ignoring votes cast for third parties, as is standard in the evaluation of districting in the United States.

Efficiency Gap: Our general measure of bias is the "shortcut version" of *efficiency gap (EG),* the difference from a seats/votes curve with no bias and slope of 2. EG is a measurement developed by opponents of partisan gerrymandering in recent legal challenges as a standard to evaluate the partisan outcome of the delegation produced by a given election. The "full" version of EG is defined as the ratio of one major party's wasted votes to the other major party's wasted votes. This simplifies into the shortcut version when turnout in every district is equal.

Responsiveness Slope: The slope of the estimated seats/vote curve at a point (i.e., the percentage of seats each party would be expected to gain given a 1% increase in vote). In line with historical average and EG, a scenario of average responsiveness would have a seats/votes slope of 2; a scenario where the slope was substantially under 2 would be considered unresponsive, and a slope substantially greater than 2 would be hyperresponsive. It is used as a measure of the responsiveness of a map under a given electoral condition.

Statewide Normal Vote: The mean two-party Republican vote share in the state over five elections: the presidential elections in 2012 and 2016 and the total congressional vote in the state in 2012, 2014, 2016, and 2018. By convenient coincidence, the national average Republican two-party vote share across these five elections was 50.0%, so it is unnecessary to adjust these statewide averages to simulate a nationally tied election environment.

Statewide 50/50 Point: This is used to estimate how likely a district is to elect a member of a certain party when each party wins 50% of the two-party vote *statewide.* Note that this is not the same as the *state's normal vote.* The statewide 50/50 point is directly important to many methods of bias analysis, and indirectly important to others such as mean/median difference.

55/45 Range: An unweighted average (of seats, EG, or slope) taken over the range in which the Republican two-party statewide vote is between 45% and 55%. This is analogous to a standard frequently used by McGann et al. (2016) in *Gerrymandering in America.*

Historically Weighted (HW) Average: A weighted average of a quantity taken over the range in which the Republican national vote is between 35% and 65%, with 99% of the weights between a range of Republican votes between 41% and 59%. The weights are derived from a normal curve where the mean of the curve is 50% and the standard deviation is 3.48%, reflecting the average deviation in national congressional popular vote over the past 50 years.

Appendix Table 6.1 Regression Analysis Using Population Weight and Control *States Weighted by CDs*

	States Weighted by CDs			
	Republican Efficiency Gap			
	Around 50/50 Point		Historically Weighted EG	
Variables	(1)	(2)	(3)	(4)
Republican Vote Advantage	–	0.28 (0.22)	–	0.39** (0.18)
Republican Map	8.37** (3.59)	9.12** (4.19)	7.18** (3.35)	9.25*** (3.30)
Rep. Vote* Rep. Map	–	–0.58 (0.40)	–	–0.98*** (0.32)
Democratic Map	–4.60 (4.85)	–8.07 (5.78)	–4.05 (4.53)	0.24 (4.55)
Dem. Vote* Rep. Map	–	–0.58 (0.44)	–	0.32 (0.35)
Nonpartisan Map	–5.12 (3.99)	–4.20 (4.05)	–0.70 (3.73)	0.56 (3.19)
Constant	5.19 (3.15)	6.24* (3.26)	2.15 (2.95)	3.61 (2.57)
Observations	35	35	35	35
R-squared	0.455	0.508	0.322	0.566

Notes: Standard errors in parentheses; *** $p < 0.01$, ** $p < 0.05$, * $p < 0.10$

Appendix Table 6.1 *Continued*

Variables	Responsiveness Slope			
	Around 50/50 Point		Historically Weighted Slope	
	(1)	(2)	(3)	(4)
Republican Vote Advantage	–	0.074* (0.042)	–	−0.0018 (0.026)
Republican Map	−0.074 (0.73)	−1.30 (0.78)	−0.75 (0.47)	−0.0036 (0.49)
Rep. Vote* Rep. Map	–	0.084 (0.075)	–	−0.12** (0.047)
Democratic Map	1.07 (0.99)	0.75 (1.07)	−0.98 (0.63)	−0.84 (0.68)
Dem. Vote* Rep. Map	–	−0.080 (0.081)	–	0.019 (0.052)
Nonpartisan Map	−0.38 (0.82)	−0.14 (0.75)	0.50 (0.52)	0.49 (0.48)
Constant	2.69*** (0.65)	2.97*** (0.61)	1.94*** (0.41)	1.93*** (0.38)
Observations	35	35	35	35
R-squared	0.078	0.317	0.292	0.480

Notes: Standard errors in parentheses; *** $p < 0.01$, ** $p < 0.05$, * $p < 0.10$

Variables	Including Controls for CDs			
	Republican Efficiency Gap			
	Around 50/50 Point		Historically Weighted EG	
	(1)	(2)	(3)	(4)
Republican Vote Advantage	–	0.11 (0.29)	–	0.81*** (0.21)
Republican Map	7.92** (3.81)	10.6** (4.74)	8.86** (3.78)	11.1*** (3.45)
Rep. Vote* Rep. Map	–	−0.43 (0.42)	–	−1.09*** (0.31)

(continued)

Appendix Table 6.1 *Continued*

	Including Controls for CDs			
	Republican Efficiency Gap			
	Around 50/50 Point		Historically Weighted EG	
Variables	(1)	(2)	(3)	(4)
Democratic Map	−7.58	−8.97*	−3.84	1.23
	(4.87)	(5.26)	(4.82)	(3.83)
Dem. Vote* Rep. Map	−	−0.37	−	−0.11
		(0.41)		(0.30)
Nonpartisan Map	−6.00	−5.73	2.99	3.39
	(4.52)	(4.60)	(4.48)	(3.35)
CDs	−0.097	−0.11	−0.10	0.12
	(0.14)	(0.17)	(0.14)	(0.12)
Constant	7.93**	7.88**	2.45	−0.48
	(3.37)	(3.62)	(3.34)	(2.64)
Observations	35	35	35	35
R-squared	0.418	0.457	0.278	0.637

Notes: Standard errors in parentheses; *** $p < 0.01$, ** $p < 0.05$, * $p < 0.10$

| | Responsiveness Slope | | | |
| | Around 50/50 Point | | Historically Weighted Slope | |
Variables	(1)	(2)	(3)	(4)
Republican Vote Advantage	−	−0.022	−	−0.086**
		(0.056)		(0.034)
Republican Map	−0.33	−1.46	−0.74	0.28
	(0.76)	(0.89)	(0.53)	(0.54)
Rep. Vote* Rep. Map	−	0.16*	−	−0.043
		(0.080)		(0.048)
Democratic Map	1.21	1.34	−0.90	−1.04*
	(0.97)	(0.99)	(0.68)	(0.60)
Dem. Vote* Rep. Map	−	0.050	−	0.081*
		(0.078)		(0.047)
Nonpartisan Map	0.25	0.16	1.40**	1.43**
	(0.90)	(0.87)	(0.63)	(0.53)

Appendix Table 6.1 *Continued*

Variables	Responsiveness Slope			
	Around 50/50 Point		Historically Weighted Slope	
	(1)	(2)	(3)	(4)
CDs	−0.062**	−0.053	−0.0071	−0.043**
	(0.028)	(0.032)	(0.020)	(0.020)
Constant	3.92***	3.87***	1.85***	2.27***
	(0.67)	(0.68)	(0.47)	(0.42)
Observations	35	35	35	35
R-squared	0.234	0.363	0.385	0.609

Notes: Standard errors in parentheses; *** $p < 0.01$, ** $p < 0.05$, * $p < 0.10$

Notes

Chapter 1

1. Approximately 5% of California congressional elections from 2002 to 2010 were decided by 10 points or fewer, compared with 13–18% of elections from 2012 to 2018 (depending on how general elections between same-party candidates under the nonpartisan primary system are counted).

Chapter 2

1. See Trickey (2017) for details of this origin.
2. Former California governor Arnold Schwarzenegger, recently a prominent national advocate for redistricting reform, also enacts a live version of this exact graphic in lectures on gerrymandering. For example, see Schwarzenegger (2019).
3. A number of scholars have explored representational trade-offs inherent in districting in varying contexts. Most notably, Butler and Cain (1992) extensively discuss some of the representational claims I describe later alongside several nonrepresentational values associated with districting (such as compactness). The idea of representational trade-offs in districting is most frequently referenced with respect to the potential conflict between substantive and descriptive representation in drawing majority-minority districts, including in Lublin (1997), Cameron, Epstein, and O'Halloran (1996), Canon and Posner (1999), Shotts (2003), and Casellas (2011). Prominent works outlining different components or concepts of representation not specific to the redistricting context include Pitkin (1967), Eulau and Karps (1977), Mansbridge (2003), and Saward (2010).
4. A "dyad" here refers to a link between two entities, in this case the voter and their assigned representative, or the principal and the agent in the representative relationship.
5. The appellate court in *Gomez* reversed the district court, holding that the plaintiff's proposed remedy for at-large districts was better than no remedy at all.
6. Though of course it has the parallel disadvantage of systematically underrepresenting or excluding minority groups or parties, especially if they are geographically dispersed (see, e.g., Nagel 2000).
7. National legislatures that employ pure proportional representation with no use of geographic districts or representation floors are very uncommon; the Netherlands is one example.
8. Assigning members to Congress based on proportional representation has been prohibited by federal law since the 1970s, but states could choose to draw single-member districts that are likely to achieve a more proportionate outcome

(e.g., *Gaffney v. Cummings* (1973)), or conversely, that are more likely to lead to hypermajoritarian/hyperresponsive outcomes (which tends to be seen in commission plans, as discussed in Chapter 7).

9. In the wave examples in Figures 2.4 through 2.7, dark-shaded districts represent districts won by Democrats, while light-shaded districts represent districts won by Republicans.

10. To the extent that we wish to measure "personal" representation, we might analogize this to the *opposite* of our competitiveness measure (as an election won unanimously would indicate that the greatest number of voters were happy with their personal representative). Modeling "discursive" representation might simply ask whether both parties are represented in the delegation, which all maps satisfy under all tides *except for the nonpartisan map*. But both of these would represent highly impoverished simplifications of the concepts of personal and discursive representation, which almost always seek to describe the quality of representation along dimensions beyond major party affiliation.

Chapter 3

1. Unable to agree on a method of reapportionment and concerned about growing political power in more urban states, Congress did not reapportion itself following the 1920 census (see Eagles 2010). A subsequent law passed in 1929 provided for automatic reapportionment in future decades.

2. Pennsylvania Republicans later corrected these population deviations, and the new map was eventually upheld in *Vieth v. Jubelirer*, as discussed later.

3. The Supreme Court case *Cooper v. Harris* (2017) which precipitated the redrawing of the North Carolina congressional districts at issue in the *Rucho v. Common Cause* case discussed in this chapter is one such example of the Court striking down a map due to the predomination of racial factors in violation of the Equal Protection Clause.

4. Stephanopoulos and McGhee (2015) do propose using "sensitivity testing" around a narrow range of deviations from the observed election outcome to show the durability of bias, and the plaintiff's experts demonstrate the historical likelihood of durability through several methods.

5. A parallel lawsuit was also filed in federal court under the name *Agre v. Wolf*, but this case was dismissed and ultimately mooted by the state court decision.

6. The plaintiff's brief was filed after the district court struck the Wisconsin map in *Whitford* but before the U.S. Supreme Court reversed this decision.

7. Note that there is no *requirement* in the PA state constitution to apply these criteria to the drawing of *congressional* districts.

8. Polsby-Popper is a measurement of district compactness based on the ratio of the area of a district to its squared perimeter. An alternate measure often used in these cases, Reock compactness, is the ratio of the area of a district to the smallest circle that would enclose it.

9. Note that although the 2011 Plan performed poorly on these metrics compared to the simulated maps, it was actually slightly *more* compact than the previous map, in place 2002–2010, which had 29 county splits and an average Polsby-Popper score of 0.162.

10. Note that the redistricting procedure outlined in the Maryland Constitution prescribed that new maps are first prepared by the governor and presented to the legislature, rather than being initiated by the legislature.

11. Cook's Partisan Voting Index (PVI) expresses how the partisanship of the district differed from the nation in an average of the last two presidential elections. A "D + 5" district voted five points to the left of the national average, while an "R + 20" district voted twenty points to the right.

12. Efficiency Gap % = GOP Seat Share - ((2*GOP Vote Share) - 50)

13. Because one race in 2018 was vacated, I excluded this one election in the delegation count.

14. Chen (2017) does find the Act 43 Wisconsin plan splits more counties and draws less compact districts than a set of simulated districts. Nevertheless, the average Reock compactness score of districts in the Act 43 plan of 0.37 is both substantially higher than the average Reock compactness of 0.278 of Pennsylvania districts struck down in *LWV*, and equal to the national average compactness of all districts during this decade (Azavea 2012).

15. The Polsby-Popper score of the 6th District declined slightly from 0.096 to 0.071 following the 2011 redistricting.

16. Recall that the average Polsby-Popper score of the Pennsylvania districts struck down in *LWV* was 0.164.

17. This 0.242 average is also larger than the 0.164 average in the PA map at issue in *LWV* and the 0.112 average in the MD map in Maryland, though smaller than the 0.324 average of the remedial map adopted by the Court in *LWV*.

18. The state's loss of a district necessitates some renumbering. The previous 19th District almost wholly became the new 4th District, and most of the 4th District was labeled as the 12th District.

Chapter 4

1. Portions of this chapter were adapted from Goedert (2017).

2. It is empirically true in the data set of congressional elections from 1972 to 2010 that nonpartisan commissions draw maps with more seats that are designed to be competitive, or at least closely balanced relative to the nation as a whole. This is demonstrated and discussed in Appendix Table 4.2. The same analysis also suggests that partisan maps draw few districts designed to be balanced when the national election is tied.

3. Figure 4.1a shows a bending in the curves for bipartisan and nonpartisan gerrymanders under extreme tides. This reflects the possibility that a wave might be so strong as to make even the safest seats in a bipartisan map competitive, or make the

closely balanced seats in a nonpartisan map noncompetitive. However, this chapter is agnostic as to whether tides extreme enough to observe these effects will be observed in the data set. Additionally, the number of nonpartisan commission states in our data set may be too small to draw strong conclusions on this question.

4. The year 1972 represents the first cycle following the first national round of redistricting post-*Wesberry v. Sanders*, and thus the first cycle in which all districts are constitutionally required to have equal population.

5. Codings, listed in Appendix Table 4.1, are mostly drawn from CQ's *Congressional Districts in the 1970s* (e.g., Moxley (1973) and subsequent volumes in this series. They were compared with the codings from research such as Glazer, Grofman, and Robbins (1987) and McDonald (2004) for robustness and supplemented by other sources where the descriptions are ambiguous. States with only one district are coded as nonpartisan. A handful of states are coded with more than one designation, most frequently where a map is chosen by a court from among those proposed by the political parties. In such cases, the districts in this state are designated as being drawn both by a court and by the party of the map chosen. This was done to recognize that some maps, while formally drawn by courts, are effectively partisan gerrymanders.

6. Maps drawn by courts serve as a separate control for which we have no particular directional predictions. Errors are clustered by district interacted with decade to account for serial autocorrelation within districts.

7. Because controls are statewide measures, the data set essentially describes the proportion of state elections that are close, weighted by the size of the delegation. An alternative specification would be to make each of these proportions a data point, weight them by delegation size (so that the impact of each individual election was still the same), and cluster by state interacted with decade (yielding 800 data points and 160 clusters). As this DV would be a proportion (rather than a binary outcome), yet not properly described by a binomial distribution, it is more difficult to determine an appropriate specification for the data formatted in this manner. Such an analysis, with the proportion of close races analyzed using OLS, is included in Appendix Table 4.3.

8. A binary variable for close races in assessing competition is used frequently in the literature (e.g., Masket, Winburn, and Wright 2012; Carson and Crespin 2004; Cox and Katz 2002; Mayhew 1974) and is chosen here because using continuous vote margin leads results to be very sensitive to imputation decisions in unopposed races. I have also tested an alternate definition of *Close Race* that additionally includes all instances of turnover, with very similar results. About 18% of all elections are *Close Races* under this alternative definition. Other variables measuring competition used in past literature, such as quality challengers and campaign finance data, are not appropriate to test our hypotheses, as these variables are largely determined before short-term electoral tides are known.

9. All three of these correlations are significant at p < 0.01 in the data set employed in the analysis.

10. This is in stark contrast with Appendix Table 4.2, showing that swing states tend to draw more *demographically* competitive districts (as opposed to districts that generate close elections).

11. As an alternative to the *Close Race* dummy, this analysis can also be run with the overall vote margin as the dependent variable. Using this DV, the effect of *National Tides* is negative and significant at $p < 0.05$ when unopposed races are excluded, and significant at $p<0.10$ when unopposed races are included and counted as a 100% vote margin.

12. Elections during the 1970s are absent from this quadrant because no states employed nonpartisan commissions at that time.

13. This result is also consistent with the analysis in Appendix Table 4.2 that nonpartisan maps draw more competitive districts at the presidential level.

14. In the case of Democratic gerrymanders, the coefficient is not significant, which is understandable given the small number of Republican-wave elections in the data set where we would hypothesize a steep slope among Democratic maps.

15. Due to the lack of Republican waves prior to 1994 and the lack of Republican gerrymanders in the 1990s, this essentially analyzes only the difference between the 2010 wave and the smaller Republican victories in 2002 and 2004.

16. Data for Democratic maps for the 1970s and 1980s are not shown because those decades had no Republican-wave elections at the congressional level. Data for Republican maps for the 1980s and 1990s are not shown because very few states had Republican-drawn districts during that period (fewer than forty total districts in any year). The number of seats changed during the 2000s due to mid-decade redistricting in Texas and Georgia.

17. This outlier suggests that competitiveness may correlate not just from absolute tides but tides in one election relative to tides in the previous election. Results are robust to inclusion of an autoregressive term for national tides in the previous election cycle. Although this term does have an independent significant effect of competition (a large *difference* in tides from the previous election correlates with more close elections), it has little or no effect on the interactions of tides and districting regimes.

18. While the estimates in this figure may appear to be linear, as opposed to the typical curves generated from probit estimates, this is merely an effect of displaying only a small portion of the feasible national tides range; the lines curve sharply under more extreme (but unobserved) partisan waves.

19. One piece that is inconsistent with the model is that nonpartisan commissions seem to have a pro-Republican bias under neutral partisan tides. The sample size for this condition is very small, and the result is not significant.

20. The impact of the most recent Democratic wave in 2018 on partisan and nonpartisan maps is examined in greater detail in Chapters 5 through 7.

21. For Tables 4.4 through 4.6, I have strictly categorized each state into only one redistricting regime, so that the number of states will sum to fifty, and the number of districts to 435.

22. As I am attempting to measure the volatility of a map, the "flip" variable includes a handful of seats that flipped to the Democrats in 2006 and back to the Republicans in 2008. As the dependent variable can never take on a value of 1 if the seat was Democratic in 2006, I have also run this same analysis on only those seats held by Republicans following the 2004 election.

23. Note that California must be excluded from this analysis because, by court order, it elected members under an entirely new map in 1974, which cannot be directly compared to the 1972 map on a district-by-district basis.

24. Southern states were much less likely to elect Republicans given their presidential partisanship than non-southern states in the 1970s. I also have not attempted to use consecutive presidential-level voting data to estimate the shifts in partisanship between 1972 and 1974; the regional strengths of McGovern and Carter as candidates are too divergent for this to be a reasonable estimate of overall partisan changes. For example, Carter won Mississippi in 1976, a state where McGovern received less than 20% of the vote. It is rather implausible to suggest that this is because Mississippi became a much more Democratic state during the four-year interim. Instead, the statewide presidential vote control represents an average of the statewide GOP margin in these two presidential elections; the national average of this variable is 10.5%.

Chapter 5

1. In Chapter 8, several other drawbacks and complications regarding the use of simulated maps as either a legal standard or a legislative proposal are discussed.

2. States with three or fewer CDs are excluded. We might also calculate efficiency gap using the actual statewide vote percentage, regardless of turnout difference or unopposed races (or some other method of imputing unopposed rates). Stephanopoulos and McGhee (2015) discuss the advantages and disadvantages of various techniques to deal with differences in turnout and opposition in EG calculations. The correlation of average statewide vote with the 75% imputation and total statewide vote during 2012–2018 is 0.97. Complete EG calculations for all states in all four election cycles using both methods are shown in Appendix Table 5.4. Note that in the 2018 calculations, the vacated North Carolina 9th District election is counted as half a Republican seat.

3. The following abbreviations are used for redistricting control in tables in this chapter: (D) Democratic; (R) Republican; (B) Bipartisan; (N) Nonpartisan; (C) Court.

4. The jungle primary system used in California, discussed further in Chapter 7, also yields an unusually high number of races lacking two-party competition in the general election, complicating EG calculations.

5. It should be noted that Stephanopoulos and McGhee (2015) suggest "sensitivity testing," where the sign of the EG is also tested over a range of hypothetical election conditions yet still centered around the observed conditions.

6. Although I believe the use of a probit or logit curve to track deviations from historical averages is slightly more accurate, especially in dealing with noncompetitive states (Goedert 2014), I choose to use EG for its recognizability and ease of calculation. EG closely tracks the probit estimate in two-party vote ranges from 35% to 65%. A contrast between these two methods and the resulting bias measures is shown in

Appendix Table 5.3, but they yield almost entirely the same substantive conclusions outlined in the next three chapters.

7. District-level data for statewide elections were drawn from a variety of sources, but the most helpful was jeffmd, "Daily Kos Elections' Statewide Election Results by Congressional and Legislative Districts," *Daily Kos*, March 23, 2021. www.dailykos. com/stories/2013/7/9/1220127/-Daily-Kos-Elections-2012-election-results-by-congressional-and-legislative-districts. In many cases, board of elections or secretary of state websites for individual states were consulted to fill in gaps in the data, as were idiosyncratic sources for specific states (e.g., the Twitter account J. Miles Coleman and www.illinoiselectiondata.com for Illinois).

8. Four of these thirty-one states have seen their map changed by court order in the middle of the decade (FL, NC, PA, and VA). In these states, I analyze only the maps drawn at the start of the decade, and only use data drawn from elections conducted while those maps were in effect.

To adjust for unopposed congressional races only, a 75% two-party vote share is imputed for any candidate that is unopposed or gets more than 75% of the vote (e.g., Seabrook 2017; Kastellec, Gelman, and Chandler 2008; Gelman and King 1994). This does generate some inaccurate estimates in extremely one-sided districts, as there do exist many districts where one party would typically receive more than 75% of the two-party vote even in opposed races. However, this imputation makes almost no difference in the overall analysis presented here, for two reasons. First, the imputation is done only for congressional races, which typically represent a small fraction of the races used in the district average. And second, any district that would vote more than 75% for one party under observed congressional conditions will never be estimated to be even slightly competitive under any of the hypothetical conditions evaluated here, and thus imputation decisions in these districts are never pivotal to the analysis.

9. Formally, the probability of a Republican win in a district D given a national Republican vote share of v_N is defined as:

$$P_{GOPwin_D}(v_N) = \Phi \left(\frac{(\mu_{D_{psc}} + \mu_{S_{psc}}) + ((v_N + (\mu_{S_{pc}} - \mu_{N_{pc}})) - .5)}{\sqrt{\sigma_{D_{ps}}^2 + \sigma_N^2}} \right)$$

$\mu_{D_{psc}}$ is the average district Republican vote share across presidential, statewide, and congressional elections.

$\mu_{S_{psc}}$ is the average statewide Republican vote share across presidential, statewide, and congressional elections.

$\mu_{S_{pc}}$ is the average statewide Republican vote share across presidential and congressional elections (used to calculate the state normal vote).

$\mu_{N_{pc}}$ is the average national Republican vote share across presidential and congressional elections (used to calculate the state normal vote).

$\sigma_{D_{ps}}$ is the standard deviation in the difference between statewide and district Republican vote in statewide and presidential elections.

σ_N is a constant reflecting average standard deviation in congressional elections nationwide.

v_N is the national congressional Republican vote in a given cycle.

Φ is the cumulative normal function.

This probability is summed across districts in the state to derive expected Republican seats, which is used to calculate efficiency gaps and responsiveness slopes at a particular national vote share. These points are weighted in likelihood by a normal function with a mean of 50% and standard deviation of 3.48% and summed to calculate the summary HWEG and HW slope measures.

10. Likely due to both the much greater number of Republican gerrymanders and geographic factors, many more states have pro-Republican than pro-Democratic bias under all measures; under no measure do more than five states have a pro-Democratic EG greater than 1%. Full results for all states are in Appendix Table 5.2.

11. Recall that we use the full HWEG method using all statewide and congressional data to estimate seats in thirty-one states, and a shortcut method using only presidential and congressional data (and a uniform size of random variance across districts) in the remaining nineteen states, including the fifteen states with three or fewer CDs.

12. All of the detailed state analysis in subsequent chapters uses congressional maps in place for the 2012 cycle. However, this projection does account for mid-decade changes in maps in Florida, North Carolina, and Virginia (prior to 2016) and Pennsylvania (prior to 2018), resulting in four to five additional projected seats for Democrats by 2018. Because the HWEG projection uses no information about individual candidate-level factors like incumbency of challenger quality, and no information about what happened in the immediately previous election, it may systematically underestimate turnover in elections with cycles with many retirements and overestimate turnover in a more status-quo cycle with fewer retirements.

Chapter 6

1. Similar to the analysis in Chapter 4, I have categorized these Deep South states separately because their maps are dominated by Voting Rights Act considerations regardless of the map-drawing party. With the exception of Georgia, this leads the map in each of these states to include one heavily Democratic Black–majority district, with each other district being heavily white and Republican.

2. Note that two significant states that arguably saw Republican gerrymanders during this decade, Florida and Texas, are not included in the graph or the subsequent averages because of ambiguous incentives and procedures in drawing their maps. While Republican legislators were in control of the map-drawing process in Florida, they were also under the constraint of a recently passed voter initiative barring the drawing of districts for partisan benefit (though the resulting map was partially struck down by the state court as overly partisan anyway). The map in Texas was the product of protracted Voting Rights Act–related litigation, resulting in what was largely viewed as an incumbent-protecting map.

3. Arkansas's map has an HWEG bias of 14.1% *in favor of Republicans,* with an extremely low HW slope of 0.4. Illinois has an HWEG bias of 4.4% in favor of Republicans, with a moderately low HW slope of 1.4. In contrast, Massachusetts, Maryland, and Oregon all have an HWEG bias of between 9% and 11% in favor of Democrats.

4. In each of Tables 6.4 through 6.6, districts in which the Republican candidate won more votes than the Democrat are shown in bold, while districts where the Republican candidate outperformed the statewide average are shown in italics.

5. Because Oregon votes entirely by mail with no voting precincts, it is difficult to acquire reliable district-level voting results in statewide races. Additionally, during this decade, almost all significant statewide races in Oregon were won by the Democrats with little significant variation in the margins. Therefore, I do not compare statewide voting results by district in Oregon as I do in the other state examples in this chapter.

6. Tennessee has a Republican gerrymander similar in many ways to Indiana and Missouri, but is not shown in the table because no recent close statewide elections had available data broken down by congressional district. Maryland presents a similar problem, as only election-day votes (excluding early and absentee votes) by congressional district are made available for statewide elections.

7. Similar results are shown in Appendix Table 6.1, alternately including controls for population and with states weighted by population, and including similar substantive results.

8. From the tripartite classification of states into competitive, noncompetitive, and extreme categories, we might expect to see some nonlinear effect of normal vote on bias and responsiveness. When we include additional interactions with the square of normal vote (which could model a nonlinear effect), the coefficients for the squared variables are in the expected direction (e.g., positive effect to Republican Vote^2*Republican Gerrymander on Republican bias), but not statistically significant, which is probably unsurprising given the small sample size and diminishing degrees of freedom as additional interactions are included.

Chapter 7

1. As nonpresidential statewide election data are less consistently available for earlier decades, I create district partisanship estimates for the 2000s and 1990s using the shortcut HWEG method applied to small states, as described in Chapter 5. That is, each district's random variance term is simply the national average of congressional election variance, and the district's mean partisanship is estimated using congressional and presidential election data only (an average of eight elections in each district). Republican normal vote, HWEG, and HW slope are estimated in the same way as described for current maps in Chapter 5.

2. See Legislative Services Agency, "Legislative Guide to Redistricting in Iowa," December 2007, www.legis.iowa.gov/docs/publications/LG/9461.pdf for further details.

3. For additional commentaries on this decision, see "Leading Case" 2015.

4. "Californians Compete for a Shot at Redistricting," *New York Times*, March 4, 2010, A18, www.nytimes.com/2010/03/04/us/politics/04redistrict.html.

5. We Draw the Lines, "Application and Selection Process," 2021, www.wedrawthelines. ca.gov/selection/.

6. A sixth criterion, nesting, is also listed but applicable only to state senate districts.

7. By contrast, Iowa, where close elections are the norm, had not elected a single woman to the U.S. House until 2018.

8. Rep. Barbara Lee (CA District 9) was the only member of Congress to vote against the use of force in Afghanistan following the attacks of September 11, 2001, while Pete Stark (CA District 13) was the only openly atheist member of Congress.

9. Competition within safe districts, promoting congruent personal and discursive representation, may also be enhanced by California's switch to a nonpartisan primary, which enables intraparty debate to occur at the higher-profile general election stage, promoting more visible primary election competition (for example, in the vigorous primary election battles between Democrats Ro Khanna and Mike Honda in the 17th District in 2014 and 2016).

10. As with all conclusions derived from HWEG, these commission maps are unbiased relative to nationwide historical average bias and responsiveness. Other scholars have drawn different conclusions with respect to maps in these same commission states, including Best et al. (2019), who find the 2010s map in Arizona biased toward Democrats, the New Jersey map biased toward Republicans, and the maps in California, Iowa, and Washington not significantly biased based on the measurement of mean/median difference compared to simulations.

Chapter 8

1. Text of Michigan Proposal 2 is available at Michigan, "Initiative Petition Amendment to the Constitution," www.michigan.gov/documents/sos/Full_Text_-_VNP_635257_7.pdf.

2. See Missouri, "Initiative Petition," filed November 23, 2016, www.sos.mo.gov/ CMSImages/Elections/Petitions/2018-048.pdf for the text of Missouri Amendment 1.

3. See https://leg.colorado.gov/sites/default/files/documents/2018A/bills/2018a_scr 004_ren.pdf for text of Colorado Amendment Y.

4. Text of Utah's Proposition 4 is available at https://elections.utah.gov/Media/Default/ 2018%20Election/Issues%20on%20the%20Ballot/Proposition%204%20-%20Bal lot%20Title%20and%20Impartial%20Analysis.pdf.

5. Text of the amendment as passed by the state legislature is available at Brennan Center, Ohio General Assembly Joint Resolution, 2017–18, https://www.brennancen ter.org/sites/default/files/legal-work/OH-Sub-SJR5.pdf.

6. See "States with Initiative or Referendum," (2021) Ballotpedia, ballotpedia.org/ States_with_initiative_or_referendum for a complete list of states permitting ballot initiatives.

7. See Brennan Center, "Overview: Virginia Redistricting Reform Amendment (HJ615/SJ306)," March 28, 2019, www.brennancenter.org/analysis/overview-virginia-redistricting-reform-amendment-hj615sj306 for further summary and House Joint Resolution 615" (2019) is lis.virginia.gov/cgi-bin/legp604.exe?191+ful+HJ615+pdf for the text of the amendment.

8. See Legiscan, Maryland Senate Bill 91, 2019, legiscan.com/MD/text/SB91/2019 for text of the proposed amendment, and Legiscan, Maryland Senate Bill 90, 2019, legiscan.com/MD/text/SB90/2019 for proposed legislation establishing the composition of the commission.

9. See Legiscan, Maryland Senate Bill 1023, 2018, legiscan.com/MD/text/SB1023/2017 for the text of the Mid-Atlantic Compact bill.

10. Unlike in Maryland, where maps must first be proposed by the governor to be approved by the legislature.

11. See Legiscan, Maryland House Bill 622, 2017, legiscan.com/MD/bill/HB622/2017 for details of the Potomac Compact proposal.

12. A previous Florida state court ruling had held that a single ballot amendment could not change both the process and the criteria for legislative districting.

13. The "splitline" method is detailed at Range Voting, "Splitline Districtings of All 50 States + DC + PR," (rangevoting.org/SplitLR.html).

14. See U.S. House of Representatives, H.R. 1, For the People Act of 2019, www.congress.gov/bill/116th-congress/house-bill/1/text for text of H.R. 1. A Fairness and Independence in Redistricting Act requiring states to adopt redistricting commissions through a more bipartisan process similar to Arizona's system has also been introduced in the House in every legislative session since 2005.

15. States unable or unwilling to create such a commission would have their maps drawn by a panel of three federal judges.

References

Abramowitz, Alan I., Brad Alexander, and Matthew Gunning. 2006. "Incumbency, Redistricting, and the Decline of Competition in US House Elections." *Journal of Politics* 68(1): 75–88.

Altman, M., and M. P. McDonald. 2011. "BARD: Better Automated Redistricting." *Journal of Statistical Software* 42(4): 1–28. http://www.jstatsoft.org.

Azavea. 2012. "Redrawing the Map on Redistricting 2012 Addendum." White Paper. https://s3.amazonaws.com/s3.azavea.com/com.redistrictingthenation/pdfs/Redistricting_The_Nation_Addendum.pdf.

Backstrom, Charles, Leonard Robins, and Scott Eller. 1990. "Establishing a Statewide Electoral Effects Baseline." *Political Gerrymandering and the Courts*: 145–70.

Barone, Michael, and Richard E. Cohen. *The Almanac of American Politics.* Washington: National Journal Group, Bi-annual Publication.

Best, R., S. Lem, D. Magleby, and M. McDonald. 2019. "Do Redistricting Commissions Avoid Partisan Gerrymanders?" *APSANET Preprint.*

Best, Robin E., Shawn J. Donahue, Jonathan Krasno, Daniel B. Magleby, and Michael D. McDonald. 2018. "Considering the Prospects for Establishing a Packing Gerrymandering Standard." *Election Law Journal* 17(1): 1–20.

Brennan Center for Justice. 2015. "Redistricting Laws Roundup." https://www.brennancenter.org/redistricting-laws-roundup-2015.

Brunell, Thomas L. 2008. *Redistricting and Representation: Why Competitive Elections Are Bad for America.* New York: Routledge.

Buchler, Justin. 2005. "Competition, Representation, and Redistricting: The Case against Competitive Congressional Districts." *Journal of Theoretical Politics* 17(4): 431–63.

Butler, David, and Bruce E. Cain. 1992. *Congressional Redistricting: Comparative and Theoretical Perspectives.* New York: Macmillan.

Bycoffe, Aaron, Ella Koeze, David Wasserman, and Julia Wolfe. 2018. "The Atlas of Redistricting." *FiveThirtyEight*, January 25. projects.fivethirtyeight.com/redistricting-maps.

Cain, Bruce E., Karin MacDonald, and Michael McDonald. 2005. "From Equality to Fairness: The Path of Political Reform since *Baker v. Carr.*" In *Party Lines*, ed. Thomas E. Mann and Bruce E. Cain, 6–30. Washington, DC: Brookings Institution.

Cameron, Charles, David Epstein, and Sharyn O'Halloran. 1996. "Do Majority-Minority Districts Maximize Substantive Black Representation in Congress?" *American Political Science Review* 90(4): 794–812.

Canon, David T. 1999. "Electoral Systems and the Representation of Minority Interests in Legislatures." *Legislative Studies Quarterly* 24(3): 331–85.

Canon, David T., and Richard A. Posner. 1999. *Race, Redistricting, and Representation: The Unintended Consequences of Black Majority Districts.* Chicago: University of Chicago Press.

Carson, James L., and Michael H. Crespin. 2004. "The Effect of State Redistricting Methods on Electoral Competition in United States House Races." *State Politics and Policy Quarterly* 4(4): 455–69.

Carson, Jamie L., Michael H. Crespin, and Ryan Dane Williamson. 2014. "Re-evaluating the Effects of Redistricting on Electoral Competition, 1972–2012." *State Politics & Policy Quarterly* 14(2): 165–77.

Casellas, Jason P. 2010. *Latino Representation in State Houses and Congress.* Cambridge: Cambridge University Press.

Chambers, Christopher P., Alan D. Miller, and Joel Sobel. 2017. "Flaws in the Efficiency Gap." *Journal of Law & Politics* 33: 1–34.

Chen, Jowei. 2017. "The Impact of Political Geography on Wisconsin Redistricting: An Analysis of Wisconsin's Act 43 Assembly Districting Plan." *Election Law Journal* 16(4): 443–52.

Chen, Jowei, and Jonathan Rodden. 2015. "Cutting through the Thicket: Redistricting Simulations and the Detection of Partisan Gerrymanders." *Election Law Journal* 14(4): 331–45.

Converse, Philip E. 1966. "The Concept of a Normal Vote." *Elections and the Political Order* 9: 39.

Cook, Charles E., and David Wasserman. 2014. "Recalibrating Ratings for a New Normal." *PS: Political Science and Politics* 47(2): 304–8.

Cox, Gary W. and Jonathan Katz. 2002. *Elbridge Gerry's Salamander: The Electoral Consequences of the Reapportionment Revolution.* New York: Cambridge University Press.

Daley, David. 2016. *Ratf**ked: Why Your Vote Doesn't Count.* New York: Norton.

Dillon, John F., Lewis Lawrence Smith, and Clinton Rogers Woodruff. 1892. "Department of Municipal Corporations and Public Law. People ex rel. Carter v. Rice, Secretary of State. Court of Appeals of New York." *American Law Register and Review* 40(12): 851–61.

Donald, Karin, and Bruce E. Cain. 2013. "Community of Interest Methodology and Public Testimony." *UC Irvine Law Review* 3: 609.

Douglas, Joshua, ed. 2016. *Election Law Stories.* New York: Foundation Press.

Dryzek, John S., and Simon Niemeyer. 2008. "Discursive Representation." *American Political Science Review* 102(4): 481–93.

Eagles, Charles W. 2010. *Democracy Delayed: Congressional Reapportionment and Urban-Rural Conflict in the 1920s.* Athens: University of Georgia Press.

Eulau, Heinz, and Paul D. Karps. 1977. "The Puzzle of Representation: Specifying Components of Responsiveness." *Legislative Studies Quarterly* 2(3): 233–54.

Ferejohn, John A. 1977. "On the Decline of Competitiveness of Congressional Elections." *American Political Science Review* 71: 166–76.

Gelman, Andrew, and Gary King. 1994. "Enhancing Democracy through Legislative Districting." *American Political Science Review* 88(3): 541–59.

Gilligan, Thomas W., and John G. Matsusaka. 2006. "Public Choice Principles of Redistricting." *Public Choice* 129(3–4): 381–98.

Glazer, Amihai, Bernard Grofman, and Marc Robbins. 1987. "Partisan and Incumbency Effects of 1970s Congressional Redistricting." *American Journal of Political Science* 31: 680–707.

Goedert, Nicholas. 2014. "Gerrymandering or Geography? How Democrats Won the Popular Vote but Lost the Congress in 2012." *Research & Politics* 1(1): 2053168014528683.

Goedert, Nicholas. 2015. "The Case of the Disappearing Bias: A 2014 Update to the 'Gerrymandering or Geography' Debate." *Research & Politics 2*(4): 2053168015622474.

Goedert, Nicholas. 2017. "The Pseudoparadox of Partisan Mapmaking and Congressional Competition." *State Politics & Policy Quarterly 17*(1): 47–75.

Golder, Matt. 2005. "Democratic Electoral Systems around the World, 1946–2000." *Electoral Studies 24*(1): 103–21.

Gopoian, David L., and Darrell M. West. 1984. "Trading Security for Seats: Strategic Considerations in the Redistricting Process." *Journal of Politics 46*(4): 1080–96.

Grofman, Bernard. 2019. "Tests for Unconstitutional Partisan Gerrymandering in a Post-Gill World." *Election Law Journal: Rules, Politics, and Policy 18*(2): 93–115.

Grofman, Bernard, and Thomas L. Brunell. 2005. "The Art of the Dummymander: The Impact of Recent Redistrictings on the Partisan Makeup of Southern House Seats." In *Redistricting in the New Millennium*, ed. Peter F. Galderisi, 183–200. New York: Rowman & Littlefield.

Grofman, Bernard, and Jonathan R. Cervas. 2018. "Can State Courts Cure Partisan Gerrymandering: Lessons from League of Women Voters v. Commonwealth of Pennsylvania (2018)." *Election Law Journal 17*(4): 264–85.

Gronke, Paul, and J. Matthew Wilson. 1999. "Competing Redistricting Plans as Evidence of Political Motives: The North Carolina Case." *American Politics Quarterly 27*(2): 147–76.

Hetherington, M. J., B. Larson, and S. Globetti. 2003. "The Redistricting Cycle and Strategic Candidate Decisions in US House Races." *Journal of Politics 65*(4): 1221–34.

Hirsch, Sam. 2003. "The United States House of Unrepresentatives: What Went Wrong in the Latest Round of Congressional Redistricting." *Election Law Journal 2*(2): 179–216.

Hood, M. V., and Seth C. McKee. 2008. "Gerrymandering on Georgia's Mind: The Effects of Redistricting on Vote Choice in the 2006 Midterm Election" *Social Science Quarterly 89*(1): 60–77.

Hunter, T. R. 2011. "The First Gerrymander? Patrick Henry, James Madison, James Monroe, and Virginia's 1788 Congressional Districting." *Early American Studies 9*: 781–820.

Issacharoff, Samuel, Pamela S. Karlan, and Richard H. Pildes. 2007. *The Law of Democracy: Legal Structures of the Political Process.* 3rd ed. New York: Foundation Press.

Kang, Michael S. 2004. "The Bright Side of Partisan Gerrymandering." *Cornell Journal of Law and Public Policy 14*: 443.

Kastellec, Jonathan P., Andrew Gelman, and Jamie P. Chandler. 2008. "Predicting and Dissecting the Seats-Votes Curve in the 2006 US House Election." *PS: Political Science & Politics 41*(1): 139–45.

Katz, Jonathan N., Gary King, and Elizabeth Rosenblatt. 2020. "Theoretical Foundations and Empirical Evaluations of Partisan Fairness in District-Based Democracies." *American Political Science Review 114*(1): 164–78.

King, Gary, and Robert X. Browning. 1987. "Democratic Representation and Partisan Bias in Congressional Elections." *American Political Science Review 81*(4): 1251–73.

Krehbiel, Keith, Adam Meirowitz, and Thomas Romer. 2005. "Parties in Elections, Parties in Government, and Partisan Bias." *Political Analysis 13*(2): 113–38.

"Leading Case: Arizona State Legislature v. Arizona Independent Redistricting Commission." 2015. *Harvard Law Review* 129: 191.

Lindgren, Eric, and Priscilla Southwell. 2013. "The Effect of Redistricting Commissions on Electoral Competitiveness in U.S. House Elections, 2002–2010." *Journal of Politics and Law 6*(2): 13.

Lowenthal, Alan S. 2019. "The Ills of Gerrymandering and Independent Redistricting Commissions as the Solution." *Harvard Journal on Legislation* 56: 1.

Lublin, David. 1997. *The Paradox of Representation: Racial Gerrymandering and Minority Interests in Congress.* Princeton, NJ: Princeton University Press.

MacDonald, Karin, and Bruce E. Cain. 2013. "Community of Interest Methodology and Public Testimony." *UC Irvine Law Review* 3: 609.

Magleby, D. B., and D. B. Mosesson. 2018. "A New Approach for Developing Neutral Redistricting Plans." *Political Analysis* 26(2): 147–67.

Mansbridge, Jane. 2003. "Rethinking Representation." *American Political Science Review* 97(4): 515–28.

Masket, Seth E., Jonathan Winburn, and Gerald C. Wright. 2012. "The Gerrymanderers Are Coming! Legislative Redistricting Won't Affect Competition or Polarization Much, No Matter Who Does It." *PS: Political Science and Politics* 45(1): 39.

Mayhew, David R. 1974. "Congressional Elections: The Case of the Vanishing Marginals." *Polity* 6(3): 295–317.

McDonald, Michael D., and Robin E. Best. 2015. "Unfair Partisan Gerrymanders in Politics and Law: A Diagnostic Applied to Six Cases." *Election Law Journal* 14(4): 312–30.

McDonald, Michael D., Daniel Magleby, Jonathan Krasno, Shawn Donahue, and Robin Best. 2018. "*A Proposal to Give Seat Effect Second Billing When Investigating Gerrymandering.*" Paper presented at the 2018 Annual Conference of the Midwest Political Science Association, Chicago.

McDonald, Michael P. 2004. "A Comparative Analysis of Redistricting Institutions in the United States, 2001–02." *State Politics and Policy Quarterly* 4(4): 371–95.

McDonald, Michael P. 2006. "Drawing the Line on District Competition." *PS: Political Science & Politics* 39: 91–94.

McGann, Anthony J., et al. 2016. *Gerrymandering in America: The House of Representatives, the Supreme Court, and the Future of Popular Sovereignty.* Cambridge: Cambridge University Press.

McGhee, Eric. 2014. "Measuring Partisan Bias in Single-Member District Electoral Systems." *Legislative Studies Quarterly* 39(1): 55–85.

McGhee, Eric. 2015. "California's Political Reforms: A Brief History." *Public Policy Institute of California.*

McGhee, Eric. 2017. "Measuring Efficiency in Redistricting." *Election Law Journal: Rules, Politics, and Policy* 16(4): 417–42.

Miller, Nicholas R. 2015. "Election Inversions under Proportional Representation." *Scandinavian Political Studies* 38(1): 4–25.

Moxley, Warden. 1973. *Congressional Districts in the 1970s.* Washington, DC: Congressional Quarterly.

Murphy, C., and Antoine Yoshinaka. 2009. "Are Mapmakers Able to Target and Protect Congressional Incumbents? The Institutional Dynamics of Electoral Competition." *American Politics Research* 37(6): 955–82.

Nagel, J. H. 2000. "Expanding the Spectrum of Democracies: Reflections on Proportional Representation in New Zealand." In *Democracy and Institutions: The Life Work of Arend Lijphart*, 113–27. Ann Arbor: University of Michigan.

Nagle, John F. 2015. "Measures of Partisan Bias for Legislating Fair Elections." *Election Law Journal* 14(4): 346–60.

Pitkin, Hannah F. 1967. *The Concept of Representation*. Vol. *75*. Berkeley: University of California Press.

Plener Cover, Benjamin. 2018. "Quantifying Partisan Gerrymandering: An Evaluation of the Efficiency Gap Proposal." *Stanford Law Review 70*: 1131.

Ranney, Austin. 1962. *The Doctrine of Responsible Party Government: Its Origins and Present State*. Vol. *34*, no. 3. Champaign: University of Illinois Press.

Ricca, F., A. Scozzari, and B. Simeone. 2013. "Political Districting: From Classical Models to Recent Approaches." *Annals of Operations Research 204*(1): 271–99.

Royden, Laura, Michael Li, and Yurij Rudensky. 2018. "Extreme Gerrymandering and the 2018 Midterm." *Brennan Center for Justice, March 23*. https://www.brennancenter.org/publication/extreme-gerrymandering-2018-midterm.

Saward, Michael. 2010. *The Representative Claim*. Oxford: Oxford University Press.

Schwarzenegger, Arnold. 2019. "Professor Schwarzenegger on Gerrymandering." YouTube, December 10. https://youtu.be/E2EnuHsRJd4.

Seabrook, Nicholas R. 2010. "The Limits of Partisan Gerrymandering: Looking Ahead to the 2010 Congressional Redistricting Cycle." *The Forum 8*(2): Article 8.

Seabrook, Nicholas R. 2017. *Drawing the Lines: Constraints on Partisan Gerrymandering in US Politics*. Ithaca, NY: Cornell University Press.

Shotts, Kenneth W. 2001. "The Effect of Majority-Minority Mandates on Partisan Gerrymandering." *American Journal of Political Science 45*(1): 120–35.

Stephanopoulos, Nicholas O., and Eric M. McGhee. 2015. "Partisan Gerrymandering and the Efficiency Gap." *University of Chicago Law Review 82*: 831–900.

Stephanopoulos, Nicholas O., and Eric M. McGhee. 2018. "The Measure of a Metric: The Debate over Quantifying Partisan Gerrymandering." *Stanford Law Review 70*: 1503.

Sterne, Simon. 1869. *Representative Government: Its Evils and Their Reform. A Lecture Delivered . . . 1869, at the Invitation and Under the Auspices of the Trustees of the Cooper Union*. CS Wescott, printers.

Tam Cho, Wendy K., and Yan Y. Liu. 2016. "Toward a Talismanic Redistricting Tool: A Computational Method for Identifying Extreme Redistricting Plans." *Election Law Journal 15(4)*: 351–66.

Tapp, Kristopher. 2019. Measuring political gerrymandering. *The American Mathematical Monthly 126*(7): 593–609.

Trickey, Erick. 2017. "Where Did the Term 'Gerrymander' Come From?" *Smithsonian Magazine*, July 20. www.smithsonianmag.com/history/where-did-term-gerrymander-come-180964118.

Tufte, Edward R. 1973. "The Relationship between Seats and Votes in Two-Party Systems." *American Political Science Review 67*(2): 540–54.

Wang, Samuel S.-H. 2016. "Three Tests for Practical Evaluation of Partisan Gerrymandering." *Stanford Law Review 68*: 1263.

Weaver, James B., and Sidney W. Hess. 1963. "A Procedure for Nonpartisan Districting: Development of Computer Techniques." *Yale Law Journal 73*: 288.

Yoshinaka, Antoine, and Chad Murphy. 2011. "The Paradox of Redistricting: How Partisan Mapmakers Foster Competition but Disrupt Representation." *Political Research Quarterly 64*(2): 435–47.

Cases Cited

Abrams v. Johnson, 521 U.S. 74 (1997)

Arizona Minority Coalition for Fair Redistricting v. Arizona Independent Redistricting Commission, No. CV 2002-004480 (Superior Court, Maricopa Co. (2004))

Arizona Independent Redistricting Commission v. Brewer, 275 P.3d 1267 (Ariz. 2012)

Arizona State Legislature v. Arizona Independent Redistricting Commission, 135 S. Ct. 2652 (2015)

Baker v. Carr, 369 U.S. 186 (1962)

Benisek v. Lamone, 138 S. Ct. 1942 (2018)

Benisek v. Lamone, 348 F.Supp.3d 493 (2018)

Bethune-Hill v. Virginia Board of Elections, 137 S. Ct. 788 *(2017)*

Common Cause v. Lewis, State of North Carolina, Wake County, 18 CV 014001 (2019), https://www.brennancenter.org/sites/default/files/legal-work/2019-09-03-Judgment.pdf

Common Cause v. Rucho, 139 S. Ct. 2484 (2019)

Common Cause v. Rucho, 318 F.Supp. 3d 777 (2018)

Cooper v. Harris, 136 S. Ct. 2512 (2017)

Davis v. Bandemer, 478 U.S. 109 (1986)

Davis v. Hildebrandt, 241 U.S. 565 (1916)

Gaffney v. Cummings, 412 U.S. 735 (1973)

Gill v. Whitford, 138 S. Ct. 1916 (2018)

Georgia v. Ashcroft, 539 US 461 (2003)

Gomez v. Watsonville, 63 F.2d 1407 (9th Cir. 1988)

Karcher v. Daggett, 462 U.S. 725 (1983)

League of Women Voters v. Commonwealth of Pennsylvania, 178 A.3d 737 (Pa. 2018)

League of Women Voters of Florida v. Dentzner, 172 So. 3d 363 (2015)

League of Women Voters of Michigan v. Benson, Case 373 F.Supp.3d 867 (E.D. Michigan 2019)

LULAC v. Perry, 548 U.S. 399 (2006)

Reynolds v. Sims, 377 US 533 (1964)

Rucho v. Common Cause, 139 S. Ct. 2484 (2019)

Rucho v. Common Cause, 318 F.Supp.3d 777 (2018)

Ohio A. Philip Randolph Inst. v. Householder, 373 F.Supp.3d 978 (S.D. Ohio 2019)

Vieth v. Pennsylvania, 195 F.Supp.2d 672 (M. D. Pa. 2002)

Vieth v. Jubelirer, 541 U.S. 267 (2004)

Voinovich v. Quilter, 507 US 146 (1993)

Wesberry v. Sanders, 376 U.S. 1 (1964)

Whitford v. Gill, 218 F.Supp. 3d 837 (W.D. Wis. 2016)

Wittman v. Personhuballah, 136 S. Ct. 1732 (2016)

Supporting Legal Documents

Petition for Review of League of Women Voters of Pennsylvania, *League of Women Voters vs. Commonwealth of Pennsylvania* (2018) (No. 159 MM 2017). https://www.brennancenter.org/sites/default/files/legal-work/Petition-for-Review.pdf. (Cited as LWV Complaint)

First Amended Complaint for Common Cause, *Common Cause v. Rucho* (2019) (No. 1:16-CV-1026). https://www.brennancenter.org/sites/default/files/legal-work/CCvRucho_AmendedComplaint.pdf. (Cited as Rucho complaint)

Complaint for William Whitford, *Whitford v. Nichol* (2016) (No. 3:15-cv-00421-bbc). https://www.brennancenter.org/sites/default/files/legal-work/Whitford-ComplaintandExhibits070816.pdf. (Cited as Whitford 1st Complaint)

Brief in Opposition of Motion for Summary Judgment by Plaintiffs, *Whitford v. Nichol* (2016) (No. 3:15-cv-00421-bbc). https://www.brennancenter.org/sites/default/files/legal-work/Whitford-BriefinOppositionbyPlaintiffsreMotionforSummaryJudgment012516.pdf.

Second Amended Complaint of Stephen Shapiro, *Benisek v. Lamone* (2018) (No. 1:13-cv-03233-JKB). https://www.brennancenter.org/sites/default/files/legal-work/D.Md_Shapiro_2nd_Amend_Complaint.pdf. (Cited as Benisek 2nd Complaint)

Index

Tables and figures are indicated by *t* and *f* following the page number